The Fettered Presidency

The Fettered Presidency

Legal Constraints on the Executive Branch

L. Gordon Crovitz & Jeremy A. Rabkin, Editors
with a foreword by Robert H. Bork

American Enterprise Institute for Public Policy Research
Washington, D.C.

Distributed by arrangement with

National Book Network
4720 Boston Way   3 Henrietta Street
Lanham, MD 20706   London WC2E 8LU England

Library of Congress Cataloging-in-Publication Data

The Fettered Presidency: legal constraints on the executive branch /
  L. Gordon Crovitz and Jeremy A. Rabkin, editors.
      p.   cm.
    Includes index.
    ISBN 0-8447-3677-5.   ISBN 0-8447-3678-3 (pbk.)
    1. Executive power—United States. I. Crovitz, L. Gordon.
  II. Rabkin, Jeremy A.
  KF5050.A75F47 1989
  342.73'064—dc19
  [347.30264]   88-31155
                                                                    CIP

AEI Studies 485

Printed in the United States of America

Contents

Foreword

Robert H. Bork

The chapters contained in this volume demonstrate that the office of the president of the United States has been significantly weakened in recent years and that Congress is largely, but not entirely, responsible. Some recent presidents have failed to defend their office's prerogatives, allowing Congress to establish easements across the constitutional powers of the presidency that time and use may make permanent. This is a deeply worrisome development, for America has usually prospered most in eras of strong presidents, and the state of today's world makes the capacity for strong executive action more important than ever. Many congressmen and commentators would, we may be sure, respond that Congress is merely reasserting its constitutional role after decades of presidential usurpation. That raises the question of how and what we should think about the two branches' constitutional powers.

Of the three branches of the federal government, the founders had least to say about the presidency. Congress was not merely carefully constituted, but in Article I, section 8, its powers were set out one by one with as much specificity as the subject allowed. Judicial power and the heads of jurisdiction were carefully designated and confined in Article III. (There is, of course, the embarrassment that the greatest of all judicial powers, the power to set aside the acts of the people's representatives in the name of the Constitution, is nowhere mentioned, but we have learned to live with that.)

In comparison with the constitutional description of the other two branches, the office of the presidency is generally and vaguely defined. The president is to be vested with "the executive Power," which means among other things, we are told, that he is to be "Commander in Chief" of the armed forces; he may require the opinion in writing of cabinet officers upon any subject relating to their duties; he may make treaties if two-thirds of the Senate concur; and he may nominate a variety of important officers and, with the advice and consent of the Senate, appoint them. He may convene Congress upon extraordinary occasions, he is to "receive Ambassadors and other public Ministers," and "he shall take Care that the Laws be faithfully executed." There is more, but none of it particularly enlightening.

So far as text is concerned, it would require a spectacular feat of interpretation to infer the scope of the president's authority to use armed force from the bare reference to him as commander in chief. His primacy in foreign affairs must be gleaned entirely from his power to negotiate treaties and receive ambassadors. But text is by no means all that counts. There is history, and that history was shaped by what in constitutional law is called structural reasoning. Reasons drawn from structure are as much a part of the Constitution as is the text, as Chief Justice John Marshall demonstrated long ago in *McCulloch* v. *Maryland*. The respective roles of Congress and the president developed according to their structural capacities and limitations. Congress, consisting of 535 members assisted by huge staffs, is obviously incapable of swift, decisive, and flexible action in the employment of armed force, the conduct of foreign policy, and the control of intelligence operations. The very number of persons involved makes confidentiality difficult, to say the least, and the attribution of responsibility impossible. That is why, as the Supreme Court said in *United States* v. *Curtiss-Wright Export Corp.*, "In this vast external realm, with its important, complicated, delicate and manifold problems, the President alone has the power to speak or listen as a representative of the nation."

It appears that the men of Philadelphia and those who ratified their work had only a general notion of what authority and functions properly belong to the new office they were creating. The president was not to be a monarch but neither was he to be the weak figurehead that many governors in the states had become. A prime reason for calling the convention, and a prime reason for ratifying its work, was intense dissatisfaction with the results of legislative dominance in the state governments. A much stronger executive was wanted in the national government, but the vision of what the executive would be and do was misty enough so that the framers and ratifiers were satisfied, or at least made do with, a fragmentary and general listing of heads of authority.

There is, nonetheless, something of a parallel between their treatment of the legislative and the executive powers. Having spelled out with considerable particularity the great powers of Congress in Article I, section 8, the Constitution concluded that subject with a provision indicating an understanding that not all things could be spelled out in advance, for the last power specified is "to make all Laws which shall be necessary and proper for carrying into Execution the foregoing Powers, and all other Powers vested by this Constitution in the Government of the United States, or in any Department or Officer thereof." In *McCulloch* v. *Maryland,* in which Congress's power to establish a national bank was upheld, Chief Justice Marshall construed that clause with some breadth, pointing out that "we must never forget that is is *a constitution* we are expounding." In language particularly appropriate to executive power, though that was not the immediate subject, Marshall said:

> This provision is made in a constitution intended to endure for ages to come, and, consequently, to be adapted to the various *crises* of human affairs. To have prescribed the means by which government should, in all future time, execute its powers, would have been to change, entirely, the character of the instrument, and give it the properties of a legal code.

It is interesting that this is precisely what Congress has been attempting to do with the president's powers under the Constitution: "to change, entirely, the character of the instrument, and give it the properties of a legal code." The War Powers Act, which disclaims any intention to alter the constitutional powers of the president, specifies in great detail what those powers are, when they may be used, and when Congress, even by its silence, may require the president to withdraw any armed forces he has committed to a region or to combat. This is the equivalent of a presidential proclamation disclaiming any intention to alter the powers of Congress but specifying in great detail what those powers are, including the power to declare war, and stating that the executive will not carry into effect any law or declaration of war that the executive deems beyond the powers the Constitution bestowed on Congress. There is no body of jurisprudence on this subject, but a president is probably under no obligation to carry out a law or declaration that he deems plainly unconstitutional. We tend to think that Andrew Johnson was right to violate the Tenure of Office Act by discharging Edwin M. Stanton as secretary of war without the consent of the Senate. That brought Johnson within one vote of conviction on impeachment in the Senate, but he was right about his powers as president and right to assert them against a congressional statute.

Since we would and should condemn a president who tried to freeze Congress's powers with such a proclamation, shouldn't we also condemn a Congress that did the same to the power of the president as commander in chief and as the nation's leader in foreign affairs to use armed forces abroad? The conduct of foreign policy often requires that troops be committed to action or be placed in areas where hostilities may commence. The president's powers are not susceptible of definition in advance. Changes in power relations, the shifting nature of alliances and adversarial postures, and, most certainly, the rapid development of military technologies mean that he must often act in ways that no one can foresee even a day in advance, much less in the ages to come.

Some of the contributors to this book express the hope that the constitutionality of the War Powers Act will be decided by the Supreme Court. I think it most unlikely that the Court will ever pass upon the act as a whole. If particular presidential actions are challenged, as was Lincoln's order to blockade the South in the *Prize Cases*, the validity of the actions will necessarily be determined by the Court's view of constitutional powers, since those are not and cannot be altered by the War Powers Act. This makes that act a very peculiar species of law, one that alters nothing. That being so, and since the president is bound to pursue his constitutional duties as the circumstances in the world dictate, the War Powers Act becomes little more than a license for congressional recrimination after the event. It is a means by which those who dislike a particular use of force but hesitate to oppose it on its merits (when it is popular, as was the invasion of Grenada) can attack the president obliquely by ignoring the merits and painting him as a lawbreaker.

While the War Powers Act thus serves no useful purpose, it does weaken the presidency and divert the public debate from the substance of policy to legalisms. Some day, I hope, a strong president will explain to the American people just what the act is, that it cannot detract from his constitutional powers, and that he intends to ignore it whenever its provisions conflict with those powers. This is a task the Supreme Court should not be asked, and if asked, should not undertake, to do for the president.

Many, probably most, Americans are under the impression that questions of constitutional powers are always questions for courts. That is, of course, not true. Some are too important or too vaguely defined to be left to judges; those are best left to the understanding of the contending branches and ultimately to the good sense of the American people. On the subject of the use of armed force, the Constitution suggests the poles of power but leaves most of the intermediate ground for political contention by the branches. The major decisions are reserved for Congress, as shown not only by its power to declare war but by its absolute control of spending. Although the president is commander in chief, Congress is under no constitutional obligation to provide him with a single private to order about. But once Congress provides the president with armed forces, it cannot interfere with his tactical decisions, and, considering that the deployment of men and materiel is often crucial to the conduct of foreign policy, in the modern world "tactical decisions" may encompass a great deal. Let me use a crude example to illustrate the extremes of power of each branch. Congress could, of course, have refused to declare war after Pearl Harbor, or, if that is too unrealistic, it could have refused to declare war on Germany. It is more debatable whether Congress could have specified that no funds should be spent in prosecuting a war against Germany until Japan was subdued. But surely it is not debatable that Congress's constitutional power would not extend to dictating the site for the invasion of Europe or to ordering that no funds be expended in the defense of Bastogne since it was better that the troops there should surrender.

The War Powers Act is merely the most dramatic example of a congressional attempt to weaken the presidency. Recent years have produced as well intrusive and debilitating congressional oversight of intelligence activities, the combination of budgets and substantive lawmaking in vetoproof continuing resolutions, the removal of part of the president's law enforcement responsibility through the creation of independent counsel in the Ethics in Government Act, vacillating incursions into foreign policy as with the five different Boland amendments that crippled policy toward the hostile Marxist regime in Nicaragua, and much more. We have heard congressmen repeatedly justify their efforts with the statement that Congress is a coequal branch. That it is, but "coequality" does not mean that Congress's functions are or should be the same as the president's any more than the judiciary's should. Each branch is designed for unique functions.

If the allocation of constitutional roles is becoming a mess, what can be done about it? No doubt the courts will occasionally be called upon to rule, but many of the questions are ill suited to judicial resolution. In any event, the Supreme Court's unsurprising but disappointing decision that the independent counsel statute is constitutional in all respects indicates that the Court is not a reliable ally of the presidency even when the president's position is constitutionally correct. The rescue of the proper powers of the presidency will have to be accomplished by strong and determined presidents who can make the case to the American people. The president must now accept the constitutionality of the independent counsel statute, but he should veto the next such enactment unless it applies to Congress as well as to the executive branch. Congress has for too long been allowed to enact legislative restrictions from which it alone is exempt.

The president must make a public issue of congressional attempts to control his legitimate powers, perhaps by refusing to accept some restrictions even at the risk of political damage. It would be a prolonged and bloody fight, but our national well-being requires that it be made.

Contributors

L. GORDON CROVITZ is assistant editor of the editorial page and a member of the editorial board of the *Wall Street Journal*. Mr. Crovitz, a lawyer, has been an editorial page writer for the domestic *Journal* and was the founding editorial page editor of the *Wall Street Journal/Europe* in Brussels.

JEREMY A. RABKIN is an associate professor of government at Cornell University. He served as a staff editor of AEI's *Regulation* magazine from 1978 to 1980 and is currently a contributing editor.

ELLIOTT ABRAMS is assistant secretary of state for inter-American affairs, his third post as assistant secretary in the Department of State since 1981. Mr. Abrams is the author of numerous essays and book reviews, which have appeared in *Commentary, The Public Interest, The American Spectator, Policy Review*, and other journals.

PAUL M. BATOR is John P. Wilson Professor of Law at the University of Chicago and of counsel with Mayer, Brown & Platt. Previously, Mr. Bator was Bruce Bromley Professor of Law at Harvard Law School. Mr. Bator also served as deputy solicitor general and counselor to the solicitor general at the U.S. Department of Justice. He is a member of AEI's Council of Academic Advisers.

JUDITH A. BEST is Distinguished Teaching Professor of Political Science at the State University of New York at Cortland. She is the author of various articles and books, including *The Case against Direct Election of the President*.

ROBERT H. BORK is the John M. Olin Scholar in Legal Studies at the American Enterprise Institute. He served on the U.S. Court of Appeals for the District of Columbia Circuit for six years. Judge Bork was solicitor general of the United States for four years. He taught at Yale Law School and practiced law with Kirkland & Ellis in Chicago and Washington, D.C.

JIM BURNLEY is secretary of the U.S. Department of Transportation, where he has also served as deputy secretary and as general counsel. Previously, Mr. Burnley was associate deputy attorney general with the U.S. Department of Justice. He also served as director of the Volunteers in Service to America (VISTA).

BARBARA HINKSON CRAIG is assistant professor of government at Wesleyan University where she teaches courses on Congress, administrative law, and constitutional law. Professor Craig has written several articles on the legislative veto. Her most recent book is *Chadha: The Story of an Epic Constitutional Struggle.*

CHARLES H. FAIRBANKS, JR., is research professor of international relations at the Johns Hopkins School of Advanced International Studies and directs the Foreign Policy Institute's Program in Soviet and American National Security Policymaking. Mr. Fairbanks has served at the Department of State as a member of the policy planning staff and as a deputy assistant secretary. He has been a teacher and researcher at the University of Toronto, the RAND Corporation, AEI, and Yale University.

LOUIS FISHER is a specialist on American national government with the Congressional Research Service at the Library of Congress. Mr. Fisher has taught at Queens College, Georgetown University, American University, Catholic University, and Indiana University. His most recent books are *Constitutional Dialogues* and *American Constitutional Law.*

SUZANNE GARMENT is a resident scholar at the American Enterprise Institute where she is writing a book about political scandal in post-Watergate Washington. She was associate editor of the editorial page of the *Wall Street Journal* and wrote a weekly column, "Capital Chronicle." She served as a special assistant to the U.S. Ambassador to the United Nations Daniel P. Moynihan.

C. BOYDEN GRAY is counselor to the vice president of the United States, George Bush. He is also counsel to the Presidential Task Force on Regulatory Relief. Before joining the vice president's staff, he was a partner in the Washington, D.C., law firm of Wilmer, Cutler & Pickering.

MORTON HALPERIN is the director of the Washington office of the American Civil Liberties Union. He is also director of the Center for National Security Studies. Mr. Halperin has held positions with the Twentieth Century Fund, the Brookings Institution, the National Security Council, the Department of Defense, and Harvard University. *Nuclear Fallacy* is his most recent book.

MICHAEL J. HOROWITZ is the managing partner of the Washington, D.C., law firm of Myerson, Kuhn & Sterrett. Previously, he was counsel to the director and chief legal officer at the Office of Management and Budget. Mr. Horowitz has taught at the University of Mississippi and Georgetown law schools.

ALAN L. KEYES was the Republican candidate for the U.S. Senate for Maryland in 1988. He is a resident scholar in foreign policy studies at the American Enterprise Institute. He is the former assistant secretary of state for international organization affairs and has also served as the U.S. representative to the UN Economic and Social Council. Mr. Keyes is working on two books, one on the relationship of diplomacy to strategic thinking and the other on the future of South Africa.

JEANE J. KIRKPATRICK is a senior fellow at the American Enterprise Institute and the Leavey Professor at Georgetown University. She was the U.S. representative to the United Nations and a member of the cabinet. Her most recent book is *Legitimacy and Force: National and International Dimensions,* and she is currently finishing a book on the U.S. role at the United Nations and in the world.

IRVING KRISTOL is the John M. Olin Distinguished Fellow at the American Enterprise Institute. He is also coeditor of *The Public Interest* magazine and publisher of *The National Interest* magazine. Mr. Kristol writes a monthly column for the *Wall Street Journal,* as well as numerous articles for other newspapers, magazines, and journals. His most recent book is *Reflections of a Neoconservative.*

CARNES LORD is director of international studies at the National Institute for Public Policy. He has taught political science at Dartmouth College, Yale University, and the University of Virginia. Mr. Lord has written extensively on military strategy, arms control, human rights, and public diplomacy. His articles have appeared in *Strategic Review, Comparative Strategy, Commentary,* and the *Wall Street Journal.*

MICHAEL J. MALBIN is associate director of the House Republican Conference. Before that, he served on the minority staff of the House Select Committee to Investigate Covert Arms Transactions with Iran. He has also been a visiting professor at the University of Maryland and a resident fellow at the American Enterprise Institute, where he remains an adjunct scholar. Mr. Malbin has written several books on campaign finance, Congress, and the First Amendment's religion clauses and contributes to AEI's biennial volume *Vital Statistics on Congress*.

THEODORE B. OLSON is the managing partner of the Washington, D.C., office of the law firm of Gibson, Dunn & Crutcher. Previously, Mr. Olson was assistant attorney general, Office of Legal Counsel, U.S. Department of Justice. He is the editor of the recently published twelve-volume *Department of Justice Manual*.

NORMAN J. ORNSTEIN is a resident scholar at the American Enterprise Institute. He is a political contributor to the MacNeil/Lehrer News-Hour and an election analyst for CBS News. His most recent book is *Vital Statistics on Congress,* now in its fourth edition. He also writes frequently for numerous newspapers and journals.

RICHARD N. PERLE is a resident scholar at the American Enterprise Institute and contributing editor to *U.S. News and World Report.* Mr. Perle served as assistant secretary of defense for international security policy and, previously, in several staff positions in the Senate.

STEPHEN P. ROSEN is a secretary of the navy research fellow at the Naval War College where he is writing books on military innovation and strategic planning. Mr. Rosen has worked in the Office of the Secretary of Defense/Net Assessment and on the staff of the National Security Council.

EUGENE V. ROSTOW is distinguished visiting research professor of law and diplomacy at the National Defense University. He has been a professor of law at Yale University Law School, under secretary for political affairs at the Department of State, and director for the Arms Control and Disarmament Agency.

GARY J. SCHMITT is visiting fellow at *The National Interest*. Previously he was executive director of the President's Foreign Intelligence Advisory Board and minority staff director of the Senate Select Committee on Intelligence. He has published numerous articles on the presidency, executive-congressional relations, and American political thought.

ABRAM N. SHULSKY is senior fellow at the National Strategy Information Center, where he is writing a book on intelligence issues. Mr. Shulsky has been visiting professor at the Committee on Social Thought and senior fellow at the John M. Olin Center, University of Chicago. He was also director of Strategic Arms Control Policy at the U.S. Department of Defense. He has published numerous articles in such journals as *The Washington Quarterly*, *The Public Interest*, and *Commentary*.

LOREN A. SMITH is chief judge of the U.S. Claims Court. He served formerly as chairman of the Administrative Conference of the United States. Judge Smith taught at Delaware Law School from 1976 to 1984 and has written numerous articles in such journals as *William & Mary Law Review* and *Duke Law Journal*.

WILLIAM FRENCH SMITH is a senior partner in the Los Angeles law firm of Gibson, Dunn & Crutcher. From 1981 to 1985 Mr. Smith served as attorney general of the United States. He is a member of the President's Foreign Intelligence Advisory Board.

ABRAHAM D. SOFAER has been legal adviser of the Department of State since 1985. From 1979 to 1985 he was U.S. district judge in the Southern District of New York. From 1969 to 1979 Judge Sofaer was professor of law at Columbia University; he has written extensively on administrative law, constitutional law, executive privilege, and the conduct of foreign and military affairs.

MICHAEL B. WALLACE is a partner of Phelps, Dunbar, Marks, Claverie & Sims in Jackson, Mississippi. Since 1984, Mr. Wallace has been a member of the Administrative Conference of the United States and served as a director of the Legal Services Corporation.

CASPAR W. WEINBERGER is publisher of *Forbes* magazine and counsel to the law firm of Rogers & Wells. Before joining Rogers & Wells, Mr. Weinberger was secretary of defense. He has been vice president, director, and general counsel of the Bechtel Group of Companies. Mr. Weinberger has also served as chairman of the Federal Trade Commission, director of the Office of Management and Budget, and secretary of Health, Education, and Welfare.

1
Introduction

L. Gordon Crovitz and Jeremy A. Rabkin

This book addresses the proliferation of legal constraints on policy making in the executive branch of the federal government and highlights the risks and dangers this poses for public policy. To some extent, this subject is as old as the republic. *The Federalist* calls "energy" in the executive branch "a leading character in the definition of good government. It is essential to the protection of the community against foreign attacks; it is not less essential to the steady administration of the laws." Energy encompasses many virtues—the ability to move quickly, to alter course, to maneuver amid changing conditions. Laws that limit executive discretion reduce the protections of individual liberty and equally cripple the efficient pursuit of national goals. Good government requires a vibrant executive branch free of improper constraints. Forming a background to this book are the grand questions that echo through our history—the proper balances to strike in government between leadership and accountability, purpose and form, law and discretion.

The focus of the book itself is more topical. Many contributors are less engaged by timeless truths than by immediate frustrations. This volume, which includes the views of many high-ranking officials in the administration of President Ronald Reagan, is also a record of the worries expressed by thoughtful participants and observers of the governmental machine in the waning months of the Reagan administration.

The timing of this publication is fortuitous. The frustrations within the executive branch expressed by many of the authors are set in sharp relief by recent events. In some contrast to the first years of the Reagan presidency, in its later years the administration seemed almost paralyzed by the bitter recriminations following the revela-

1

tions in the fall of 1986 that it had secretly sold arms to Iran and channeled funds to the contra forces in Sandinista-ruled Nicaragua. These "scandals" dominated congressional and media attention through much of 1987; their snowballing effect for a time evoked comparisons with the Watergate scandal of the early 1970s. Although the storm had abated a good deal by the spring of 1988, the Reagan administration seemed to have lost its earlier sense of energy and direction, evoking comparisons with the last year of the Jimmy Carter administration.

Much of the discussion, therefore, is weighed down with the oppressive sense that after all its earlier successes, the Reagan administration, too, had finally fallen victim to the mysterious political curse that had brought down each of its predecessors of the previous two decades. This curse, of course, relates to the general theme of a fettered executive branch and how legal constraints adversely affect its performance and thus the performance of government generally.

The purpose here is not to evaluate the policy record of the Reagan administration but to explore the institutional obstacles it faced in implementing those policies. From this point of view, it was appropriate that many of the contributors are generally sympathetic or at least not determinedly hostile to the policy aims of the Reagan administration. Though the majority of the contributors had been actively involved in the major policy battles of the 1980s, the discussion did not revive the acrimony of those struggles. Debate tends to focus, as we had hoped, not on the propriety of the administration's goals but on the soundness of its tactics and methods given the institutional and political realities of the 1980s. The true center of attention is not the Reagan administration itself but the character of this larger operating environment for executive policy.

We believe the papers and comments made at an American Enterprise Institute conference in April 1988 have important lessons and suggestions for the administration of George Bush. This volume draws on experiences in a wide range of policy fields, from the high cost of the system of Pentagon weapons procurement and the constraints on covert intelligence operations to the policy convolutions in the regulation of automobile fuel consumption standards and the provision of legal services to the poor. The contributors were a mixture of engaged policy makers and academic observers, specialists and generalists, skeptics and idealists. And for better or for worse, perceptions of what happened in the 1980s are bound to have a decisive influence on the perspectives that Washington policy makers take with them into the 1990s. This volume may thus be of immediate interest in a presidential election year.

Excessive Legalism

In this book, we sought to concentrate particularly on what seemed to us a disturbing trend toward excessive reliance on legal standards in the formulation or control of public policy. William French Smith's paper on the practical difficulties of independent counsel to investigate possible law breaking by executive branch officials and Stephen P. Rosen's paper on one cause of the Pentagon's unwieldy weapons procurement system are good examples of what we had in mind. To deal with genuine but secondary concerns—preventing corrupt dealings or conflicts of interest in both law enforcement and military procurement—we have erected an extensive and elaborate set of restrictions that greatly hobble the main concerns of, respectively, doing justice to individuals in enforcing the law and securing effective and reliable military hardware at the lowest feasible cost. One contributor, former Assistant Attorney General Theodore B. Olson, himself lived under the threat of indictment by an independent counsel for nearly three years, during which time he amassed a legal bill approaching $1.5 million. Mr. Olson had been accused in a congressional committee report of having unlawfully defended executive privilege during 1983 testimony in an Environmental Protection Agency controversy. The independent counsel concluded that there was no evidence that Mr. Olson had committed any crime.

Michael Malbin's paper on the congressional response to the Iran-contra "scandal" documents another cost of excessive legalization. Once the charge was raised that the Reagan administration had broken the law, virtually all congressional and public policy debate centered on technical questions of legality instead of on the policy merits of what had been done or what might be done differently in the future. Although everyone realized that vital interests were at stake in the Persian Gulf and in Central America, the wrangling of lawyers—what Lt. Col. Oliver North described in his compelling congressional testimony as the "criminalization of policy differences"—almost totally displaced further consideration of the policy options. This surely exacerbated the confusion and indecision of American policy in these vital regions.

These consequences appear most perverse if one stands back from the immediate controversies and looks at the structure of institutions and debates as aspects of a single, overall machine for the administration of public affairs. Once one does adopt this sort of managerial perspective on governmental decision making, it is natural to focus on the results of the process. And it then seems equally natural to reason back from distressing results to the conclusion that

3

defectively working parts must have put the machinery of government out of kilter.

From this perspective, then, the question of how much to rely on fixed rules—on laws—in the conduct of government business seems only a somewhat more complicated version of ordinary management questions encountered in all collective endeavors. Every good manager knows that some rules are needed for ordering and coordinating complex undertakings, but every good manager also knows that there are limits to the range of subordinates' activities that can be fixed by preestablished rules. Good managers understand it is frequently necessary to trust decisions to the discretion of subordinates and to bend or adapt existing rules to new problems and circumstances. As experience over time suggests the need for modifications in particular rules, so it may also suggest the need for shifting operations toward a greater or lesser reliance on rules themselves. As Richard Perle comments in this book, "Executive authority means the discretion to exercise judgment in the face of uncertainty; and if this discretion means anything, it must include the discretion to make mistakes."

This perspective on government operations is hardly the invention of modern systems analysts in political science or their predecessors among management gurus in commerce. Government *is* an instrument for achieving public purposes, and it is never pointless to inquire whether an instrument is well designed to achieve its purposes. That is why *The Federalist* could speak of the "administration of government, in its largest sense," as a concern that "comprehends all the operations of the body politic, whether legislative, executive or judiciary," and still "safely pronounce that the true test of a good government is its aptitude and tendency to produce a good administration." From this perspective, it is results that count.

Of course this perspective abstracts from the central problem that the public—for whom the machine of government presumably operates—is not a single, collective entity. To take the most obvious example, a regulatory agency may, by exceeding its statutory authority, secure valuable benefits for the general public, and this result may seem to outweigh the harm imposed on an individual victim. The victim will have a view of the costs and benefits different from the general public, however, and a regulated firm will thus insist that government regulators must not interfere with its affairs any more than the law allows. Courts are separated from the rest of the policy-making process to provide the victims of government decisions with some assurance that their rights will be respected. Courts and the lawyers who represent clients in the legal process display strong tendencies therefore to resist the management perspective, and to

4

fasten instead on the moral imperatives of "the law."

Those quotation marks underscore the general realization that the law itself now purports to regulate behavior that may not be susceptible to legal control. Courts are not just the model but indeed the source for much of the legalization of policy making in contemporary Washington. Over the past two decades, more and more aspects of public policy making have come under judicial control. Twenty years ago, challenges to government policy were largely limited to claims by property holders protesting improper government interference with their property rights and expectations. By the early 1970s, long established judicial doctrines—such as who can sue for what kinds of alleged harms—had been radically transformed to allow new kinds of claimants to press their concerns before the courts. So, for example, environmental groups were allowed to challenge the award of operating licenses to nuclear power plants, building permits for new highways, and zoning permits for new urban developments.

In fact, not only self-styled public interest advocacy groups but an entire range of specialized interests found new opportunities to press their claims through litigation. In one famous early case, computer companies were allowed to file suit against the comptroller of the currency to block a new rule authorizing the provision of data processing services by commercial banks—their potential business competitors. By the 1980s, it was routine for trucking firms to file suits against the Interstate Commerce Commission to block the extension of deregulation policies that accorded new opportunities to competitors. A specialized court was even created for domestic manufacturers to file suit demanding the imposition of import barriers against "unfair competition" from foreign imports. Labor unions regularly sued the Occupational Safety and Health Administration to demand more rigorous or extensive safety standards outside the traditional context of labor-management negotiations.

Interests that stand to benefit—or think they do—by one or another interpretation of the law can thus try to enforce their favored interpretation through the courts. Indeed, this is the essential purpose of broadening access to the courts. But there is an inevitable consequence to the operations of government. Once legal standards are brought into litigation, they naturally acquire a judicial gloss restricting or elaborating their meaning. The very fact that more and more administrative decisions can be and are challenged in the courts means over time that the relevant legal standards acquire added layers of complexity, making the job of administrators correspondingly more difficult. In this way, administrative discretion is increasingly limited by the claims of private claimants. Thus, as the system provides more and more legal leverage for the claims of special interests, administrative agencies have less and less scope to act in what they conceive to be the public interest.

This perspective on the problem of excessive legalization of policy making is well developed in Paul Bator's paper addressing the main themes of the book. This problem will be one for future administrations to confront as the trend continues. Interestingly, however, the authors devoted relatively little attention to this problem of government operations as it appears from the general, managerial perspective. This is perhaps because it is very difficult to remain fixed in the abstractions of the managerial perspective in the face of the immediate issues of policy making and political results. Indeed, this difficulty may itself be one of the central lessons of this volume.

The U.S. constitutional scheme presents another great challenge to the managerial perspective on public policy, quite apart from issues raised as part of protecting private claims under the law. From the managerial perspective, questions of law versus discretion seem to be for managers to resolve in response to changing conditions and new evaluations of performance by subordinates. The problem with applying this to the federal government is that the governmental machinery has two distinct top managers—with one managerial hierarchy running to the White House and another running to Congress. Questions of law versus discretion, then, are not mere questions of management but key stakes in the ongoing struggle for power between Congress and the president.

Virtually all contributors to this volume were mindful of this reality, often giving little attention to other aspects of the problem. Many tend to treat law as essentially a shorthand term for the power of lawmakers in Congress and discretion as power under the control of the president. The abstract issue of law versus discretion thus is often treated as the balance of power between the two political branches. The frustrations of the Reagan administration are generally described in terms primarily of an excess of congressional muscle flexing or an excess of congressional ambition to manage the details of policy rather than as an excess of "law."

Yet even this formulation of the institutional power battle may put the point in an overly abstract and institutional way. The underlying reality of the Reagan years, as for most of the past two decades, has been that the president is the leader of one political party and Congress is dominated by the opposing political party. So even re-characterizing the issue as Congress versus the president rather than law versus discretion still conceals the underlying tension here—Democrats versus Republicans. Much of the authors' frustration might be interpreted as the cries of one set of partisans against the institutional leverage of their partisan opponents. Many of the presentations were explicitly of this nature.

There is more here than the mere ups and downs of politics, however—certainly more than mere partisan frustration with a constitutional scheme that divides power at the top and an electorate that has reinforced this division (with some help from incumbent-protection laws and gerrymandering, no doubt) by routinely splitting its votes in elections for federal offices. We are now at one of the keys to the issue: the two political parties are not simply parallel coalitions of interests. Rather, each party in modern times has relatively distinct aims and characteristics of its own. Their institutional strangleholds also have distinctive capacities and limitations. If Republicans seemed especially gloomy about the trend of the mid-1980s, there was more to this gloom than just disappointment at their failure to capture power at both ends of Pennsylvania Avenue.

The particular configuration of power in Washington during the 1980s was unfavorable to Republican aims and more conducive to Democratic priorities. This point, implicit in much of what was said at the conference, deserves to be made more explicitly. The liberal majority in the Democratic party was generally skeptical if not outright hostile toward the exercise of U.S. strength in world affairs. Holding fast to what a majority in the party supposed to be the "lessons of Vietnam," most Democrats favored a more cautious, passive, or "multilateral" approach to foreign affairs than the Republicans. In the nature of world affairs and our constitutional scheme, an active foreign policy requires an active president. Even were Congress eager to see an interventionist foreign policy, it could do little to achieve this beyond leaving the president a great deal of maneuvering room and urging him to use it. But a Congress inclined toward passivity and restraint in foreign affairs is inherently better situated to achieve its ends because legal constraints on the executive branch can certainly inhibit action. For liberal Democrats in Congress in the 1980s, the ambitions of their party were very well matched with the opportunities afforded by their institutional place.

This was nowhere clearer than in the regional conflict that dominated much of the Reagan years. Led by the Republican president and backed by Republican congressmen, one national policy was to aid the democratic resistance in Nicaragua, the contras. Led by Speaker of the House of Representatives Jim Wright, the Democratic policy was more ambiguous. The inconsistent policy of support for the contras, then hostility to them, then humanitarian aid only, then military aid, then again no explicit funding was symbolized by the five Boland amendments. At no time was there a clear policy from Congress that no aid should go to the contras. For significant periods, the compromise between the two branches was that aid to the contras would be limited to the efforts of the executive branch acting unilaterally. The risk, which occurred, was that these unilateral acts would later be renounced by Congress. In the end, political accountability was muddled by the failure to pressure the Sandinistas into democratic reform.

Something similar has been true in domestic affairs. For well over fifty years, the Democratic party has stood for the expansion of federal spending and the enlargement of federal controls on the economy. Republicans have generally championed the opposite cause. The Democrats, moreover, have generally embraced a far more heterogeneous coalition than have the Republicans, and they maintain this coalition in part by promising a diverse array of governmental benefits for the various elements in this coalition—in the vernacular, special-interest politics. Log rolling and pork barreling, of course, find their natural home in Congress, where hundreds of independent decision makers must be cajoled into support for each successive bill. Discipline and restraint are much more readily imposed by the executive branch, where only one person at the top needs to be persuaded to impose a veto and, at least in theory, this person has the power to remove any subordinates who oppose his policies.

Here too, then, the institutional interests of Congress were particularly congenial to the political priorities of the Democrats. The opposing objectives of Republicans would have been served by a strong presidency, and a Democrat-controlled Congress therefore had every incentive to resist presidential strength: hence the maneuvers in Congress to circumvent the presidential veto power with new budgeting techniques, including vetoproof, last-minute, and all-in-one continuing resolutions. These and other techniques are well described in the papers by Judith Best, Michael Wallace, and Barbara Hinkson Craig.

In earlier decades, the institutional proclivities of the political parties were less clear. For one thing, through most of this century Democrats championed a more active or internationalist foreign policy, while Republicans urged caution. Even in domestic affairs, Democrats had a considerable stake in a strong presidency when their agenda called for ambitious new legislative programs at a time when only presidential leadership seemed capable of rallying broad enough support for such measures in Congress. To this day, the great Democratic administrations of this century are remembered by the slogans of their legislative programs—the New Deal, Fair Deal, New Frontier, and Great Society. Republican administrations, less eager to embrace ambitious new programs, have left no such rhetorical legacy. The most enduring programmatic slogan of any Republican administration in this century has been President Harding's pledge of a "return to normalcy," a return not then thought to require great exertions of legislative leadership.

For the most part the Reagan administration has adhered to this historical Republican pattern. The tax cuts and early deregulation successes were significant exceptions, using strong Republican presidential leadership to reverse the legacy of earlier Democratic presidential leadership. The Reagan administration, however, never developed much of a legislative agenda despite its great policy ambitions. The administration might well have set its sights higher if it had enjoyed the chance to work with a Republican-dominated Congress. As it was, Reagan policy initiatives were often designed to work around Congress. In effect, this meant that the Reagan administration chose to rely less on the political resources of the presidency than on the institutional prerogatives of the executive branch. But given the partisan configuration of the 1980s, this vastly increased the incentives of Congress to cut down the institutional prerogatives of the executive branch—hence, the Iran-contra "scandal" and budget making by continuing resolution.

The circumstances of the 1980s conspired to tilt the balance quite heavily against executive discretion in favor of legal controls. More than this, it encouraged an especially nasty, sniping sort of legalism where executive branch officials faced the prospect of going to jail for working against the will of some in Congress—even when taking actions that they had every reason to believe were within the legitimate prerogatives of the executive branch. This new trend of prosecutorial politics is illustrated by the independent counsel law, described by Suzanne Garment and former Attorney General William French Smith, and the inflated dudgeon of the Iran-contra hearings described by Michael Malbin.

Restoring Presidential Discretion

What can be done? One can urge the common interest in effective government—in effect, urge everyone to lay aside partisan sympathies and revert to a managerial perspective on governmental operations. The prospects for such a change did not seem very bright at the end of the Reagan presidency and seemed to run counter to the strong trend of the past decades. Some authors of this book counsel patience and the hope that a less skewed partisan alignment in Washington will eventually generate a more receptive political alignment for com-

9

plaints about excessive legalization.

Others urge an appeal to constitutional standards as the ultimate safeguard of executive branch authority. Eugene Rostow, for example, urges litigation to establish the unconstitutionality of congressional constraints on the presidential war powers. It is true and indeed remarkable that there has been no definitive judicial inquiry into the War Powers Resolution, now nearly fifteen years old, or its progeny, including the Boland amendments. Likewise, Judith Best and Barbara Hinkson Craig advocate constitutional appeals to resurrect the presidential veto power from devices that seek to establish direct control of spending or regulatory decisions by Congress and sometimes by its committees alone. Again, it is startling to realize that there has been no constitutional challenge to the Budget and Impoundment Control Act of 1974, which purported to prohibit the traditional power of the president to impound, or refuse to spend, appropriated funds as a tool to control the budget.

The plausibility of this approach derives from the fact that—as Judith Best, Louis Fisher, and others emphasize—the framers of the federal Constitution hoped that their institutional arrangements would protect managerial competence in government. The framers went to considerable lengths to render the chief executive independent of Congress and did so not merely or even primarily because they feared the tyrannical impulses of an overly powerful Congress. From their experience under the Articles of Confederation, where Congress hired and fired all administrative officials on its own initiative, the framers were at least equally mindful of the incompetence and confusion produced by legislative government. They thus sought to develop a system allowing for strong, independent executive action.

Two hundred years later it remains a very plausible—and perhaps proven—argument that the executive branch is more capable of developing consistent and considered policy direction than Congress. The top officials of the executive all owe their allegiance to the winner of one national election; Congress derives its authority from 535 local elections, and none of its members can easily force the others to cooperate in a common scheme. This argument for forceful executive authority is at its strongest, however, only where the actual direction of public policy is already agreed on by all concerned. This is not an argument likely to impress those who strongly disagree with the policies of the incumbent administration. But then, of course, appeals to constitutional requirements are appeals precisely intended to avoid partisan differences. A constitutional system presupposes that legal obligations will be honored by all parties, regardless of the immediate consequences.

Many contributors, however, urge equally plausible objections to such reliance on abstract constitutional principles as a way to rescue executive authority. Many predict that Congress will always be inventive or contriving enough to achieve new forms of control. Secretary of Transportation Jim Burnley emphasizes this congressional creativity in his account of the appropriations control devices that have replaced the formal legislative veto the Supreme Court invalidated in the *Chadha* case. Others warn that leaving discretion or policy initiative to the executive branch would, in practice, often simply entrench the power of career bureaucrats. Alan Keyes even argues that in serious policy battles, an "energetic" executive may find it particularly advantageous to enlist congressional legislation as a force against bureaucratic inertia. Both objections are embraced in more general terms by those who note that the White House is often willing to compromise with Congress rather than stand on principles or presidential prerogatives, to gain policy ground on more immediately pressing issues. This same point is made from somewhat opposing perspectives by Michael Horowitz, who served as chief legal officer in the Reagan Office of Management and Budget, and Louis Fisher of the Congressional Research Service. The argument here is that appeals to constitutional obligations are at best uncertain escapes from the coils of legalism because such appeals have a legalistic rigidity of their own.

For many contributors, then, the best solution is to build up the political strength of the presidency, not to litigate the constitutional rights of the office. The further one follows this logic, of course, the further one gets from defining the issue as one of legislative versus executive powers. The issue immediately becomes a direct confrontation between rival parties and competing partisan interests. Appeals are made to the cause of the president's followers, not to the prerogatives of the office. This strategy looks most attractive to those persuaded that the president and his party can ultimately rally the most popular support; it looks least attractive to those who fear that the president will lose in such confrontations and carry to defeat not just his own policies but also the institutional preconditions for any president successfully implementing his policies: that is, both the president and the presidency will lose. This partisan strategy risks sacrificing the managerial capabilities of the executive required for effective government.

The dilemma need not be this stark because no administration is obliged to pursue one strategy to the complete exclusion of the other. But neither are the underlying tensions likely to disappear. To some extent, they are built into the constitutional scheme, which invites presidents to act simultaneously as administrative chiefs and political

11

leaders. The framers were perfectly well aware that the president would have a personal or political stake in his managerial prerogatives. As the formulation in *The Federalist* put it, the constitutional scheme connects "the interest of the man" to the "constitutional rights of the place." The framers recognized that without a considerable amount of presidential assertiveness, no textual delineation of duties and powers could secure the conditions of "energetic" government. Whatever legal points the president may win in or out of court regarding his constitutional powers, what counts in the end is an administration's political will and capacity to exercise those powers.

Like it or not, the president must be a politician as well as a manager. The framers intended a president who would manage the government; yet they understood the inherent difficulties in managing a nation that is not naturally a single community with entirely harmonious interests. Inevitably, only a president who is an able politician will enjoy the freedom and discretion necessary to carry out his administrative responsibilities. The executive has many inherent powers at his disposal to protect against the legal constraints that cripple effective policy making. The lesson of the past eight years is that these powers must be used with greater vigor and resolve if the presidency is to fulfill its intended role.

PART ONE

Foreign Policy and Defense

2

Separation of Powers and the Use of Force

Abraham D. Sofaer

The subject of separation of powers is of fundamental importance. It goes beyond examining the powers assigned each branch of our federal government, or those concerning particular areas of governmental activity. The separation of powers deals with the broader question of what the assigned or implied powers of particular branches mean when the powers of all three branches are considered together. To answer this question, one must ask what intentions or purposes are implied from the particular assignments of power in the Constitution about the *relative* authority of the branches.

The Constitutional Plan

In designing the Constitution, the framers gave broad authority to the president to conduct the nation's foreign affairs. *The Federalist* explicitly subscribed to an arrangement that would enable the president not only to act with authority, but to act effectively and to negotiate with "secrecy and despatch."[1] At the same time, however, the framers granted Congress powers that they knew would enable Congress—or the Senate alone—to control the president and to frustrate executive objectives. As Corwin put it in his memorable summation, reciting the relevant provisions "amounts to saying that the Constitution, considered only for its affirmative grants of powers which are capable of affecting the issue, is an invitation to struggle for the privilege of directing American foreign policy."[2]

The views expressed here are those of the author alone.

Actually, the Constitution is more than an invitation to struggle. It is a license to do so, which the framers expected and intended to be used, even at the cost of efficiency and effectiveness. The framers had a higher priority—the prevention of tyranny.

In *The Federalist*, Madison responded specifically to the objection that the Constitution failed to separate properly the powers it distributed. He argued that Montesquieu never intended a strict separation of powers, because he had modeled his theory on the British system, which consisted also of a "blend[ing]" of powers.[3] The concept of blending—of giving traditionally executive power to the legislature and vice versa—was designed to protect liberty, which Montesquieu believed would be effectively "subverted" if one branch of government exercised the *whole* power of the other branches.[4] Blending was indispensable, in fact, Madison argued, to maintain a sufficient degree of separation. "Parchment barriers"—even the specific enumeration of powers in a constitution—could not control the conduct of politicians; and appeals to reason, to the public interest, or to the people, had proved impractical or unreliable. The solution attempted in the Constitution, he wrote, was to create an "interior structure" for government with constituent parts that would keep one another in their proper places. "Ambition must be made to counteract ambition. The interest of the man must be connected with the constitutional rights of the place." Madison recognized that, "in republican government, the legislative authority, necessarily, predominates"; but he praised the division of the legislature into two houses, and the veto, as devices intended to protect the executive from being overwhelmed.[5]

This constitutional design was based—as can clearly be inferred from Madison's commentary—on an unflattering view of human nature. Hamilton, commenting on his own criticisms of the anti-Federalists, showed a degree of self-scrutiny and skepticism that remains refreshing:

> We are not always sure that those who advocate the truth are influenced by purer principles than their antagonists. Ambition, avarice, personal animosity, party opposition, and many other motives not more laudable than these, are apt to operate [equally on both sides].[6]

Madison echoed this sentiment in his classic analysis of faction, "the latent causes" of which he found were "sewn in the nature of man."[7] People had good qualities, too, such as compassion, honor, and decency, without which no government, however well devised, could succeed. But these qualities could not be relied on to ensure security or to render the clash of interests "subservient to the public good."[8]

16

The only solution was to control the "effects" of faction through a representative government of divided powers, rather than a democracy, to adopt "this policy of supplying, by opposite and rival interests, the defect of better motives."[9] After all, as he put it, "what is government itself but the greatest of all reflections on human nature?"[10]

Separation of Powers in Practice

American politicians have behaved as Madison and Hamilton anticipated; and the theory of separation of powers the framers advanced has functioned as intended.

• The Congress has, from time to time, demonstrated its ultimate authority to prevent executive initiatives or policies, and to shape national objectives for the executive to pursue. Congress's use of the appropriation power to compel the withdrawal of U.S. forces from Vietnam and to prevent aid to Angola is an example. In general, however, Congress has allowed or authorized the executive to exercise considerable discretion in pursuing national objectives.

• The executive has taken the initiative, especially in foreign and military affairs, relying sometimes upon constitutionally assigned powers and sometimes upon authority granted or allowed by statutes, treaties, or other legislative actions. Often the president has deployed forces on his own constitutional authority, but thereafter relied on express or implied congressional authorization (through funding actions or otherwise) to sustain it.

• Each branch has repeatedly pressed its powers as far as the other allowed or was unable to prevent. Competition for authority—the struggle for control—has been a persistent characteristic of American government.

• The "mixing" of legislative and executive powers and the overlapping jurisdiction of each kind of authority have required the two political branches to share both power and responsibility to enable the United States to act effectively.

In the area of war powers, as in other areas, Congress has from the outset exercised its ultimate authority through the appropriation power by providing or denying the means for conducting military actions; by indicating the policies it insists should be pursued, such as the protection of American commerce, installations, and personnel, or the defense of allies from attack or subversion; by prohibiting various forms of conduct; and by establishing rules for oversight. These legislative actions have left the president with broad powers to use force or to make the use of force more likely because of diplomatic or military activities. Presidents of both parties, both before and after the UN Charter, have repeatedly exercised military power to protect Americans abroad, to protect U.S. property, to defend international rights, and to protect our allies. As Justice Robert H. Jackson said in his profound concurrence in *Youngstown Sheet and Tube*, "Congressional inertia, indifference or quiescence may sometimes, at least as a practical matter, enable, if not invite, measures on independent presidential responsibility."[11]

The resulting pattern reflects the nature of the branches designed by the Constitution. The executive, designed to be effective in conducting the nation's affairs, has utilized express and implied statutory and constitutional authorities, and filled the vacuum created by the absence of legislative regulation. The Congress, given the capacity to check executive authority, but representing diverse factions and having neither the incentive nor the capacity to assume responsibility for particular military initiatives, has allowed the president wide authority to act to achieve commonly held aims, while at the same time second-guessing, criticizing, and placing responsibility upon the executive for initiatives that fail.

The War Powers Resolution

The War Powers Resolution was adopted on November 7, 1973, over President Nixon's veto, just a few days after the "Saturday night massacre." Even at this ebb of executive authority, the resolution recognizes that executive initiative in military affairs for a period of at least sixty days is an expected form of activity in the constitutional framework, though the resolution declares that such authority exists only in limited circumstances.[12] The resolution is faithful to the Constitution's scheme in calling for reports and prior consultation when possible. Congress is entitled to have the information necessary for it to exercise its assigned authority, as well as the opportunity to do so, whenever possible.

The resolution attempts in some other ways, however, to alter the historic pattern of separation of powers in this area:

• It seeks to set a time limit on the president's power to place U.S. forces in the midst of hostilities or in imminently hostile situations, even if, when the president acts, Congress fails to adopt a law ordering the president to stop. Congress has the power, for example, to adopt laws that would prevent the president from using the armed forces in the Persian Gulf. But the War Powers Resolution attempts to achieve that end without requiring Congress to legislate, thereby circumventing the president's power to veto.

• The resolution also attempts to expand Congress's power to control the president by ordering compliance with any concurrent resolution, not subject to veto, that the president cease a military action. Again, Congress has the power to control the president, but it cannot limit otherwise legitimate executive action without passing a law subject to the veto.

• Finally, the resolution attempts to define for all future situations involving hostilities the meaning of legislative consent. Unless Congress passes a law authorizing a specific action with explicit reference to the resolution itself, the resolution asserts, that action has not been authorized.[13] The Congress cannot, however, effectively deprive itself of the power to delegate authority or approve actions in any lawful manner, including, for example, by paying for them.[14] And the resolution cannot constitutionally deprive any sufficient form of legislative approval of its normal legal effect.

The War Powers Resolution has been ineffective in its effort to impose these unprecedented controls on presidents. It has nevertheless had seriously adverse consequences on the effective functioning of both the executive and the legislative branches:

• It has focused attention on legal issues, and away from the merits of particular uses of force. Congress has extensively debated, for example, the sufficiency of prior consultations, the propriety of the form in which reports are submitted, whether U.S. forces are or were in situations of imminent hostilities, and the claimed impropriety of the president's commencing or continuing an operation without specific legislative approval. Debate on these nonsubstantive issues diverts attention from the policy questions, and ultimately from the tough issue of whether Congress should assume clear responsibility by acting to approve, disapprove, or otherwise regulate the action involved.

• These debates reduce the effectiveness of executive action. They can signal a divided nation, giving our adversaries a basis for hoping that the president may be forced to withdraw, or at least may be pressured to do so. In fact the debates often represent only interbranch or partisan rivalry. Our adversaries may be misled in such situations into assuming an absence of national resolve, and thus into making miscalculations that escalate the military and political risks.

• The resolution also reduces the potential effectiveness of the legislature's role. Congress has become a prisoner of the resolution's insistence that the president seek specific legislative approval to continue a regulated action beyond the designated time limits. Since presidents have refused to seek such authority, Congress has been forced to debate or adopt laws authorizing executive actions to avoid appearing to have allowed the president to evade the resolution's requirements. In the most recent of these exercises—the Persian Gulf operation—although many legislators insisted that U.S. forces were in a situation of imminent hostilities, Congress allowed many months to pass without taking any action to authorize or limit this presidential initiative. In such situations Congress is made to seem ineffectual when in fact it has the ultimate power over military actions.

As Senator Sam Nunn, among others, has noted, the resolution is "riddled with defects."[15] These defects all reflect an underlying failure. The resolution is an attempt to change the fundamental nature of American government, the planned separation of powers. Those who support this change are motivated by the desire to rein in the executive—to alter the president's traditional role—in a world they believe is very different from the one that existed in 1789.[16] I disagree with this premise. The need for a strong, effective executive is as great today as ever in our history.

More fundamentally, however, in this our Constitution's bicentennial we should be especially sensitive to the importance of avoiding efforts to advance particular political perspectives by changing the balance of powers the framers so carefully crafted. The Constitution already enables Congress to control the president, when the legislative consensus to do so actually exists. Congress needs no War Powers Resolution to assert this ultimate authority. But when Congress does not form a definitive judgment, for whatever reason, the Constitution was designed to allow the president to act. Hamilton said in *Federalist* No. 23, the authorities essential to the "common defense . . . ought to exist without limitation; *because it is impossible to foresee or define the extent and variety of natural exigencies, or the correspondent extent and variety of the means which may be necessary to satisfy them.*"[17] Congress was not intended to assume primary responsibility for military initiatives, especially those short of war, and that it has seldom overcome the reluctance to do so has characterized its conduct throughout American history.

To accept the War Power Resolution's pattern of regulating military activities, moreover, would justify in principle the same form of regulation in other areas of governmental activity. Instead of an executive capable of protecting the nation's interests, in the absence of legislative direction, the vacuum that exists when Congress is inert, indifferent, or quiescent would remain a vacuum. Real consequences would occur by default, with neither the president nor the Congress accepting clear responsibility for the policy reflected by inaction.

Finally, changes of this sort in the basic structure of our government jeopardize the president's ability to withstand congressional control over all executive powers, making possible the legislative tyranny that Madison, Hamilton, and the other framers worked to prevent. In considering arrangements such as the War Powers Resolution—to the extent they are effective—a great deal more is at stake than whether we should act militarily in one situation or another. Our legislators are no less aggressive in the endless battle for power than are presidents and those who serve the executive branch. Nothing has happened in history to suggest that the unflattering view of human nature shared by men as diverse in their views as Madison and Hamilton is no longer justified. To the contrary, we now realize that our moral perversity goes beyond even our conscious capacity to perceive.

So the basic structure, conceived by the framers, must be preserved. I celebrate it. It helps ensure, through the balanced conflict of the political branches, that we will remain free of the tyranny that would result from unbalanced government, however well intended.

Notes

1. *The Federalist*, J. Cooke, ed. (Middleton, Conn: Wesleyan Univ. Press, 1961), No. 70, p. 472.
2. Edward S. Corwin, *The President: Office and Powers*, 5th ed. (New York: New York University Press, 1984), p. 201.
3. *Federalist* No. 47 (Madison), p. 332.
4. Ibid., pp. 325–26.
5. *Federalist* No. 51 (Madison), pp. 342–49.
6. *Federalist* No. 1 (Hamilton), p. 34.
7. *Federalist* No. 10 (Madison), p. 58.
8. Ibid., p. 60.
9. *Federalist* No. 51 (Madison), p. 349.
10. Ibid.
11. Youngstown Sheet and Tube Co. v. Sawyer, 343 U.S. 579, 637 (1952) (Jackson, Robert H., concurring).
12. War Powers Resolution sections 2(c), 5(b), 50 U.S.C. sections 1541(c), 1544(b).
13. Ibid., section 8(a)(1), 50 U.S.C. section 1547(a)(1).
14. See, for example, Massachusetts v. Laird, 451 F.2d 26 (1st Cir. 1971); DaCosta v. Laird, 448 F.2d 1368 (2d Cir. 1971); Orlando v. Laird, 443 F.2d 1039 (2d Cir. 1971) (all holding that Congress's appropriation of funds for prosecu-

tion of the Vietnam War was constitutionally sufficient authorization of the president to continue the war).

15. Senator Sam Nunn, *Democratic Leadership Council Speech* (Williamsburg, Va., February 29, 1988), p.4.

16. Louis Henkin, "Foreign Affairs and the Constitution," *Foreign Affairs*, vol. 66 (1987), p. 284.

17. *Federalist* No. 23 (Hamilton), p. 147 (emphasis in original).

3

Executive Leadership and Congressional Activism in the Success and Failure of U.S. Policy toward the United Nations

Alan L. Keyes

During the 1970s not only did America lose effective influence at the United Nations but that influence passed into the hands of forces hostile to the interests of the United States and its friends. In a system where results depended on amassing a majority of votes for or against a position, the United States found that it could not reliably sway any bloc of votes. In the give and take of the United Nations's political game, it seemed that we had nothing to give.

This is, of course, a somewhat oversimplified view. The developing countries that controlled the majority bloc of votes in the United Nations were interested in greater access to the financial and technological resources of the Western countries. Through such devices as the New International Economic Order (NIEO) and the proposal for comprehensive global negotiations on economic issues, they attempted to create structures that would allow them to use the majority-dominated political process of the United Nations to win material concessions from the West (including Japan). Theoretically the desire of the developing countries for economic concessions might have been used to coin political capital for the West—that is, to gain the votes of the developing nations on political issues at the United Nations in exchange for Western concessions on the economic issues.

In fact, however, this trade-off was not feasible. Most of the developing countries, particularly the more weighty ones (Brazil, India, and Mexico), believed they could secure better economic terms

23

by dealing with Western countries on an individual basis. For many developing countries, the United Nations seemed more attractive as an arena in which to work off the domestic political costs of these close Western ties—to posture as vocal supporters of radical or "progressive" international views. By cooperating with the more radical Soviet aligned states of the majority bloc on political issues that served Soviet interests, they could avoid, or at least postpone, the day when those forces would target them as candidates for internal agitation or subversion. Where this was not a threat, the United Nations could still be used to placate left-leaning elements of a governing coalition that might otherwise make more trouble at home.

The Western countries also lacked the interest or coherence to engage in such a strategy. Given their power in the world at large, they had no reason to prefer dealing with economic issues in an environment that exaggerated the power of the developing countries. Moreover, the Europeans preferred to deal individually with political issues, using their own influence when their interests were directly affected, feeling little need or inclination to show solidarity with the United States as a matter of course. Some, like the Scandinavian countries and Ireland, affected a stance of practical nonalignment on political questions. Others, like Greece, could often be found blatantly aligned with the majority bloc in an anti-U.S. stance.

The lack of a cohesive Western bloc damaged America's influence at the United Nations more than it affected that of the other Western countries. With fewer international interests or commitments, to begin with, the other Western countries could more readily approach international issues through bilateral negotiations on the side. France, for instance, could exert leverage on the West Africans when threatened with UN censure for its actions toward its Pacific territories. Britain could mobilize some activity among the Commonwealth developing countries. The United States, however, found itself in the ineffective position of treating everything as important, while leaving the distinct impression that nothing was so important that a country's attitude toward the United States would affect its relations with the United States in the world at large.

Thus neither the preponderance of Western global economic power nor the importance to most countries of their ties with the United States provided a basis for effective U.S. influence in the United Nations. The United States had one further potential source of influence—its role as the chief contributor to the UN budget. But a reverent habit of decades had invested the UN contributions with a privileged status in the U.S. budget. Successive administrations intoned ritual phrases about America's treaty obligations, without seriously examining just what they were. Congress nodded respectfully and sent the money along.

The forfeiture of U.S. influence at the United Nations resulted at least in part from the fact that few policy makers in the U.S. government were interested in retaining it. Apart from those moments when serious crises in the Middle East or elsewhere momentarily spilled into the Security Council, the United Nations's activities seemed to be an unimportant, though occasionally annoying, sideshow. Ambassador Daniel Patrick Moynihan breathed life into America's UN representation long enough to witness and condemn one of the General Assembly's ugliest attacks on Israel. As secretary of state, Henry Kissinger had a brief and lamentable burst of interest during the mid-1970s when, among other things, the NIEO was born. During the Carter administration UN Ambassador Andrew Young explored the United Nations as a platform for domestic strains of anti-Americanism. None of these periods saw a sustained effort to understand the UN political game in its own terms. In none of these periods was there any effort to explore the ways and means of increasing America's ability to deal effectively with the United Nations.

The U.S. Mission under Reagan

Under Jeane Kirkpatrick's leadership, President Reagan assembled a team at the U.S. Mission to the United Nations determined to make such an effort. Kirkpatrick and her colleagues undertook to understand the language and logic that prevailed at the United Nations and to use that understanding to combat the campaigns being waged against the United States, its policies, values, and friends. This required, among other things, a thoughtful effort to articulate for others in the U.S. government and for the American public at large, a clear analysis of the threat to American interests posed by events at the United Nations. Though this effort encompassed a number of areas, including human rights and economic issues, it focused especially on the political issues, highlighting in particular the campaign being waged against the legitimacy of the state of Israel and of America's relations with Israel.

Congressional actions with respect to the United Nations must be viewed in the context of the assertive leadership that came from the administration, and especially from the U.S. delegation to the United Nations, during the first Reagan administration. This leadership sparked and guided congressional interest, enabling key congressional actors to identify opportunities for legislative action that would strengthen the leverage, influence, and bargaining power of the U.S.

delegation. These opportunities fell into three broad areas:

- congressional actions that served notice on the United Nations as a whole that certain excesses would induce a tough American reaction, with broad bipartisan political support in the United States
- congressional actions that made clear to all the member states that their actions in the United Nations were under scrutiny and could have consequences for their bilateral relations, including foreign assistance, with the United States
- congressional actions that made use of the leverage implied by the sizable U.S. share of the UN budget to express U.S. displeasure with particular UN actions or to impel the organization to address fundamental institutional imbalances

The first area involved what proved to be the highly effective U.S. strategy to deflect efforts to expel Israel from the UN General Assembly. This effort was the prospective culmination of the campaign to delegitimize Israel by reducing it to the same pariah status the United Nations had more or less successfully imposed on South Africa. Early in President Reagan's first term, the United States scotched the momentum of the expulsion effort with a diplomatic campaign that argued forcefully that it violated the UN Charter's fundamental principles. The administration punctuated this diplomacy with the declaration that, should Israel be expelled from the United Nations, the United States would also withdraw. Congress initiated this step with a joint resolution that made clear that U.S. withdrawal would involve the suspension of U.S. contributions until such time as Israel was reinstated.

The congressional initiative buttressed the credibility of the U.S. government's stand. It made clear that the United Nations would pay a heavy financial cost if the warning were ignored. It also prevented antiadministration elements among the UN delegations and in the UN Secretariat from weakening the impact of the declaration by portraying it as an extreme stance whose implementation could be complicated or blocked by political controversy in the United States. The effect of this congressional action was important not only in this instance but for the success of the entire more assertive approach adopted by the administration.

Resistance to the Administration's Approach

It is appropriate to note here that within the U.S. government itself the approach undertaken by the Kirkpatrick team met with resistance.[1] Bureaucratic inertia partly accounted for this, as well as a fundamentally different view of the United Nations and America's role in it. Career professionals in the International Organization (IO) bureau were unaccustomed to the idea that the UN arena was an ideological battleground where adverse results represented damaging defeats for the United States. Some regarded the new assertiveness as unnecessarily confrontational. They feared that the tactics it implied would provoke criticism from America's Western partners and damage UN institutional processes. Congressional actions that required a firmer U.S. stance served as a useful counterpoise to these hesitations and doubts. In some instances they also imposed legal requirements that usefully goaded and structured the bureaucracy's activities.

One such instance was the legislative requirement for an annual report, prefaced by the U.S. permanent representative, on the voting practices of UN member states. The requirement gave rise to an annual exercise that focuses the attention, first of the bureaucracy and then of the public at large, on the comparative performance of other member states vis-à-vis the United States. Not only the IO bureau but also each of the regional bureaus in the State Department must annually devote attention to UN voting results.

The specter of informed congressional interest in the voting behavior of the member states explains the attention that the bureaucracy, albeit reluctantly, devotes to the report. The resources Congress provides for foreign assistance, as well as the decisions it can take affecting terms of trade and other bilateral economic relations, loom large in the minds of at least some of the State Department's regional offices. To the African bureau especially these resources matter, as signals that reinforce or undermine the bilateral political relations the bureau seeks to maintain with particular governments.

As yet there have been no specific instances in which congressional action on such matters was explicitly based on the information provided by the voting practices report.[2] This does not mean, however, that it has had no impact. Other member states, particularly those who receive significant amounts of U.S. assistance, have shown serious interest in the report and have been at pains to react to any unfavorable impression it creates. In many instances the release of the report is the occasion for a discussion between the U.S. ambassador and the foreign minister or head of state about a country's UN record. In that discussion the possible consequences of the record are more credible than in the past, thanks to the knowledge on both sides that Congress possesses information on the basis of which individual members could make specific legislative proposals. Some states, such as Brazil and Mexico, have even undertaken voting studies of their own as a basis for responding to U.S. criticisms based on the report.

The annual report on UN voting behavior begins to breach the firewall that separates UN and bilateral affairs. It includes information that could be a useful catalyst for congressional action with respect to specific countries that reinforces the perception that a country's UN behavior has consequences. Such action should respond to positive as well as negative behavior. Smaller countries, for which U.S. assistance can be a significant financial boost, may be especially susceptible to a judicious combination of punishments and rewards directly linked to their UN voting records.[3] An argument can be made, however, that this approach has unavoidable limitations. Decisions affecting U.S. relations with a given country must take account of a variety of interests. The role of countries like Egypt and Pakistan in U.S. policy toward sensitive areas may be rightly judged to be more important than any negative or positive contribution they make in the United Nations. Particular circumstances affecting U.S. influence in a country may also preclude a tough reaction to a negative pattern of UN behavior. The State Department's regional bureaus try to erect these concerns into a blanket objection to the linking approach, but their misuse of the arguments does not mean that they can simply be ignored.[4]

It would be a mistake, therefore, to rely exclusively on efforts to link bilateral and multilateral behavior as the means to enhance U.S. influence in the UN arena. U.S. efforts to influence the behavior of individual countries at the bilateral level must be augmented by efforts to make use of the collective interest member states have in the United Nations itself. Apologists for the organization sometimes point out that smaller, less powerful countries have a greater stake in the United Nations than the United States because they see it as an opportunity to play a role on the world stage that would otherwise be unavailable to them. By organizing into voting blocs, certain groups of countries (particularly the Africans and the Arabs) have used (or misused, as the case may be) the United Nations to focus international attention on issues and problems they consider critical.[5] Given such interests, these countries (which are the majority of the UN membership) want the organization to survive. They realize, however, that it could not survive without the active support and participation of the United States.

The Kassebaum-Solomon Language

The third category of congressional actions made use of the leverage implied in this situation. Congress began to impose conditions on the authorization and appropriation of these funds. In some instances these conditions were meant to express disapproval for specific activities of groups recognized and supported by the United Nations. In other instances they were meant to stimulate administrative and management improvements in the UN bureaucracy. This approach culminated in the well-known Kassebaum-Solomon language in the State Department's fiscal year 1986 authorization bill, language that became the basis for a strategy aimed at altering the balance of power between the United States and the UN majority.

During the early Reagan years Congress became more aware of, and concerned about, the UN role in several areas that aroused passionate political interest. The disregard for UN Charter principles that emerged in the campaign against Israel, the countenancing of acts of international terrorism by the Palestine Liberation Organization (PLO) and others, and the abuse of UN practices and diplomatic status by the Soviets and other East bloc states aroused angry sentiments. This shattered the tradition that had shielded the U.S. contribution to the United Nations from the usual vicissitudes of the legislative process. The Congress enacted language requiring that the U.S. contribution to UN organizations be reduced by its proportionate share of any funds going to organizations that practiced or supported terrorism, in particular the PLO or the Southwest African People's Organization (SWAPO). In effect this legislation forced the State Department to seek, for the first time, a full and general accounting of UN expenditures for these organizations. Though the amounts involved were small, the automatic reductions put the United Nations on notice that any enlargement of its involvement with these groups would mean a corresponding reduction in financial support from the United States. Like the threat of U.S. withdrawal in the event of expulsion, these congressional actions deterred further intensification of the negative trends in the organization.

As the congressional role evolved, legislation moved from deterrence to compulsion. One UN agency (the UN High Commissioner for Refugees) had to submit to an external audit or risk a reduction in U.S. support. Another faced tough scrutiny over its possible role in encouraging violence among the school-age Palestinian refugee population. Not every congressional concern produced legislative proposals, and most of the legislative proposals were not enacted into law. But the United Nations had become fair game.

A number of factors that contributed to this trend were not exclusively related to the United Nations or UN policy. Like most parts of the foreign assistance budget, the UN appropriation had no strong domestic constituency. Its anti-American image made it a suitable whipping boy for politicians who wanted to demonstrate their fiscal severity while taking a popular swipe at America's foreign critics and enemies. In addition, the U.S. government entered a period of intense concern over budget deficits. This intensified the haphazard annual search on Capitol Hill for expedients that could result in real or paper savings. Once the lid was removed from the UN pot, the temptation to dip into it in favor of other, more politically salient priorities, became politically irresistible. The congressional internationalists who might once have defended the UN contribution out of personal conviction were reluctant or embarrassed to take a stand that might be seen as abetting the organization's antisemitic, anti-American, pro-Soviet character.

Given these factors, by the time the Kassebaum-Solomon language passed into law, pressures were building for significant cuts in overall funding for the United Nations. Proposals were floated that would have required that the U.S. contribution be cut back to a level equal to that of the Soviets, that it be no more than 10 percent of the UN budget (down from 25 percent), and the like. In the end, the Kassebaum-Solomon authorizing language mandated, beginning in fiscal year 1987, a 20 percent reduction in the overall U.S. contribution to the United Nations until there was a fundamental change in the way the General Assembly made its decisions on budgetary matters. Instead of the majoritarian principle, the language demanded that voting power on budgetary matters be in proportion to a government's financial contribution to the organization. The language represented a major shift in both the aims and the methods of the congressional approach to the United Nations. In fact, in the guise of another tactical contribution, the Congress dictated a major shift in U.S. strategy toward the organization. The new strategy aimed to achieve a major breakthrough in the U.S. position at the United Nations, one that would alter the organization's political power structure completely. It was a bold step. With care, persistence, and a rare combination of toughness and adaptability, it had a good chance of success. Unfortunately, neither the Congress, which initiated it, nor those at the very top in the State Department, where its implementation had to be worked out, had the understanding or seriousness of purpose needed to make it work.

The congressional action had a considerable impact within the UN system. Disbelief and evasiveness gave way to a short-term but very real sense of urgency when the congressionally mandated short-fall in the U.S. contribution took effect.[6] In the wake of the legislation, the General Assembly established a high level group of experts to make proposals for reforms in UN administrative and decision-making procedures. Faced with the likelihood of large cuts in available cash, the secretariat made plans to reduce its projected outlays. The secretary general appealed to other member states to make their contributions early. He called for a special session of the General Assembly to deal with the organization's fiscal crisis.

This is not the place to review the details of the negotiating process that unfolded in the United Nations during the next year. By September 1986 the congressional initiative had been translated into a major U.S. effort to change the UN budget decision-making process, an effort that dominated the General Assembly's 1986 session. That effort resulted in an agreement by which the General Assembly approved, in modified form, some of the personnel reductions and administrative reforms recommended by the high level group of experts. More important, the assembly agreed to language that had the potential to shift the UN budget decision-making process from majority rule to a consensus-based process, in which the United States could have exercised a virtual veto over displeasing elements of the UN budget.

Here the emphasis is on the word *potential*. The results of the 1986 General Assembly did not in fact achieve the shift in the balance of power envisaged by the Kassebaum-Solomon language. It had created a beachhead from which the United States could advantageously launch its effort to secure that basic shift. The "big stick" had produced a big opportunity. At this point, it became necessary to play upon the hopes, as well as the fears, of those who felt the greatest stake in the future of the United Nations. Congress needed to demonstrate that movement toward its position could have a positive effect but without reducing the short-term financial pressure on the United Nations. The recipe for achieving this was quite simple—authorize and appropriate the funds needed to meet the full U.S. contribution to the United Nations but make satisfactory completion of the basic decision-making reforms the condition for actual payment of part or all of the appropriation. Movement along these lines in 1987 would have produced maximum pressure for a satisfactory outcome at the

1987 session of the General Assembly.

Things did not turn out that way, however. Neither the key actors in Congress nor the highest-level officials in the State Department had a concept of the goal of U.S. policy commensurate with the instruments being employed. The Kassebaum-Solomon language rolled out a major threat for the sake of a major restructuring of power. Yet key figures in the Congress and the administration spoke as if the aim of it all was to eliminate a few UN jobs and achieve some significant but easily reversible reductions in the UN budget. Given this failure to appreciate the overall goal implied in the congressional initiative, it was hard for these actors to understand or articulate the reasons for giving the UN policy special attention in the budget process. Through most of 1987 it appeared, therefore, as if the Congress would not relent (that is, the severe budget pressure on the United Nations would continue). Yet at the start of the 1987 General Assembly it began to seem that Congress would restore funding but at the wrong time and for the wrong reasons. This combination squandered the opportunity created by the Kassebaum-Solomon initiative.

Reasons for Failure

I believe that several things account for this failure. One explanation is a lack of serious, competent judgment among the highest-level decision makers in the State Department. Another had to do with the shift in the balance of power within the bipartisan congressional coalition on UN issues that followed the 1986 congressional elections. This latter contributed to a third, which surfaced in the intensification of congressional micromanagement of policy during the 1987 budget process.

The failure of judgment at the helm of the State Department resulted from a special combination of weaknesses. On the one hand, top officials simply could not take UN policy at all seriously. This meant that they did not appreciate the institutional changes at stake in the U.S. reform effort. On the other, they were susceptible to the influence of UN apologists who believed that U.S. pressures were illegal, counterproductive, or already effective enough to be removed. Moved by these influences, they periodically signaled the UN leadership that the whole U.S. effort aimed to produce a "fig leaf" that would provide the excuse for revising an ill-advised congressional maneuver.

These attitudes sowed the seeds of inconsistency, confusion, and misunderstanding on Capitol Hill. The best example of this is the bureaucratic maneuvering that surrounded preparation of the administration's proposal to amend the Kassebaum-Solomon language in light of the results of the 1986 General Assembly session. Prior to subcommittee deliberations in the House, efforts were made to dilute the language tying payment of the appropriated funds to satisfactory implementation of the decision-making reforms.[7] In fact, after formal agreement had been reached in the department, the diluted language was stealthily substituted for the other and sent to Capitol Hill. In the end, behind-the-scenes negotiations on Capitol Hill led to a House version in line with the originally agreed approach, but the inclinations of some in the State Department had been clearly revealed, though they lacked the confidence to display them openly.

Despite the initial success of the congressional strategy, therefore, a covert desire existed at the upper levels in the State Department to back away from this high-stakes strategy. After the 1986 elections this desire gained strength on Capitol Hill. Weakened by the electoral outcome, some Republican actors gradually reduced their interest and shied away from the larger goals they had originally articulated. Others remained unconvinced that the reforms produced at the 1986 General Assembly offered real advantages to the United States. On the Democratic side, some simply wished to deny the Reagan administration or its allies in the Congress the chance to claim a success.

The main problem with the Democrats, however, was the fact that any UN policy considerations were subordinate to the larger struggle with the administration with regard to general budget priorities. As part of this struggle the newly consolidated congressional majority resorted to detailed micromanagement, probably as a means of fragmenting bureaucratic interests and decreasing whatever ability the president had to impose discipline on the various departments and agencies. In the UN accounts, this expressed itself in moves toward full earmarking of all the subelements in the account—an approach that made it far more difficult to adjust the U.S. government's response to the character and situation of each UN agency.

In retrospect, I believe that congressional activism in recent years made a positive contribution to U.S. policy toward the United Nations. The preconditions for that success must, however, be clearly understood. Congress acted in response to executive leadership. During the period of its greatest success, congressional action came in partnership with the executive. The legislation it enacted created or reinforced the leverage and influence of those implementing policy. It also provided a sense of the overall direction of policy acceptable to the Congress and to the people it represented.

When the executive leadership weakened, the partnership lost much of its energy.[8] Ironically, it had sufficient momentum to produce a significant breakthrough in 1986, but the fruits of that victory have fallen by the wayside. If there is a lesson to be drawn from the experience, it may be that the chief asset of the executive branch is the clear purpose and quality and political strength of its own leadership. If the executive has a clear purpose, the skill to pursue it, and the will to build the political strength to back up that skill, congressional activism can be an asset.

Notes

1. In the maneuvering that preceded congressional passage of the legislation concerning Israeli expulsion, for instance, individuals in the State Department tried to get the language on U.S. contributions amended to provide for payment of U.S. contributions to an escrow account during the period of U.S. withdrawal. The United Nations would have faced no permanent loss in the event the General Assembly proceeded with the expulsion.

2. This is not to say that UN behavior has never been linked to a cut in U.S. assistance. In the wake of the Security Council sessions on the Soviet shooting of KAL 007, the administration cited Zimbabwe's displeasing performance as part of the rationale for a reduction in the requested U.S. aid. It was, however, one of a number of factors contributing to a deterioration of U.S.-Zimbabwe relations at that time.

3. It is especially important that smaller countries that are supporters or potential supporters of the United States be made to see their UN performance as an opportunity for attracting favorable attention that they would otherwise be unable to hope for.

4. The best approach would probably be to make an example each year of several of the most egregious (and vulnerable) offenders, as well as several of our most faithful friends.

5. For several years running, for instance, the Africans were able to use the United Nations as a platform for directing world attention and action toward their economic plight. The humanitarian passions aroused by the effects of drought, famine, disease, and infestation were magnified and more effectively mobilized as a result.

6. A step that Congress had taken for reasons of expediency some time before also increased the impact of the Kassebaum-Solomon withholdings. To achieve a one-time savings, Congress shifted the payment of U.S. contributions from one fiscal year to the next. This meant that U.S. obligations for calendar year 1986 came out of the FY 1987 budget. It also meant that the U.S. payment was delayed until the beginning of the fiscal year in October. By the time the United Nations received the U.S. payment, it was critical to the organization's cash flow. This naturally increased UN anxiety at the prospect of large reductions in U.S. support.

7. The difference was over whether, in response to the failure to implement the reforms, the United States should simply continue the Kassebaum restrictions or toughen them. The United Nations had already adjusted to the

Kassebaum levels. In fact, actual shortfalls in U.S. contributions for FY 1987 (calendar year 1986) exceeded the Kassebaum levels. Merely continuing the Kassebaum restrictions might therefore have meant an increase in actual U.S. payments in response to inaction on reform. By tying performance to a proportion of the funds appropriated, one ensured that the United Nations would pay a penalty for nonperformance, no matter what level of funding the Congress decided on. This made it difficult for the organization to develop a plan for absorbing or circumventing U.S. financial pressure. It guaranteed that there would be no business as usual until U.S. concerns were addressed.

8. The departure of Ambassador Kirkpatrick began this process. The loss of the Senate in 1986 accelerated it. The prevalence of poor judgment at the top of the State Department completed it.

4

Commentaries and Exchanges on Foreign Policy

Commentary by Elliott Abrams

Let me start, as seems appropriate for this topic, with the words of Alexander Hamilton. In *Federalist* No. 71 he wrote:

> The tendency of the legislative authority to absorb every other has been fully displayed and illustrated by examples. . . . In governments purely republican, this tendency is almost irresistible. Representatives of the people in a popular assembly seem sometimes to fancy that they are the people themselves, and betray strong symptoms of impatience and disgust at the least sign of opposition from any other quarter, as if the exercise of its rights — by either the Executive or the Judiciary — were a breach of their privilege and an outrage to their dignity. They often appear disposed to exert imperious control over the other departments and as they commonly have the people on their side, they always act with such momentum as to make it very difficult for the other members of the government to maintain the balance of the Constitution.

The road is a long one from there to the Foreign Assistance Act of 1989, one passage of which bears quotation here:

> **Sec. 702, Subsection A, "Military Aircraft Transfers."** During fiscal years 1988 and 1989 the authorities of Part 2 of the Foreign Assistance Act 1961, and the Arms Export Control Act may not be used to make available any helicopters or other aircraft for military use and license may not be issued under Section 38 of the Arms Export Control Act for the export of any such aircraft to any country in Central America, unless the Committee on Foreign Affairs and Committee on

Appropriations of the House of Representatives, and the Committee on Foreign Relations and the Committee on Appropriations of the Senate are notified, in writing, at least 15 days in advance. . . .

Subsection B: Military aircraft provided by other countries during fiscal years 1988 and 1989. The Secretary of State shall promptly notify the committees designated in Subsection A whenever any helicopters, or other aircraft for military use are provided to any country in Central America by any foreign country.

What we see here is an assertion of power by the legislative branch. This was predictable. Indeed, it was predicted. This measure exemplifies precisely the sort of constitutional distemper that Hamilton warned about in *Federalist* No. 71. This sort of struggle over policy between the legislative and executive branches has been going on for a very long time. To some extent it is built into our system of checks and balances, but there is also something new in this.

What is new, I would argue—and what makes the system in some respects not only different but much worse—is the infusion of ideology and partisan politics into the struggles between the legislative and executive branches, so that the struggle between the branches today is also, in many areas, a struggle between left and right. The reason for this is not hard to find. It is that the Democratic party essentially controls the legislative branch and has for quite a long time and the Republican party has controlled the executive branch for sixteen of the past twenty years. This partisan imbalance has changed the situation for the worse.

The roots of the ideological conflict that now divides the parties can be traced back to Vietnam. This can be illustrated with another quotation:

The source of an effective foreign policy under our system is presidential power. It is my conviction that for the existing requirements of American foreign policy we have hobbled the president with too niggardly a grant of power. It is highly unlikely that we can successfully execute a long-term program for the taming or containing of today's aggressive and revolutionary forces, by continuing to leave vast and vital decision-making powers in the hands of a decentralized, independent-minded, largely parochial body of legislators.

That was said in 1961 by J. William Fulbright. Later he came to a different view—the view for which he is now remembered as a champion of legislative prerogatives against an "imperial presidency." Fulbright came to this later view, I would suggest, for ideological reasons. Like many in the Democratic party, he turned against presidential power when he turned against the Vietnam War in the mid-1960s. This view came to prevail in Congress when the political left realized that Congress could be used to thwart an active, anti-Communist foreign policy and that Congress could be relied on to do this, because of the virtually permanent control of the Democratic party over the House of Representatives and indeed—for most of the past twenty years—over the Senate.

Others have emphasized that the assertion of congressional power against the executive has been accompanied by an increasing legalization of policy making. But the ideological factor—the struggle between left and right—has added particular force to this trend in relation to foreign policy. We have seen a vast increase in statutory restrictions on the power of the president to conduct foreign policy. This does not happen just because congressmen like to be powerful. It happens, too, because today's congressmen seek to pursue a political or ideological agenda in foreign affairs. And they pursue it pretty well.

In the past few years, there has been a new twist. It has occurred to people in Congress that their assertions of power are, after all, laws and that officials in the executive branch can therefore be punished for violating them. Congress, then, can do more than simply yell at executive officials when it finds fault with their decisions; it can accuse them of committing crimes. That is the latest chapter in this twenty-year struggle for control of foreign policy—not just the legalization of policy disputes but the criminalization of policy decisions.

What is to be done about this? I have no simple answers. But it is obvious that, were one party—either party—to have control of both the legislative and executive branches for as much as eight years, much of the current pattern would dissipate. Perhaps then the ideological conflict that inflames so much of the current struggle between Congress and the executive would also settle down. Perhaps then we might return to the more routine disputes between the branches that our system of separated powers and checks and balances must always entail. Although I would prefer the Republican party to control the two branches, even a period of unified control by the Democrats would be a good thing for the health of our system, because it would take much of the partisan and ideological venom out of the current disputes between the branches.

This ideological venom in the relations between Congress and the executive makes it particularly difficult to conduct a sensible foreign policy. There will always be some friction between Congress and the president; but foreign policy was not, in earlier times, so entangled in ideological struggles between the parties, and it need not always be like this in the future.

Commentary by Eugene V. Rostow

Our constitutonal order has extremely powerful built-in stabilizers, and the American people—who are generally more sensible than their leaders—have thus far prevented the emergence of anything like a mindless government, dominated by the passions of the mob. I believe this will always be so, but only on one condition: that we elect presidents who are willing to fight for the prerogatives of the presidency, not only in Congress and before the people but also in the courts.

I agree with much of the current criticism of excessive reliance on litigation and the proliferation of judicial power. But when it comes to keeping the constitutional balance between Congress and the president in the field of foreign affairs, the courts are now the only branch of government capable of effective action, because the overriding institutional loyalties of most members of Congress are to their own team or their own tribe, that is, to Congress itself. Thus it is utopian to imagine that Congress and the president can work out any sort of compromise that will restore the presidency to the position it had for a very long time in our national life.

The declining power of the executive in foreign affairs is often linked to the reactions to our experience in Vietnam. But I believe it is tied up with the reaction to a more profound and far-reaching development. That is the evolution of the international system in the twentieth century, which has changed the foreign policy burdens of the United States profoundly and permanently. It shocked Americans in this century, when they noticed that the nineteenth century had ended, that the security of the United States could no longer be protected by the Concert of Europe and the British fleet. We continue to resist this development. We fight it all the time and try to pretend it has not happened. But it has happened, and it entails all sorts of responsibilities and activities alien to the myth we cherish about the nature of our foreign policy. This has provoked a real rebellion against the constitutional order.

Congress has responded to the national unease about foreign policy by promising to curb the wicked "imperial president" who craves adventure and glory abroad. Congress has promised the people immunity from wars and other troubles by wise legislation. We tasted the bitter fruits of such folly at Pearl Harbor nearly fifty years ago. In the 1930s, as the danger of war increased, we tried to head it off with neutrality and embargo legislation—when the very opposite was needed. We have not learned the lessons of that era. The encroachments of Congress on the executive power in foreign affairs have nearly brought us to a paralysis in foreign policy. This can have very serious consequences, even when we do not face challenges on quite the scale of the 1930s.

Let me offer one example from my own experience in the Lyndon Johnson administration—from the era when the contemporary unease about presidential power in foreign affairs began to attain its paralyzing force. In the last years of the administration a crisis loomed in the Middle East—the crisis that finally brought about the Six-Day War of June 1967. It began in the previous year and reached a climax in May when President Gamal Abdel Nasser of Egypt closed the Strait of Tiran to Israeli shipping. This act was in violation of promises made by Egypt to the United States in 1957, as part of the settlement of an earlier war between Egypt and Israel. Free passage through the Strait of Tiran was of great strategic importance to Israel; it had been agreed in 1957 that Israel would be justified in responding with force if the strait was ever again closed to its shipping by force. War in the Middle East thus seemed inevitable unless some way could be found to reverse Nasser's decision.

To head off this threat, the United States, Great Britain, and other countries assembled naval vessels in the Red Sea, just outside the Strait of Tiran. We thought that by escorting a convoy of ships through the Egyptian blockade, we could force the reopening of the strait and avert an escalation of the crisis. As a matter of law, I think it is clear that the president did not need congressional approval for this maneuver, which constituted a limited use of force in self-defense and did not require a declaration of war. Furthermore, Congress had already affirmed, in 1957 and again in 1961, the readiness of the United States to resort to force to keep the Strait of Tiran open. But by 1966 President Johnson was deeply embroiled in controversy over the war in Vietnam, and it was therefore judged politically indispensable for him to get congressional approval before taking decisive action in the Middle East to carry out Eisenhower's promise.

The result was that no decisive action was taken by the United States. We were delayed by the complexities of arguing and drafting such a resolution, and before it could be voted on, the situation on the ground had drastically changed. Attention shifted from the closing of the Strait of Tiran to the mobilization of the Egyptian army. Finally

Israel launched a preemptive attack to cope with a threatened invasion from Egypt, Jordan, Syria, and Iraq. Constitutional controversy between Congress and the president delayed American action at a time when quick and energetic action was urgently needed. While we delayed, the war exploded.

Today we are experiencing a somewhat different form of congressional overreaching, arising from the efforts of Senators Sam Nunn and Joseph Biden and others to bind the president to particular interpretations of treaties in the course of Senate ratification. At best this seems to me an exercise in jurisprudential naiveté. A treaty, like a statute or a constitutional provision or any law, inevitably grows and develops through time, as the broad purposes of its draftsmen—and those who voted for it—are adapted to new and often unforeseen circumstances. It is in the spirit of King Canute to try to tell the president that a treaty or any other law will mean A rather than B or C forevermore. The learned senators are struggling in vain. What they are trying to do is simply contrary to the nature of law.

Such efforts also seem to me a clear violation of constitutional limitations, for they seek to establish what is, in effect, a legislative veto on the president's authority—an authority he must exercise every day in interpreting and applying treaties and statutes. The president is responsible for enforcing and executing hundreds, perhaps thousands, of treaties. Every time the president instructs our UN ambassadors how to vote on a resolution before some organ of the United Nations, for example, he is interpreting the UN Charter—a legally binding treaty—and applying it to a new situation. The problem is exactly the same in dealing with international aviation problems, fishing, telecommunications, trade negotiations, and hundreds of other treaty obligations. For the Senate to try to keep control over the evolution of a treaty forever is to cross the boundary between the legislative power and the executive power under the Constitution.

I blame our presidents, in considerable part, for allowing things to reach this extreme. They have hesitated to go to the courts for protection. Some presidents have ideological inhibitions about using the courts to handle such problems. Others have simply preferred to treat this as an entirely political problem and to solve it, issue by issue, through political deals with Congress. But there are some subjects on which deals are not possible, and in such instances it is necessary to invoke constitutional standards. In many cases, such as the Senate's current bid for control over the interpretation of treaties, I think a forceful presentation of the president's claims would have a good chance of rallying public opinion. But presidents must also be prepared to consider the use of the courts to try to restore the balance.

Appeals for better consultation with Congress will not solve the problem. Of course, Senator Arthur Vandenberg spoke with much sense in the late 1940s when he urged presidents to consult with Congress before "taking off" on a foreign policy initiative if they wanted Congress to remain on board for the landing. This is elemental political prudence. But "consultation" is not a term of any fixed constitutional meaning, and it cannot be legislated into practice. It is a matter of political intuition and of discretion. President Johnson caught this exactly in musing on why Senator Vandenberg's maxim had failed him in Vietnam. He had not only consulted with Congress but obtained congressional endorsement for his Vietnam policies in vote after vote. "I thought," he said, "I had them with me on the takeoff because I wanted them with me for the crash landing. But I forgot one thing—parachutes."

That is the essence of the problem—responsibility. The president has the prime responsibility under the Constitution for the conduct of foreign affairs. He cannot exercise his responsibility if he does not defend his powers.

JEREMY RABKIN: Dean Rostow's suggestion that the courts should be brought in to arbitrate disputes between Congress and the president over foreign affairs seems to me a very problematic notion. Whatever might be said for congressmen playing a role in foreign policy, the judiciary seems terribly ill equipped to settle large questions in this area. Isn't legalism more often the problem than the solution?

MR. ROSTOW: I would not say that for a moment. The Supreme Court has always decided questions about the allocation of power between the branches. It does not have to go into the substance of the underlying policy issues at all. The Court has had no trouble in recent years deciding extremely sensitive questions about the separation of powers on issues involving voting rights and many other things. The *Chadha* case, for example, came along in 1983 without any prompting from the top of the government. In deciding that challenge to a legislative veto provision, the Supreme Court went out of its way to declare unconstitutional some 200 statutes with such provisions, provisions that have been accumulating since 1932. Congress has since lived in a state of contempt of court or, more politely, of civil disobedience on this question, treating other legislative veto provisions as if they were still valid. But this does not change the legal force of the decision.

I regret the unwillingness of the Reagan administration to pursue these issues. When 101 congressmen brought a suit demanding enforcement of the War Powers Act, the administration, instead of seizing the occasion to argue the unconstitutionality of that act, fought the suit on jurisdictional grounds. I am all in favor of bipartisan cooperation between the president and Congress in foreign policy, but part of the president's power to lead in achieving cooperation with Congress depends on congressional recognition of the president's constitutional authority and the limits it imposes on what Congress can do.

Commentary by Jeane J. Kirkpatrick

The separation of powers is at the foundation of our constitutional system. In our times it has become entangled with some new and unfamiliar elements. One party and one ideological orientation have become anchored in the legislative branch and the other party and ideological orientation in the executive. There has been a marked expansion in the role of courts and law in policy making and most recently a trend not only toward legalizing but toward criminalizing policy differences. Out of this syndrome of structural and ideological elements we must fight our way through to coherent policy. We must also work our way back to coherent positions on the appropriate roles of the different branches of government.

This requires us to think about the roles of those branches apart from their current partisan character. One of my old professors, Robert MacIver, used to say that in considering a constitutional system and the placement of power in the system, you should begin by imagining that your bitterest opponents might eventually control it. That is what I try to do. Imagining my strongest opponents in that branch of government where I would otherwise vest the most power makes me very, very cautious.

I start with the assumption, then, that not only the president but Congress too has a legitimate and important role to play in the making of foreign policy. The Constitution ensures a legitimate role for Congress, and I believe it deserves to be important. For while constitutional theory may present presidential power as the alternative to Congress, in practice the power of the executive often turns out to be exercised by the bureaucracy. Just as war is too important to be left entirely to the generals, foreign policy is too important to be left entirely to the bureaucracy. Bureaucracies develop corporate interests of their own, distinct from the interests of the nation. Bureaucracies develop distinctive perspectives, which may fairly be described as biases in some areas. Bureaucracies develop various other institutional shortcomings. We need some kind of counterbalance to all these shortcomings. The Constitution has provided that counterbalance in Congress. My own experience is that Congress can play an extremely constructive role in the elaboration of foreign policy.

Clearly the fact that Congress can do some things, even some very important and constructive things, does not mean that Congress can do everything. I think it is manifest that Congress has, in recent years, attempted a kind of micromanagement of U.S. policy that is quite dysfunctional from the point of view of the national interest. The War Powers Act and the Boland amendments might be cited as among the most obvious cases of this.

In the earliest days of the Reagan administration we had serious discussions in the cabinet about the possibility of a legal challenge to the War Powers Act. A decision not to proceed was made on the grounds that it would be difficult to bring the question before a court on the appropriate issue. But I think we might have proceeded.

With regard to the Boland amendments, I also have some vivid memories of deals being made between particular congressional committees and particular representatives of the White House and the State Department on what would be an acceptable reach and wording for these restrictions. Some of us thought they were very bad deals at the time, and sometimes the deals came undone anyway. After congressional leaders had made a deal with the administration, Congress imposed two or three additional requirements on its own, almost as an afterthought. Some of us thought then that these were manifestly unconstitutional encroachments on executive power and argued for a direct challenge to the authority of these amendments.

Such challenges might have been made through the courts. Or they might have been pursued in the forum of public opinion, by going public with the disputes and letting the people decide. The Reagan administration decided to do neither. I regretted that at the time, and I regret it now. This administration should have made a head-on fight against congressional efforts to micromanage foreign policy, and the next administration should also fight this trend head-on, because it is finally incompatible with all the requirements for effective conduct of American foreign policy.

I do not say this simply because Congress lacks expertise. Foreign policy, I repeat, cannot simply be left to experts in the bureaucracy, because foreign policy ultimately turns on the most fundamental values in our society. Foreign policy must be rooted in democratic politics. But here again detailed policy management by Congress presents real problems. A democratic policy must emerge from a

45

process that establishes responsibility because democratic government requires accountability; it requires that we be able to identify who did it to us and then be able to throw the rascals out. When policy is made by Congress, the question always arises, Who really speaks for Congress? We say "Congress" imposed these requirements. But it is not clear who speaks for Congress, and it is not always clear, even afterward, what "Congress" really means when it enacts detailed requirements. That is why micromanagement is not conducive to democratic accountability any more than to coherent policy in this area.

Questions of foreign policy are more remote, they are more ambiguous, they are more complex than those we encounter in domestic policy making. But in today's interdependent world, we must finally deal with foreign policy questions, and we must find appropriate democratic means to deal with foreign policy as well as with domestic affairs. Congress does have an important role to play in clarifying the broad themes through resolutions and general enactments and in focusing attention and debate through oversight. Remembering that a future White House may adopt policies we very strongly oppose, we should not be too quick to exaggerate the dangers of immobilism from interbranch tensions—or too quick to minimize the dangers of unilateral executive action. A divided government may be better for all over the long run than an overunified, willful government. But we need to find the right balance. Congress can be an important counterbalance in the system, particularly in relation to entrenched bureaucracies, but it cannot be the managerial center, trying to direct the smallest details of implementation in foreign policy. We need to have full debate over basic questions. In the long run we also need to remember that foreign policy depends on policy—on the well-considered adaptation of means to ends—and not merely debate.

QUESTION: What about the feasibility of enforcing the Logan Act, which forbids unauthorized negotiations with foreign powers? If the legislative branch is seeking to criminalize political differences, why doesn't the executive branch take action on what seems to be criminal or treasonous behavior on the part of legislators—such as extensive dealings with the Sandinistas by prominent figures in Congress?

MS. KIRKPATRICK: This may very well reflect a deliberate decision by the executive not to engage in the criminalization of political disputes. If this is the reason for not enforcing the Logan Act, I think it is a legitimate decision. But I believe that the administration has an alternative, which is a political pursuit of these activities, attempting to delegitimize rather than criminalize them. This administration has not been as determined as it might be in defending executive powers through such methods. A separation of powers can only work when each branch is pulling as hard as it can to maintain its own position. I do not think the executive branch has been doing that—and this may be another example.

Commentary by Charles H. Fairbanks, Jr.

I have left it to others to discuss the "big picture," the major legislative constraints on executive authority that concern important headline issues. What I want to talk about now is the small picture, that is, legal restraints on executive authority that do not get into the headlines but that nevertheless may have a significant cumulative effect on the quality of U.S. foreign policy. I want to talk about the interaction between these minor legal constraints and other features of the American policy-making system, particularly the predominance of the bureaucracy in the system.

The small picture is worth considering carefully because it is usually neglected by top policy makers. Within the foreign service, people making policy often assume that on large, controversial matters—like the law requiring the State Department to certify the human rights progress of strategic countries like El Salvador—the executive branch cannot do much to rescue policy from such legalistic burdens. But there is a tendency to assume that on the minor, detailed questions—the kind of questions that do not get covered in the newspapers—the executive can do what it likes. Is this really true? It is worth thinking about.

To begin, we might think for a minute about foreign trade. Who has the advantage in creating influence through foreign trade—the Soviet Union or the United States? That may seem a silly question, given the vastly greater output of the United States, but the answer is a bit complex. The Soviet Union is able to make individual trade deals very shrewdly. In trading gold, for example, the Soviet Union has gold that it can produce very cheaply, and it has the necessary mechanisms in place to manage big transactions in international gold sales very expeditiously. The problem for Soviet foreign trade comes in the details. Soviet goods are shoddy, their availability is unpredictable, and the foreign purchaser of them usually must go through endless paperwork to carry on a trade transaction with the Soviet

Union. The United States thus seems to be a much more attractive trading partner for foreign countries.

To secure policy influence through foreign trade, however, a government must be able to control trade patterns in ways that further its own objectives. From this point of view the comparative advantage between the United States and the Soviet Union is again less obvious. Many people—including many high officials of the Reagan administration—believe that the general American trade advantage can be applied to arms sales and security assistance. They think, that is, that the United States is particularly well situated to advance Western or American influence in the third world by offering superior security assistance to third world countries seeking such aid. This is where the small picture is worth considering carefully.

I will try to illustrate the difficulties facing the American system in this area with a single story, which I call "The Long Arm of the Law." It begins in the middle of the 1950s, when the United States was trying to restore a devastated Europe. One of its instruments was something called the Military Assistance Program, essentially a program offering gifts of military equipment to American allies. As part of this program, the United States gave several hundred M-47 tanks to Italy. The United States began phasing out this tank from the American army in the 1960s, and Italy began phasing it out in the early 1970s. So the United States had passed along to the Italians several hundred tanks that would soon be obsolete. As in all American security assistance programs, the original transfer was made with a stipulation that the Italians would not pass the tanks along to any other countries without express American approval.

The world changed a great deal, however, during the lifetime of those tanks. By the mid-1960s Italy, like our other European allies, had become a very prosperous country capable of making or paying for its own weapons. Since our European allies no longer needed gifts of American weapons, the Military Assistance Program was abolished. By the middle 1970s Western security concerns had shifted to new parts of the world, and our story must shift to a new scene—to the Horn of Africa, the back door to the Middle East and to the strategically vital Persian Gulf.

When Emperor Haile Selassie, the last feudal ruler in the world, was overthrown in the mid-1970s, Ethiopia was plunged into a civil war among its various subjugated nationalities—the Eritreans, Tigreans, Oromo, Somalis, and others—and various factions of the Ethiopian left. U.S. security assistance to Ethiopia was cut off by American human rights legislation forbidding such aid to oppressive regimes. The new rulers of Ethiopia thus turned to the Soviet Union.

The Soviets had previously been helping Somalia against Ethiopia, because in the context of the larger struggle within Ethiopia, neighboring Somalia had tried to recover parts of Ethiopia that were inhabited by ethnic Somalis and that had been held before World II by Italian Somaliland. When the Ethiopians appealed to the Soviets for assistance, the Soviets promptly switched sides and abandoned the Somalis. The Somalis then tried to make their own switch, appealing for Western aid against the Soviet-backed Ethiopians.

This border war between Ethiopia and Somalia is still going on today. But the main war—the war to determine whether Ethiopia would disintegrate entirely—was decided in the mid-1970s by the scale of Soviet assistance to the Marxist government in Addis Ababa. Over a ten-year period, the Soviet Union gave $4.5 billion in security assistance to Ethiopia, including the most modern tanks and jet fighters. Half was provided as outright gifts, and the debts owed on the other half have since been forgiven. Before the American aid cutoff the United States had given only $122 million to Ethiopia in the 1970s—so there was always a great disproportion in the willingness of the two superpowers to devote resources to security assistance in this part of the world.

In the course of the 1970s this area assumed greater strategic importance for the West, as the Western position worsened. In the mid-1970s the OPEC cartel successfully restricted international oil supplies, triggering an energy crisis in the West. The shah was overthrown in Iran and replaced with an anti-Western government. Then the Soviets invaded Afghanistan, bringing Soviet forces within close striking distance of the Persian Gulf. By 1980 the Somalis, having suffered continuing setbacks in their war with Ethiopia, were desperate for assistance. The United States, which had refused any aid to Somalia in 1978 and 1979, finally agreed to provide $20 million in assistance in 1980; but the Somalis needed more.

They turned to Italy, the former colonial master of Somaliland. Italy still had several hundred of the M-47 tanks it received in the 1950s. These tanks were clearly the property of Italy—as they had been for twenty-five years. Since they had already been phased out of the Italian forces, they were not needed at all by Italy. They were just sitting in Italy, offering an easy way to help the Somalis at no cost to anyone. The Italians proposed to give them to beleaguered Somalia, but it turned out that this was not so easy.

The U.S. State Department scented an infraction of American legal rights. Somewhere through the cable traffic State Department officials picked up the fact that these tanks, though Italian property for the past quarter-century, had been given to Italy under the Military

Assistance Program and that this program, though long since abolished, entitled the United States to pass on the retransfer of those tanks. The State Department reminded the Italians that they were obliged to seek American permission for their gift to Somalia, and on April 4, 1980, Italy submitted a formal request for U.S. approval for the transfer of those tanks.

What was the American reply? "We are not sure. We are studying the issue." A great bureaucratic struggle ensued, continuing over four years—that is why this story is called "The Long Arm of the Law." U.S. legal constraints from the mid-1950s thus reached out in the early 1980s to take a death grip on Italy's gift of its own tanks to a third country. It is not quite accurate, however, to say that these legal constraints reached out on their own to exert this effect. Someone in the bureaucracy had to remember them and invoke them. That is the key point to remember in thinking about the small picture that this story is meant to illustrate. Legal constraints on executive discretion do not operate in a vacuum; they operate only through interaction with the bureaucracy. Perhaps we can stipulate this as an axiom of political science—legal constraints put weapons in the hands of bureaucrats.

The final acts of this story illustrate the axiom all too well. The Italians submitted their formal request and were told to wait while the State Department studied the issue. Italy's assistance to Somalia would now turn on a struggle within the American bureaucracy. In Rome in 1981 the Italian foreign minister pursued the question directly with Alexander Haig, the new secretary of state. Haig endorsed the transfer, but this did not settle the issue, because Haig's endorsement would not commit the Department of State. Late in 1981 proponents of this tank transfer within the U.S. government won a bureaucratic victory: not an actual agreement to approve the transfer of the tanks but an agreement to send a team to Italy to check on the condition of the tanks to see if the issue were still relevant, so that the issue *could* be decided when the team returned, *if* it turned out that the issue were still relevant.

On December 22, 1981, I received a briefing by the U.S. Army official team that had carefully inspected each tank in Italy. What they told us was this: in the eighteen months since Italy decided to give the tanks to Somalia, they had sat out in the rain at Caserta, near Naples, with their hatches open, and they had rusted through. Now they were junk. Their treads would not turn. Their gun barrels were blocked. Their sights were blinded. Remember these rusted tanks sitting outside Naples as a metaphor for the effects of legal restraints on security assistance.

The story did not end with these rusted tanks. The Somalis went elsewhere and obtained weapons from Romania, Kuwait, and Iran—all countries close to the Soviet Union. Meanwhile, the Italians were so embarrassed by the rusting of their gift tanks that they found some workable tanks elsewhere. The U.S. government then became embarrassed about holding up the transfer for four years and in 1983 consented to this new transfer. In 1984 the Somalis finally got their obsolete tanks, but by then they had already pulled back entirely from the Ogaden province, which had been the main focus of their war. To understand the cumulative effect of legal restraints on executive discretion in foreign affairs, this particular incident must be multiplied at least a thousandfold, for there are many such stories in the annals of contemporary foreign policy.

The United States often conducts a very strange foreign policy. Most of the time we do not seem to care what will help our friends or thwart our enemies. We do not seize opportunities to extend our influence, nor do we allow our allies to seize such opportunities for us. Legalism is not the ultimate source of this strange approach to foreign policy, but it is frequently the mode through which it proceeds. Perhaps the main way it does so is by imposing interminable delay in foreign policy decision making. Because of a law from the 1950s, the United States took four years to approve Italy's decision to transfer its own obsolete tanks to a third country, in an arrangement essentially quite favorable to American interests. The Soviet Union, by contrast, was able to extend $2 billion worth of high-quality military equipment to Ethiopia in the first nine months of their relationship.

There is, of course, a place for cautious deliberation. The framers of the American Constitution took it for granted that calmness, prudence, and deliberation were necessary attributes of legislative action, but they assumed that secrecy and dispatch would be necessary for the executive in matters like the conduct of foreign policy. The contemporary network of legal constraints on executive policy makers forces them to adopt the very slow institutional pace of legislative deliberation. By importing some of the intransigence of legislative debate into the executive, it simultaneously exacerbates partisan warfare within the bureaucracy. We thus get an executive bureaucracy with more and more aspects of a democratic legislature. The question is whether this is a suitable institutional structure for the conduct of foreign affairs. With all our other advantages, doesn't this structure risk putting us at an institutional disadvantage vis-à-vis the Soviet Union, a disadvantage that may prove cumulatively quite burdensome?

We should consider, too, whether this is what was really intended by the framers of the American Constitution. As an epilogue to this story, I would like to go back to the eighteenth century. We tend to think of the American president as a head of state like most heads of state. We forget that the prime minister in Britain has only recently become a personal ruler rather than a first among equals in the cabinet. The British Constitution, the constitutions of other Western countries, even of third world countries, have all developed under the influence of American arrangements. If we look at the powers of the presidency in the perspective of historical experience before 1780, we can see that the American president is given greater constitutional powers than any republican ruler in history—greater than the stadtholder of the Netherlands in the seventeenth century, greater than the Roman consuls in ancient times. Indeed in *Federalist* No. 70 the president is compared to a Roman dictator, that is, an executive during a period of deep crisis rather than a governor of ordinary times. That is the original conception of executive power in the American Constitution. On the big public issues there are always powerful political constraints on the executive. The question is whether, even on small matters, the kinds of legal constraints illustrated by the Somali tank deal are not dangerously deflecting this original conception.

Ms. KIRKPATRICK: Two questions occurred to me when I heard this story. The first is, Who discovered that American approval was required for the transfer of those tanks? When I say who, I don't mean what branch of government. I mean what person discovered that and passed the fact on up to the point where it became authoritative U.S. policy? Second, why did the Italians go along? They are not always so sensitive to American preferences. They are not always so sensitive even to what we claim as our rights. They have, for example, raised real obstacles from time to time about our use of NATO bases in the face of prior agreements.

MR. FAIRBANKS: On the question why the Italians allowed us to hold things up for four years, the answer is revealing. Countries in a comparable position—like the Turks in Cyprus or the Israelis in Lebanon—do not always pay so much attention to American legalities. This reflects a general truth about the operation of such legal constraints, that when a country is involved in an issue that it regards as very important—rather than merely a favor to a former colony, as the Italians seem to have considered the tank transfer to Somalia—American rules do not have much effect. Our legal restraints generally affect only the very biggest issues, like the certification of human rights progress in El Salvador—where a general rule may not be appropriate —or else they affect the very low-level issues, which are often those the rule was never intended to affect. In this sense legislating restrictions on the conduct of foreign policy is rarely effective.

ALAN L. KEYES: You have still left out an explicit discussion of one very important point, which was the point that Jeane Kirkpatrick was hinting at when she asked who raised this issue within the American bureaucracy. This issue was plainly employed as an instrument in a larger policy process. You mentioned only in passing that during those four years, while the tank transfer was debated in Washington, the Ogaden war receded. This was of more than incidental importance. Whoever raised this legal issue did not want to have those tanks delivered when they could still have been relevant to the outcome of that war. So even here the legal problem was subordinate to the serious problem, which was the lack of clear policy purpose or the unwillingness to decide exactly how we should respond to that war for our own strategic purposes. We backed away from the tank transfer because we were still preoccupied with how we could affect a reconciliation with the Ethiopians.

MR. FAIRBANKS: I agree, but I think that legal constraints do make a difference. When a bureaucracy, pursuing its own agenda, comes across a legal standard like this, it provides a hook for its own aims, a way of connecting with other sources of power to pursue those aims with greater vigor.

MR. KEYES: Yes, but only if there is a congruence of interests. In this case the State Department bureaucracy had an interest in not delivering those tanks, but I think the Italians also had an interest in not delivering the tanks while still appearing willing to help. In effect, everybody was cooperating to prevent what they did not want to happen—the strengthening of the Somalis in the war with Ethiopia.

Commentary by Alan L. Keyes

My perspective may be a little different from that expressed by others, because my experience in the Reagan administration has given me some understanding and appreciation of the potential role of Congress in foreign policy. I have seen Congress play a very helpful role in relation to policy toward the United Nations. At one point the essential policy of the United States toward the United Nations was based on a congressionally mandated strategy.

I am not sure Congress fully understood that it had mandated this strategy; but its actions did amount to the mandating of a general strategy, and by and large that strategy was successful and effective. It did this by invoking its power of the purse to force the American government to exert a similar, latent leverage at the United Nations by conditioning its annual contributions on the satisfactory conduct of that organization. I do not want to get into the legalities of all this, since I am here interested in prudence rather than jurisprudence. But the United States was concerned about a range of disturbing trends at the United Nations—the continuing efforts to expel Israel from the General Assembly, the United Nation's support for specific terrorist organizations, the increasingly anti-American tone of UN proceedings—which violated at least our own notions of international right. Congressional actions were very important in the struggle to reverse these trends, both in initiating particular policies and in providing continuing support for them.

It is particularly important to notice, too, that this congressional role was conditioned by a clear assertion of executive leadership in this area in the early years of the Reagan administration. When the full record is revealed—which probably cannot be for quite some time—it will be clear that the level of congressional interest in this area and the informed nature of that interest owed very much to this prior assertion of executive leadership. That leadership involved many particular policy suggestions to Congress but also something more important. It is that extra something that needs most of all to be emphasized.

That extra dimension of leadership was the articulation of a broad understanding of what the United Nations was about, of the dangers it posed to the fundamental interests of the United States, and of why those dangers had to be taken seriously. It led to the articulation of broad strategies for effective action, both by Congress and within the executive branch, to meet those dangers and to protect those threatened national interests. This ultimately produced a significant breakthrough in the UN General Assembly in 1986. But I fear the fruits of the policy have been thrown away in the past year by the failure of the State Department to follow through on our initial successes. This experience reinforces my sense that the chief asset of the executive branch is the clear purpose, the quality, and the political strength of its top leadership.

If the executive branch has a clear purpose, the skill to pursue it, and the will to build the political strength to back up that skill, congressional activism can be an asset to foreign policy. People who complain about congressional interference see the problem as one of institutions rather than leadership. They find fault with the arrangements that establish something of an adversary relationship between the branches of government. Some suggest that the basic problem is that society as a whole is entangled in conflict, so that the underlying problem is "ideology." This view makes it seem that if only we could do something about the partisanship of the nasty Congress, we could move on to a healthy foreign policy. I do not think this is the proper perspective on the problems of recent years.

Partisanship is simply endemic to political situations, and so is the conflictive nature of governance. That was the fundamental insight of our founders and of the classical liberal thinkers whom they read. That is the fundamental insight on which the American regime was founded. To put the point most bluntly, this insight is that politics is an extension of war and to engage in politics is to engage, to a certain degree, in a transformed and transmuted art of war. But in this war the Reagan administration has begun to seem like David facing the Philistines. When they offered David the armor of King Saul, remember, he found that it was too big for him, and he refused it. But at least David then picked up his slingshot. Complaints about the separation of powers seem to me like complaints about oversized armor, complaints about the tools and instruments available. The complaint has a hollow ring from people who are not willing to pick up other tools to continue the struggle.

Much of the complaint seems to reflect a general weariness with the struggle. We are weary of the notion that politics is conflict and weary of the obligation to be good political warriors. Hobbes said that war is a running away on both sides. But in many of the political battles of recent years, it has seemed to be a running away on one side only—a running away by the forces of the present administration. This reflects, I think, a refusal to face the fact that conflict and struggle are inevitable in politics. If this is so, the underlying problem is not the inadequacy of our institutions but the inadequacy of the people now trying to operate these institutions.

The traditional understanding was that democratic government requires a certain fit character in the people. But a leadership that does not understand the inescapable nature of political conflict is unable or unwilling to appeal to the people. We carried a successful policy toward the United Nations for a time because we did understand the need to persuade and move public opinion. At the same time, we tried to move Congress to understand the problems we faced in the

United Nations and the strategy we needed to cope with those problems.

I sensed during my time in the State Department, however, that the career bureaucrats did not fully appreciate the need to forge a domestic basis for foreign policy. For this reason, the bureaucracy did not always accept the leadership of those who could effectively engage in the political struggle, starting with the White House and including others who came to foreign policy battles from the political arena. It is silly to imagine that an effective foreign policy can be conducted by career officials in isolation, because at the end of the day they cannot formulate policies that take account of domestic political opinion. More important, they cannot form the necessary political coalitions to sustain their policies.

On the whole, our policy toward the United Nations shows that effective political leadership can make a decisive difference. Leadership made the difference, not the lack of ideology or the lack of congressional involvement. Effective leadership from the executive made it possible to turn congressional activism—which was potentially dangerous here as elsewhere—into a very useful tool of U.S. policy. In thinking about policy failures in other areas, then, perhaps we should be giving less attention to the institutional setting and more thought to why similar executive leadership was not forthcoming in dealing with Congress on other issues.

QUESTION: Is it possible to undo the ineffectiveness of this administration or the apathy of this administration and still go back and challenge the Boland amendments and the War Powers Act?

MR. KEYES: I think the desire to take these things into court is really a desire among the elite in the government to avoid an appeal to the people. The desire to avoid an appeal to the people is becoming endemic in our society, and a dysfunction is developing between the electoral process, which is based on one set of issues, mostly false, and the real issues that divide the participants in the decision-making process. If you want to punish your opponents in political wars, you cannot send them to jail or haul them into court. You have to punish them by focusing the power and authority of the people against them. That requires a campaign that is not fought in the courts, that is not conducted by deal making with Congress, but that attempts to infuse, once again, a sense of substance into the political process of choice that takes place before the judgment of the people.

QUESTION: It does appear that the executive has lost zeal or leadership on such foreign policy issues as our approach to the United Nations. Why does that seem to be the case? What are some of the constraints on the executive besides Congress? The press? Timing? Are the constraints self-imposed?

MS. KIRKPATRICK: I do not think there are any structural constraints. There is a lack of political will.

MR. KEYES: I would add that, apart from a lack of political will, there is a very deep difficulty, which the executive branch shares with the public, and that is the unresolved confusion about what the ends and means of our foreign policy should be. I would go further and say the problem involves a failure of political rhetoric—in the high sense of the term. In order to have a fight over policy, we have to have a common frame of reference. There must be some concepts on which we agree so that we are not simply talking past one another. Over the past ten or twenty years we have lost that common frame of reference. We no longer speak politically in a common language. Our statesmen no longer move us with symbols that have a common emotive power. That is not because the symbols do not exist. It is because they are no longer taken seriously. Our politicians fail us because they no longer have the background, the knowledge, the understanding, the sense of statesmanship to engage in that kind of struggle.

5

The Theory and Practice of Separation of Powers: The Case of Covert Action

Gary J. Schmitt and Abram N. Shulsky

The prevalent view of the intended division of national security powers between Congress and the president is captured by Edward Corwin's famous statement that the Constitution is "an invitation to struggle for the privilege of directing American foreign policy."[1] Its underlying premise is that the object of separation of powers—the framework on which the Constitution rests—is to confound in practice the unilateral and coherent use of power. Optimally, the framers had designed a system with "an inherent tendency toward inertia."[2]

If struggle or stalemate was the goal, the Constitution's architects should have cared less about precisely how the national security powers were separated than ensuring that they were sufficiently fractured. So understood, powers might be divided for politically capricious reasons as easily as not. According to Louis Henkin, the powers over foreign affairs are "not determined by any 'natural' division."[3] Indeed, they "appear not so much 'separated' as fissured" and, in the final analysis, owe more to the "dissension, vacillation and compromise at the Constitutional Convention" than to a reasoned analysis of what is required to conduct an effective foreign policy. Altogether, the constitutional arrangements for handling foreign policy are hardly "worthy of celebration."[4]

This paper represents the personal views of the authors and does not necessarily represent those of any institution or agency with which they have been or are associated.

If this in fact was how the framers came to understand and to implement the doctrine of separation of powers, it is a striking departure from how that doctrine was set forth in its principal original form by John Locke in *Two Treatises of Government*. Locke believes that separation of powers is useful for restraining tyrannical tendencies in government; however, his full explication reveals that this is to be achieved by separating powers not arbitrarily, but along functional lines.[5] In fact, Locke attributes "the original right and rise of both the Legislative and Executive Power" to the fundamental tasks of passing laws and executing them.[6]

This functional aspect of separation of powers is also obvious in Locke's analysis of the third of the principal powers existing in government, the "federative."[7] His discussion of it begins and ends on a functional note. He describes the genesis of the federative power as rooted in the fact that states, as such, can themselves never escape the state of nature. Unlike individuals, who may avoid the arbitrary use of power by others by establishing a proper government, nations will continue to exist in a situation in which they will be threatened by other nations and from which there is no supreme civil appeal. As depicted by Locke, the domain of foreign affairs is largely a lawless one in which a state's capacity to make domestic laws or execute them is essentially irrelevant. What a government requires is a distinct capacity to react to the inconstant and recalcitrant behavior of other states.[8]

In defining the federative power as he has, Locke is careful not to dissipate it in practice by suggesting it might be housed with the legislature. Put succinctly, such power "admits not of a plurality of governors."[9]

Although concern with effectiveness leads Locke away from conjoining the federative power with the legislative, the same concern moves him to accept the conflation of the federative with the executive. Though distinct in theory, the two are composed of "the force of the Society" and, as such, are "always almost united" in practice.[10] When not united, that force would necessarily be of two minds. In times of crisis, when division and debate can least be afforded, separating the executive power from the federative is an invitation to "disorder and ruin."[11]

In sum, the framers would hardly have learned from Locke that the singular purpose of separation of powers was the safe dispersal of power, unfettered by any requirement for its effective use.

Nevertheless, if they examined Locke's *Second Treatise* closely, the framers would also have noticed that in associating the great and active prerogatives of foreign affairs with the domestic capacities of the chief executive, Locke had created an office that implicitly challenges his own initial description of the legislature as the "Supreme Power."[12] Locke obliquely reminds his readers that tension between the two—while not an "invitation to struggle"—is indeed possible. There is no attempt to resolve the tension. The tension is inevitable because it is intrinsic to any properly constructed government whose origins dictate the need for the rule of law, but whose continued existence requires executive discretion.

Possible clashes between the legislature and the executive, however, are not to be settled in just any manner. Montesquieu's *Spirit of the Laws*, the most famous discussion of separation of powers, rejects a legislative check on the executive that impairs the functional advantages of a unified executive office. Sharing executive power with the legislature or giving it a "stay" over the executive, according to Montesquieu, is "not proper." The legislature is "not fit" as a body to carry out the required tasks or to act with the requisite decisiveness and dispatch.[13] The check discussed by Montesquieu is the legislature's control of the public purse. It is a power that has the advantage of ultimately controlling the executive but of doing so in a manner that leaves the institutional efficacy of his office intact.

There is every reason to believe that the Constitution's architects did not turn their back on Locke and Montesquieu's conception of the doctrine of separation of powers. Experience under both the Articles of Confederation and the state constitutions had confirmed in their minds "the belief that kinds of power are best exercised by particular kinds of bodies."[14] By the time of the Constitutional Convention,

> The adoption of the principle of separation of powers as interpreted to mean the exercise of different functions of government by departments officered by entirely different individuals, also seemed insistently demanded as a *sine qua non* of governmental efficiency.[15]

By culling out executive from legislative power and housing it in a largely independent and unitary office, the framers were signaling their intent to move decisively away from the incompetence of congressionally dominated government, particularly in the areas of war and foreign affairs.[16] They wanted "more decision, more dispatch, more secrecy, [and] more responsibility." And those were more likely to be found "where single men," not "bodies" exercised power.[17]

Operating on that theory, President George Washington moved decisively to assert executive branch control of the national security affairs of the young country. Proclamations of neutrality and offensive military campaigns against the Indian nations of the Northwest are

61

just two examples of "Washington's decision to assume control of government operations and policy-making over a range of activities, including foreign affairs and the conduct of military operations."[18] There is little evidence that Congress opposed Washington's decision. To the contrary, provisions for a "special activity" fund and the large delegation of power granted the president under the newly created Departments of War and State reinforce the view that congressional deference to the executive branch in these matters was expected.[19]

Viewed in the context of the current debate, it appears that neither the Constitution's framers nor the republic's first officials saw the relationship between Congress and the president as being necessarily adversarial; they did not see each branch as existing principally to check the other. Rather, Congress appears to have understood its power to "make all laws . . . necessary and proper for carrying into execution . . . all other powers" as mandating that it "facilitate the exercise of executive power in the realm of foreign affairs." Although the potential of Congress to trim legitimate executive discretion has never simply abated, constitutionally (as Corwin himself notes) the presidency "possesses unity and is capable of acting with greatest expedition, secrecy, and fullest knowledge—in short, with greatest efficiency."[20] Those attributes made it both likely and constitutionally appropriate that in the area of foreign affairs the president would be first among equals. Although the Constitution created separate but equal branches, its framers never intended those branches to be equal in the same way, about the same matters, and at the same time.

History of Congressional Oversight

It is in this constitutional and historical context that we must analyze the country's experience with covert actions. After the enactment of the National Security Act of 1947 (which created the Central Intelligence Agency [CIA]) and the CIA Act of 1949 (which gave the director of central intelligence [DCI] various powers required to run it), Congress addressed the subject of congressional oversight in 1955, when Senator Mike Mansfield introduced a resolution to form a Joint Oversight Committee (modeled on the Joint Atomic Energy Committee) with responsibility for intelligence activities. This proposal came after the CIA covert action programs in Guatemala and Iran had received some publicity and was to some extent in response to it. Its immediate impetus, however, was a recommendation in the second Hoover Commission (the Commission on the Organization of the Executive Branch of the Government) that oversight be expanded.

Opposition to Mansfield's resolution came from several sources.

A major source was the reluctance of the leadership of the Armed Services and Appropriations committees to give up their jurisdiction over intelligence activities. There also seemed to be a sense that intelligence activities were, by and large, an executive branch matter for which congressional responsibility was limited. Thus, as Senator Leverett Saltonstall said in the course of the floor debate, he was reluctant

> to seek information and knowledge on subjects which I personally, as a Member of Congress and as a citizen, would rather not have, *unless I believed it to be my responsibility to have it* because it might involve the lives of American citizens. (Emphasis added.)

The resolution was vigorously opposed by the Senate giants— Richard Russell (chairman of the Armed Services Committee), Carl Hayden (chairman of the Appropriations Committee), and Saltonstall (a prominent minority member of the Armed Services and Appropriations committees)—and soundly defeated, 59 to 27. (It did, however, lead to the formation of CIA subcommittees in the Armed Services and Appropriations committees.) A similar bill introduced in 1961, after the Bay of Pigs fiasco, also failed.[21]

Congress's next major expression of concern about covert action came during the late 1960s, after *Ramparts* magazine exposed the CIA's support for the international activities of the National Student Association (NSA).[22] The revelations appeared in 1967 and led to the severing of confidential relationships between the CIA and various educational and private voluntary groups, which had served as conduits for CIA funds for NSA and other organizations.

At this point, there were proposals to replace CIA funding with a new mechanism for overt governmental support. Legislation was introduced by Representative Dante Fascell, among others, to create an "Institute of International Affairs" for this purpose.[23] Nothing came of the proposal at the time. In 1973, though, after Senator Clifford Case publicly confirmed CIA funding of Radio Free Europe and Radio Liberty, Congress decided to replace the covert funding mechanism with overt U.S. government support through a newly created independent federal agency, the Board for International Broadcasting.

Before 1974, congressional oversight of covert action was formally exercised by the CIA subcommittees of the Appropriations and Armed Services committees; in fact, it appears that the oversight process was quite informal and effectively involved only a few key members of those committees. After the revelation of the CIA's covert action in Chile, Congress at the end of 1974 passed the Hughes-Ryan

Amendment (to the Foreign Assistance Act of 1961); this amendment constituted the first statutory requirement that the president inform Congress about covert action.

Although it was passed by the Senate in a manner that Senator John Stennis correctly described as "casual,"[24] the Hughes-Ryan Amendment represented a major change in the way covert action programs were handled within the U.S. government.[25] As it finally emerged from a House-Senate conference, its major elements were as follows:

1. Each covert action required an explicit presidential "finding" that the operation was "important to the national security of the United States." This did away with the notion of "plausible deniability" as far as the president was concerned. Although the phrase "important to the national security" was too vague to substantively limit the president's use of covert action, it does suggest that covert action ought not be used as a routine tool of foreign policy.

2. The president was required to report, in a "timely" fashion, "a description and scope" of any covert action operation to the "appropriate committees of the Congress," including the Foreign Relations and Foreign Affairs committees of the Senate and the House, respectively. This new statutory congressional right to be informed of covert action put the Foreign Relations/Affairs committees into the intellience oversight business. The amendment recognized that covert action was a foreign policy tool; at the same time, its provisions spread knowledge of sensitive activities to an ever larger circle of congressmen and their staffs.

As Senator Harold Hughes made clear, he regarded his amendment as a stopgap measure pending some more formal congressional legislation that, from his point of view, would have banned all peacetime covert action:

> The amendment I offer should be regarded as only a beginning toward the imperative of imposing some order and structure to the means by which the American people, through their elected representatives, can exercise a measure of control over the cloak-and-dagger operations of intelligence agencies of the U.S. Government.
>
> I would admit that circumstances might develop in which covert action would be justified in time of war.
>
> I find it impossible, however, to envisage any circumstances in time of peace that would justify them.[26]

In addition, Senator Hughes referred to reports that Secretary of State

Henry Kissinger and Director of Central Intelligence William Colby had said that no covert action programs were under way at that time.

Paradoxically, the Hughes-Ryan Amendment provided the first explicit congressional recognition of covert action and allowed the CIA to argue, as it did during the congressional investigations of 1975–1976, that it authorized the CIA to conduct covert action.[27] In the final version that emerged from the Conference Committee (and that adopted the language in the House bill), this point is less clear than in Senator Hughes's original version, which explicitly stated:

> the President may authorize and direct that any covert action operation be resumed, or that any other covert action operation be initiated, and funds may be expended therefore, if, but not before, . . .[28]

In any case, the proposals "for improving congressional oversight of intelligence activities" that were under study at the time, and to which Senator Hughes referred when introducing his amendment, were soon to be preempted by the creation of special House and Senate committees (chaired by Representative Otis Pike and Senator Frank Church) to investigate the activities of the intelligence agencies.

In the context of congressional assertiveness with respect to its foreign policy role, and faced with the specific arguments about the disadvantages of secrecy in foreign policy formulation and implementation, the Church Committee considered prohibiting all covert action;[29] it favored instead enhanced congressional oversight coupled with various statutory limitations that were to be included in proposed (but never enacted) intelligence charter legislation.

Thus, the statutory regime governing covert action remained the same from December 1974 (when the Hughes-Ryan Amendment was enacted) until 1980, when the general intelligence oversight authority of the permanent House and Senate Select Committees on Intelligence was given the force of law. (Until that time, the requirement that the committees be kept "fully and currently informed" of intelligence activities other than CIA-conducted covert action rested solely on presidential executive orders.)

Nevertheless, the political reality changed drastically during this period, primarily because of the Church and Pike Committee revelations. In fact, Congress received advance notice of covert action in almost all cases; Admiral Stansfield Turner has testified that, during his four years as DCI, there were only three times—all in connection with attempts to rescue Americans from Tehran in 1979–1980—when this was not done.[30]

In 1980 the Hughes-Ryan requirement to notify the "appropriate" congressional committees (in practice, eight committees: the intelligence, foreign relations or affairs, defense, and appropriations committees of both the House and the Senate) was relaxed so that only the two intelligence committees need be briefed.[31] (In "extraordinary circumstances affecting vital interests of the United States," notification may be further limited to the "Group of Eight," the chairmen and ranking minority members of the intelligence committees, and the leaders of each party in each house.) At the same time, the Hughes-Ryan requirement for "timely" notification was tightened to prior notification, subject to the president's invoking constitutional authority to delay it.[32] Furthermore, the notification requirement, which under Hughes-Ryan applied only to CIA activities, was broadened to all "significant anticipated intelligence activities," which presumably includes covert action undertaken by other agencies of government.

In the wake of the Iran-contra affair and investigation, public discussion in 1988 focused on various proposals for tightening up the executive branch procedures dealing with covert action and for strengthening congressional oversight, rather than on proposals for banning covert action altogether or regulating its scope or content. The general thrust of these proposals resembled those put forward by President Reagan in a letter to Senator David Boren, chairman of the Senate Select Committee on Intelligence (SSCI),[33] as well as the recommendations of the House and Senate Iran-contra committees in their report.[34] Particular controversy centered on a proposal to require that Congress be notified of *all* covert action findings within forty-eight hours of the president's making them.

Some of the issues deal with the manner in which the executive branch handles covert action internally. Thus, the president's letter in August 1987 stated his support for the following "concepts" and his intention to incorporate them in appropriate executive documents:

- all findings to be in writing, except in cases of "extreme emergency"
- oral findings to be reduced to writing within two days
- findings not to be retroactively authorize or sanction covert actions
- findings to be required for covert action undertaken by agencies other than the CIA
- all findings to be made available to members of the NSC (National Security Council)[35]

In January 1988, the SSCI reported out Senator William Cohen's Intelligence Oversight Act of 1988 (S. 1721), which included, with minor differences, all but the last of the president's proposals noted above.[36]

In addition, as originally proposed by Senator Cohen, the bill would have required that the written finding specify "any third party, including any foreign country . . . who it is contemplated will be used to fund or otherwise participate in any way in the special activity."[37] In the bill as reported by the SSCI, this provision was watered down to a requirement to specify *whether* such a third party will be involved.[38] As explained in the committee report on the bill,[39] this change may be less significant than it first appears:

> The finding itself need state only whether such use is contemplated, without actually identifying the third party (or parties) concerned. Additional information concerning the involvement of such third parties would be provided to the intelligence committees in accordance with subsection 503(b).

Since the written findings will have to be provided to Congress, it is unclear to what extent foreign services, unused to the notion of legislative oversight of intelligence, will be willing to cooperate with U.S. covert action under these conditions.

More controversial are likely to be the issues that deal with the relationship between the executive branch and Congress. The Iran-contra affair has uncovered several major ones, which may become the focus of heated debate.

First is the question of requiring prior notification of Congress of *all* covert action. Prior notification is now the general rule.[40] According to officials of the Carter and Reagan administrations, there have been only four cases in the past eleven years when it was not given. The first three related to attempts in 1979–1980 to rescue the Americans held hostage in Tehran, including support activities for the "Canadian caper"[41] (in which six Americans who had taken refuge at the Canadian Embassy were successfully spirited out of Iran). The fourth was, of course, the arms sales to Iran in 1985–1986.[42]

On the grounds that prior notification of Congress would have prevented that fiasco, the proposed legislation eliminated the president's option to provide only "timely" notice. S. 1721 would require that, in general, the president notify Congress before a covert action program is initiated but, in any case, within forty-eight hours of his determination to proceed with it.[43]

The bill would preserve the provision in current law that allows the president to limit notification to the "Group of Eight" if he deems it essential. It further would have provided him with a new option: he may notify only the four leaders of the two houses. In this latter case, however, he must determine weekly (and inform the "Group of Four") that the limitation of notification is still required.[44]

The Question of Congressional Oversight

As the history of the Hughes-Ryan Amendment shows, the present system of congressional oversight of covert action came into being as a temporary stopgap measure. The ensuing Church Committee report considered, but rejected, an outright ban on covert action, but its own proposal—the regulation of covert action by means of detailed provisions—failed when the SSCI's effort to enact an intelligence charter in which they were contained was abandoned. Thus, there is no single place to look, no grand debate to turn to, for a statement of the purpose of congressional oversight that authoritatively reflects the views of those who placed it on the books.[45]

Nevertheless, it is not difficult to reconstruct the basic arguments in favor of congressional oversight of covert action. The main argument proceeds that, because of the absence of public debate about covert action, the administration lacks a reliable mechanism to tell it whether the means being adopted are generally regarded as justified by "public opinion," let alone to force it to be guided by this judgment. Thus, it has been argued, programs are adopted and, when they finally come to light, are rejected by the public as inconsistent with its values and principles.[46]

This point may be somewhat more subtle than it first appears, however, if the problem is seen as due not to the bad character or atypical views of the individuals who deal with covert action but rather to systemic factors. These factors have been said to include: (1) the limitation of knowledge and therefore debate about covert action to a small group of officials, cutting out the public, most or all members of Congress (before Hughes-Ryan), and many executive branch officials as well, and reducing or eliminating the outside checks on most foreign policy decisions; (2) the intelligence community's supposed "can do" mentality, which does not want to admit that some results are beyond its ability to achieve; and (3) the supposed unwillingness of executive branch officials to oppose presidential wishes. In such a situation, there would be a tendency to adopt goal-oriented measures regardless of other, more principled concerns; the argument has been made that presidents would choose covert action techniques precisely to avoid having to balance the various points of view and concerns that would otherwise come into play.[47]

Thus, a major purpose of congressional notification of covert action (and indeed, of *prior* notification) is to allow the intelligence committees to serve as a sounding board, a surrogate for the much wider debate (intra-executive branch, congressional, and public) that would usually accompany an overt foreign policy initiative. Although in principle congressional notification does not imply that the committees possess a veto power over covert action programs, strong objections from committee members may cause revision or even cancellation of a proposal if it appears that the political cost will exceed the program's expected results.[48] Thus, one purpose of prior notification might be described as the testing of a proposal against an (admittedly quite restricted) cross section of political opinion, represented by individuals independent of the president, to see if it appears out of line with fundamental beliefs or values.

Despite the absence of a formal congressional veto, an individual committee member who is vehemently opposed to a covert action project could attempt to stop it by threatening to leak it to the press (or by actually doing so). Implementing such a threat would violate congressional rules, and so the entire question has been shrouded in discreet silence. (Of course, any member of Congress, relying on the constitutional protection of congressional debate, can say anything he wishes;[49] while immune from prosecution, he could, however, be censured or, in extreme cases, expelled by action of the Senate or the House. This, however, has not been a problem in practice.[50]) Senator Biden's reported claim to have stopped two covert action programs in this manner is an unusual, if not unique, public reference to this issue.[51]

Beyond this sounding-board function spreading the knowledge of covert action to members of Congress creates the opportunity for Congress to exercise its "power of the purse." This power can be exercised by the intelligence committees themselves, or it can involve full-scale debate on the floor of the Senate and House of Representatives, as in the case of the various Boland amendments restricting or prohibiting aid to the Nicaraguan resistance.

The fundamental claim on behalf of congressional oversight of covert action is that it combines the advantages of checks and balances on the one hand with those of secrecy on the other. Committee consideration serves as a surrogate for the full-scale public debate and democratic decision-making process, which is of course incompatible with secrecy. The validity of this claim has been attacked in both practical and theoretical terms.

Practically, the issue is whether congressional oversight leads inevitably to public revelation of the information, regardless of what the rules say. The Iran-contra hearings spawned much discussion of the source of the frequent leaks about covert action operations, as well as other intelligence matters. Members of the executive branch frequently assert or imply that the Congress is the source of most leaks about covert action,[52] which members of Congress just as frequently deny. In fact, there is very little hard information available about the source of leaks.[53]

Given the importance journalists place on not revealing their sources, this is not surprising. Furthermore, even the information that we do have may be misleading: a reference in an article to a "congressional source" or an "administration official" may not indicate who first tipped the journalist off; the original source may have spoken on "deep background," precluding any reference to him at all.[54] Thus, the article could well refer to a source who confirmed the story in some fashion, not to the one who originally leaked it.[55]

In any case, there is no doubt that congressional oversight increases the number of people with access to information about covert action; many of these people are not used to dealing with classified information, and they work in a more political setting than the average intelligence official. The need to brief Congress probably leads to the involvement of an additional number of people, almost as great, within the executive branch itself. In most cases, the number of people with access is sufficiently high that the increase due to congressional oversight probably does not significantly increase the risk of a leak; in special cases, such as that referred to by Admiral Turner, the difference could have a considerable impact.[56]

Although much of the public debate about congressional oversight centers on the question of leaks, the theoretical question is whether Congress's adopting secret procedures as a routine matter is proper and can be effective.

Before the Church Committee, Morton Halperin argued against congressional oversight:

> [Better forms of control] cannot succeed in curing the evils inherent in having a covert capability. The only weapon that opponents of a Presidential policy, inside or outside the executive branch, have is public debate. If a policy can be debated openly, then Congress may be persuaded to constrain the President and public pressure may force a change in policy. But if secrecy is accepted as the norm and as legitimate, then the checks put on covert operations can easily be ignored.[57]

This prediction has proved excessively dismissive of what congressional committees can achieve in quiet negotiation with the executive branch (the threat to "go public" remaining in the background); it does, however, contain a kernel of truth. In major disagreements such as over "covert" aid to the Nicaraguan resistance, the norm of secrecy has been abandoned, and the issue has given rise to full-scale, and public, congressional debate.

Thus, the notion of congressional oversight conducted in secrecy seems to contain an inherent flaw: if followed to the letter, it would put the intelligence committees in the role of mere advisory boards, unable to block an action of which they disapproved (at least until the next year's budget was being considered).[58] Nevertheless, if the action fails in an embarrassing and public way, the committee members are likely to be held politically responsible for not having done something to stop it. They seem to have responsibility without authority; to assert any authority, they typically have to act in a public manner, thus sacrificing secrecy.

Aside from the practical questions, there are constitutional issues that any requirement of prior notification necessarily raises. In 1980 the Carter administration took the position that an absolute prior notice requirement would be an unconstitutional infringement on the president's Article II powers;[59] as a result of negotiations between his administration and the Senate Select Committee on Intelligence, the current law qualifies the prior notification requirement with preambular language that refers to "authorities and duties . . . conferred by the Constitution on the executive . . . branch of the Government" and provides that the president give "timely" notice of all covert actions for which prior notice was not given.[60] Similarly, the Reagan administration has warned the SSCI that the president would have vetoed any requirement for forty-eight hours' notice.[61]

In a memorandum addressing this issue, the Reagan administration implied that a requirement of prior notice would be an unconstitutional infringement on the president's inherent constitutional authority to conduct foreign policy.[62] The key issue seems to be whether such a requirement could, as Admiral Turner asserted in the case of the hostage rescue mission, prevent the president from undertaking some foreign policy activity he believed to be vital to the national security. Although this question has some empirical aspects to it (for example, to what extent does notification of Congress increase the probability of a leak?), the real constitutional issue would seem to be whose judgment of the question is decisive.

In its report on the Intelligence Oversight Act of 1988, the SSCI discusses the constitutionality of requiring prior notice.[63] Most of the arguments it adduces, however, are irrelevant to the issue of *prior* notification; at most, they demonstrate that Congress requires information about covert action in order to fulfill its own responsibilities (i.e., "timely" notification). This claim is not contested by the administration, but neither does it identify any constitutional basis for a congressional demand for prior notification of covert actions.

Thus, although Congress's oversight powers, including its power to demand information, which derive from its general legislative power (the "necessary and proper" clause[64]) and its power of the purse, may require that Congress be notified of covert actions, they do not seem to require prior notification. Notification after the event, for example, in the course of the annual budget cycle, would appear to be sufficient to support their exercise. Indeed, S. 1721 would retain from current legislation the proviso that the Intelligence Committees' approval is not a "condition precedent to the initiation of such [intelligence] activities."[65]

The only conceivable basis for a demand for *prior* notification would seem to be the possibility that Congress could intervene legislatively to cut off funds for the covert action before it could be initiated (or completed). This seems to be the meaning of the report's contention that

> notice of special activities [covert action] should be given *prior* to undertaking such action in order to provide Congress with an *opportunity to exercise its responsibilities* under the Constitution. When [this can not be done], such notice must be provided as soon as possible thereafter, again to *maximize Congress' opportunity to play an effective role with respect to the execution of such activity*[66] [Emphasis added].

Given that legislative action would almost certainly require overriding a presidential veto, the possibility is remote that this could be accomplished in time to affect the execution of the covert action.[67] If, however, the committee is thinking of a long-term covert action, then there seems to be no justification for requiring notification within forty-eight hours rather than, for example, ten days.[68] In any case, if the president believed the situation to be a significant threat to U.S. national security, it is not clear that he would obey such a congressional injunction any more than Franklin D. Roosevelt did when, in 1941, he ordered the occupation of Iceland.[69]

Rather than being a serious attempt to enable Congress to exercise its constitutional responsibilities and authority, the prior notification requirement seems to reflect a desire on the part of the intelligence committees to become a kind of advisory council for the intelligence community.[70] Indeed, the provisions for notifying the Group of Eight or the Group of Four can hardly be understood otherwise, given that these groups, if they obey the implied prohibition against informing their colleagues, are not in a position to initiate any legislative action at all. Thus, the SSCI report defends these provisions by citing the "benefit" to the president of a "broader range of opinion from carefully chosen representatives of the House of Representatives and the Senate."[71] The report seeks an "effective voice" in the covert action approval process, although it notes that the president "would be free to carry out any special activity he determined was necessary, even in the face of unanimous disapproval from the Committee."[72]

There is no doubt that the congressional power of the purse—the requirement that funds be drawn from the U.S. Treasury only "in consequence of appropriations made by law"[73]—gives Congress an important role to play in all aspects of government, including the conduct of intelligence activities. In addition, the Constitution's "necessary and proper" clause suggests that Congress's power cannot be read narrowly.[74]

It does not follow, however, that in return for appropriating funds for a given purpose (such as covert action), Congress is entitled to impose any condition it wishes on how the funds are spent (such as prior notification of all covert actions). Thus, although Congress may appropriate funds to support an army or not, as it sees fit, it cannot make its appropriation conditional on the president's acquiescing to someone other than himself becoming commander in chief. He could legitimately ignore any legislative attempt to accomplish this goal indirectly, such as by creating an advisory council with which the president is bound to confer before exercising command. To the extent that the president considered a prior notice requirement an obstacle to undertaking any covert action he believed necessary, he would likewise be free to ignore it.

Today's Situation

Few people are happy with the current congressional oversight process as it pertains to "special activities." Largely depending on at which end of Pennsylvania Avenue one sits, it is typically described as being either too much or too little.

Making judgments about this debate is not easy. On the one hand, given the political environment, it is probably impractical to challenge the present mechanisms. On the other hand, to accept them is to invite a continuation of the problems and controversies that have marked political life in this area since the early 1980s.

Moreover, assessing the constitutional merits of the various proposals for covert action is somewhat frustrated by the fact that the Constitution does not explicitly address the topic. Judgments about what is constitutionally correct are not to be reached by a conclusive reading of a particular phrase or clause of that document but from the logic of the Constitution's framework. Separation of powers ultimately defines how we should think about these matters. Understanding both the strengths and the weaknesses of that system helps explain current difficulties and provides insight into what might be done to correct the present situation.

As argued earlier, one reason why the framers implemented the separation doctrine was that they saw a need for the national government to have at all times an effective executive force. As far as was institutionally possible and consistent with republican principles, it was to be a power whose existence would never be in doubt—a point embodied in the fact that the president's office is also his home.

The Constitution erected a system of government that would to the extent feasible ensure an executive power capable of meeting the evolving necessities of international affairs, while at the same time providing institutionally separate means for moderating that power with due legislative deliberation. In contrast, governments of the parliamentary type tend to reflect one of two political extremes: either stalemate or overwhelming concentrations of political power. As James Ceaser has written, the "American system . . . purchases the security of ensuring the existence of the essential executive power at the cost . . . of having the possibility of a highly energetic and unitary policy-making system."[75] So, although it is true that large-scale and long-term policy programs (such as the Caribbean Basin Initiative) may not fare well at times in a system of separated powers, it is precisely that separation that frees a president to act with the requisite dispatch and decision to protect American interests abroad (as in the case of Grenada).

Of course, it is one thing to know in theory the strengths and weaknesses of the American constitutional system and another to discipline the system's participants so that they act with them in mind. In some key respects, the two branches have turned matters on their head.

Congress, through legislation and the oversight process, has infused its own institutional tendencies to compromise and deliberate into a mechanism whose design should be to maximize secrecy, decision, and dispatch. The requirement that presidents certify with written findings that each covert action is "important to the national security" and report the same to the intelligence committees acts as a disincentive to conducting a foreign policy that is strategically decisive and tactically agile.

At the same time, the executive branch has occasionally been seen as using covert action to put in place broad new policy initiatives. Absent a clear consensus about foreign policy objectives, it is unrealistic to expect implementation of a program like the Reagan Doctrine to be free of controversy and the inevitable political turmoil that accompanies it. It really does not matter whether the accusation that administrations choose the covert route in order to avoid the more difficult task of building consensus for a policy is correct.[76] Covert programs will rarely, if ever, be sustained if they operate outside the general sense of the nation's perceived interest regardless of the kind of oversight that is exercised. The heyday of American covert action, the 1950s, was not only a result of "relaxed" congressional oversight but, more important, the product of an era of overwhelming unanimity about the country's foreign policy objectives.

In contrast, the prospect today for successfully rebuilding a foreign policy consensus is uncertain at best. The decline of discipline within the political parties, combined with the fragmentation of the power within Congress, makes forging a working alliance between the two branches a seemingly fruitless task.[77]

The effect of this dysfunction in the body politic is the creation of temporary congressional majorities determined by the lines of least political resistance. Or, in the absence of any coherent consensus, Congress will at times pass legislation that amounts to little more than an accumulation of individual policy preferences, preferences marked more by their value for domestic politics than for foreign policy. As a practical matter, then, the field available for covert programs seems well circumscribed and somewhat bedeviled by changing boundaries. So, though prudence suggests that "special activities" should stay within the foreign policy consensus, that consensus is not always easily defined.

But the political and constitutional problems would not end even if a public consensus could be resurrected. The necessities of national security will inevitably outrun the conventions of the day. There is no inextricable link between what might be required and what public opinion believes. As the example of Roosevelt's covert assistance to Great Britain in the years immediately preceding World War II suggests, this is not a theoretical speculation.[78]

Notes

1. Edward S. Corwin, *The President: Office and Powers* (New York: New York University Press, 1957), p. 171.

2. Arthur M. Schlesinger, Jr., *The Imperial Presidency* (New York: Houghton Mifflin, 1974), p. 9. The "doctrine of separation of powers was adopted by the Convention of 1787, not to promote efficiency but to preclude the exercise of arbitrary power." Justice Brandeis, Myers v. United States, 272 U.S. 52, 293 (1926). See also, Woodrow Wilson, *Constitutional Government in the United States* (New York: Columbia University Press, 1961), pp. 54-57.

3. Louis Henkin, *Foreign Affairs and the Constitution* (New York: W. W. Norton, 1975), pp. 32–33.

4. Louis Henkin, "Foreign Affairs and the Constitution," in *Foreign Affairs* (Winter 1987/88), p. 284.

5. John Locke, *Two Treatises of Government*, ed. Peter Laslett (New York: New American Library, 1960), Book 2, chap. 12, sec. 143.

6. Ibid., chap. 9, secs. 124, 126, 127.

7. Ibid., chap. 12, secs. 145, 146.

8. Ibid., sec. 147.

9. Ibid., chap. 8, secs. 108. See also chap. 14, sec. 160.

10. Ibid., chap. 12, secs. 147, 148.

11. Ibid., sec. 148.

12. Ibid., chap. 14, secs. 160, 166.

13. Montesquieu, *Spirit of the Laws* (New York: Hefner, 1949), Book 11, chap. 6, pp. 155–158, 61. Montesquieu appears to accept Locke's opinion that the power over foreign affairs is the executive's when he defines the "executive power" as the power "to make peace or war, send or receive embassies, establish public security, and provide against invasions." Ibid., p. 151.

14. Ann Stuart Diamond, "The Zenith of Separation of Powers Theory: The Federal Convention of 1787," *Publius* 8 (Summer 1978), p. 59.

15. Charles C. Thach, Jr., *The Creation of the Presidency: 1775–1789* (Baltimore: Johns Hopkins Press, 1929), p. 74.

16. Louis Fisher, "The Efficiency Side of Separated Powers," *Journal of American Studies* (August 1971), pp. 113–31.

17. Alexander Hamilton, *The Papers of Alexander Hamilton*, ed. Harold C. Syrett, 26 vols. (New York: Columbia University Press, 1961–1979), vol. 2, p. 245.

18. Abraham D. Sofaer, *War, Foreign Affairs and Constitutional Power: The Origins* (Cambridge, Mass.: Ballinger, 1976), p. 129.

19. See Edward F. Sayle, "The Historical Underpinnings of the U.S. Intelligence Community," *International Journal of Intelligence and Counterintelligence* 1, no. 1 (1986), p. 9; Statutes at Large of the United States of America, 1789–1873, vol. 1, pp. 28, 49.

20. See L. Peter Schultz, "Separation of Powers and Foreign Affairs," in Robert A. Goldwin and Art Kaufman, eds., *Separation of Powers—Does It Still Work?* (Washington, D.C.: American Enterprise Institute, 1986), pp. 124 ff;

and Edward S. Corwin, *The President's Control of Foreign Relations* (Princeton: Princeton University Press, 1917), p. 205.

21. See Senate Select Committee to Study Governmental Operations with Respect to Intelligence Activities (hereafter, Church Committee), *Final Report*, Book IV (1976), pp. 51–55. Sen. Saltonstall's remarks are cited on p. 54.

22. Ibid., Book I, pp. 184–88 for a discussion of this situation.

23. H.R. 7484, 90th Cong., 1st sess. (1967).

24. *Congressional Record*, October 2, 1974, p. S 33490.

25. The amendment applied only to the CIA: a covert action to be carried out by some other part of the U.S. government would not be covered.

26. *Congressional Record*, October 2, 1974, p. S 36488.

27. Church Committee, *Final Report*, Book I, p. 135.

28. Amendment offered by Senator Hughes, October 2, 1974, *Congressional Record*, p. S 33488.

29. See, for example, the prepared statement to the Church Committee of Morton Halperin, advocating that the U.S. renounce "as a matter of national policy" covert action as well as a career service for any clandestine intelligence activity, including collection. *Final Report*, Book I, pp. 520–23.

30. See his testimony in *Hearings before the Subcommittee on Legislation, Permanent Select Committee on Intelligence*, House of Representatives, "H.R. 1013, H.R. 1371, and Other Proposals Which Address the Issue of Affording Prior Notice of Covert Actions to the Congress" (1987), pp. 44–47. Reported in "Wright Urges Requiring Disclosure of Covert Acts," *New York Times*, April 2, 1987, p. A21.

31. Originally introduced as a separate bill, the intelligence oversight provisions are contained in Section 407 of the "Intelligence Authorization Act for Fiscal Year 1981" (P.L. 96–450).

32. Whether the president had such constitutional authority was a major bone of contention between the branches during the drafting of the legislation. The final result was an "agreement to disagree" in which Congress, without conceding that such authority existed, nevertheless recognized that a president might invoke it. This "agreement to disagree" was recorded in the "preambular clause," which subjected the prior notification requirement to the following language:

> To the extent consistent with all applicable authorities and duties, including those conferred by the Constitution upon the executive and legislative branches (Section 501(a) of the National Security Act of 1947, as amended in 1980).

33. "Reagan Pledges New Steps to Keep Congress Informed about Covert Operations," *New York Times*, August 8, 1987, p. 1.

34. Report of the Congressional Committees Investigating the Iran-Contra Affair (1987), chap. 28, pp. 423–427.

35. "Reagan Pledges New Steps to Keep Congress Informed about Covert Actions," *New York Times*, August 8, 1987, p. 1. It would appear that the fourth item (findings for non-CIA covert action programs) was already required by Executive Order 12333.

36. Representative Louis Stokes's proposed "Intelligence Oversight

Amendments of 1987" (H.R. 1013) included a requirement that the written covert action findings be furnished to the members of the National Security Council, thereby imposing a duty on the president toward his subordinates. This provision seems particularly dubious constitutionally; in a letter to the House Permanent Select Committee on Intelligence, Professor William van Alstyne, who believes that the Constitution establishes Congress as *primus inter pares* even in respect to foreign affairs, opined that the "subordination" of the president to members of his cabinet violated the separation of powers. Letter, "Hearings on H.R. 1013," March 2, 1987, Permanent Select Committee on Intelligence, House of Representatives, pp. 212–14.

37. Proposed amended reading of Section 503(a)(4) of the National Security Act of 1947.

38. Proposed amended reading of Section 503(a)(4) of the National Security Act of 1947, according to S. 1721, as reported out of the SSCI on January 27, 1988.

39. Senate Select Committee on Intelligence, "Intelligence Oversight Act of 1988," Senate Report 100–276, January 27, 1988, p. 33.

40. Under current legislation passed in 1980, the president must invoke inherent constitutional powers to avoid prior notification. The legislation included vague language that reflected the disagreement between Congress and President Carter as to the existence of such a power.

41. See letter from former DCI Admiral Stansfield Turner, *Hearings on H.R. 1013*, p. 217.

42. Testimony of Under Secretary of State Michael Armacost, in *Hearings on H.R. 1013*, pp. 167–68.

43. The Senate bill allows oral findings in cases where "immediate action . . . is required and time does not permit the preparation of a written finding"; the oral finding must be reduced to writing within forty-eight hours. In either case, notification must be provided within forty-eight hours of the initial (written or oral) "determination."

44. Proposed amended section 503(c)(3) and (4) of the National Security Act of 1947.

45. Given the importance the Hughes-Ryan Amendment plays in the history of congressional oversight of covert action, it is surprising to see how little attention it received at the time. The provision was added to the Foreign Assistance Act by voice vote. Although the bill itself was surrounded by controversy (after being recommitted to the Foreign Relations Committee, final passage was by a vote of forty-six to forty-five), this had nothing to do with the Hughes-Ryan Amendment; thus, Senators Joseph Biden, Frank Church, and George McGovern all voted against the bill. (*Congressional Record*, December 4, 1974 P.S 38151.)

46. The Church Committee laid great stress on this point, but not entirely fairly: it tended to judge past behavior by what it believed were the public's current (that is, post-Vietnam) standards.

47. Henry Kissinger's discussion of the origins of the Chilean "Track II"— the promotion of interference by the Chilean military to block Allende's selection—provides an extreme example of the scenario implied here:

Nixon was given to grandiloquent statements on which he did not insist once their implications became clear to him. The fear that unwary visitors would take the President literally was, indeed, one of the reasons why Haldeman controlled access to him so solicitously.
See Henry Kissinger, *The White House Years* (Boston: Little, Brown & Co., 1982), p. 674.

48. The 1980 intelligence oversight legislation explicitly provides that "the foregoing [notification] provision shall not require approval of the intelligence committees as a condition precedent to the initiation of any such anticipated intelligence activity [i.e., covert action]." 50 USC 413(a)(1)(A).

49. U.S. Constitution, Article I, section 6.

50. On June 29, 1971, Senator Mike Gravel relied on this provison when he read part of the text of the *Pentagon Papers* into the record of a Senate subcommittee: at that point, it was still unclear whether the courts would allow newspapers to continue publishing stories based on these documents.

51. According to Brit Hume, "Biden says he 'twice threatened to go public with covert action plans by the Reagan administration that were harebrained,' and thereby halted them." "Mighty Mouth," *The New Republic*, Sept. 1, 1986, p. 20.

52. Even such a strong believer in congressional oversight of intelligence as former DCI William Colby expressed this view:

Sadly the experience [of briefing Congress on covert action] demonstrated that secrets, if they are to remain secret, cannot be given to more than a few Congressmen—*every* new project subject to this procedure during 1975 leaked, and the 'covert' part of the CIA's covert action seemed almost gone.

William Colby, *Honorable Men: My Life in the CIA* (New York: Simon and Schuster, 1978), p. 423, emphasis in original.

53. Jim Lehrer was quoted by *Radio TV Reports* in March 1987, as making the following comment:

I think the House and Senate Intelligence Committees are colanders of leaks, and it comes from the staff. It doesn't come from the principals. . . . Let me tell you, when you're 30 years old or 34 and you're carrying all that wisdom and heavy stuff in your head, they are going to go tell it.

Coming from someone in a position to know, such a comment about sources, even in generalized form, is very rare.

54. Leon V. Sigal, *Reporters and Officials: The Organization and Politics of Newsmaking* (Lexington, Mass.: D. C. Heath and Company, 1973), pp. 113–14, discusses the use of "deep background" to help an official establish an alibi.

55. Once a reporter has the original lead, he can often force other officials to comment by threatening to run the story anyway; thus, the official faces the choice of having the story appear in print in a version that reflects the view of the original leaker (who may be his bureaucratic adversary) or of providing additional information (thereby confirming the basic facts), in order to have the published story be more "balanced" from his point of view.

56. See note 41.

57. Church Committee, *Final Report*, Book I, p. 522.

58. The difficulty is even more extreme with respect to notification of the Group of Eight or the Group of Four, as authorized by the intelligence oversight provisions of 1980 or proposed in the Intelligence Oversight Act of 1988. The logic of these provisions implies that the notified members of Congress will not tell their colleagues; but if they do not, then they are limited to giving advice that cannot be backed up by any exercise of power at all.

59. Admiral Turner testified to the SSCI in 1980 that

statutory requirements [for prior notice of covert action] would amount to excessive intrusion by the Congress into the President's exercise of his powers under the Constitution. . . . Prior reporting would reduce the President's flexibility to deal with situations involving grave danger to personal safety, or which dictate special requirements for speed and secrecy.

U.S. Senate, *National Intelligence Act of 1980, Hearings before the Select Committee on Intelligence*, 96th Congress, 2nd session, 1980, p. 17.

In 1987, Turner testified:

When a similar [prior notice] provision was discussed in 1980 in connection with the Intelligence Oversight Act of that year, I recommended to President Carter that he veto such a bill if it did pass the Congress. I believe the President was inclined to do so at that time.

U.S. House of Representatives, *H.R. 1013, H.R. 1371, and Other Proposals Which Address the Issue of Affording Prior Notice of Covert Actions to the Congress, Hearings before the Subcommittee on Legislation, Permanent Select Committee on Intelligence*, 100th Congress, 1st session, 1987, p. 45.

60. Section 501(b) of the National Security Act of 1947, as amended.

61. "Carlucci Warns of Veto On Covert-Action Notice," *Washington Post*, December 17, 1987, p. A8.

62. Office of Legal Counsel, Department of Justice, Memorandum for the Attorney General, *The President's Compliance with the "Timely Notification" Requirement of Section 501(b) of the National Security Act*, December 17, 1986.

63. *Senate Select Committee on Intelligence*, Report 100-276, pp. 19–25.

64. "Congress shall have the power . . . to make all laws which shall be necessary and proper for carrying into execution . . . all other powers vested . . . in the government of the United States, or in any department or officer thereof." U.S. Constitution, Art. I, sec. 8.

65. Proposed amended Section 501(a) of the National Security Act of 1947.

66. Ibid., p. 21.

67. As noted above, it raises additional questions about the congressional intent with respect to the "Group of Eight" and "Group of Four" notification options. If the notified members of Congress play by the rules, then even this possibility seems to be foreclosed.

68. A floor amendment to this effect, introduced by Senator Chafee was rejected, 60 to 32. "Senate Votes to Restrict Covert Acts," *Washington Post*, March 16, 1988, p. A1.

69. Congress, in raising and supporting the army in 1940, provided that

U.S. troops not be used outside the Western Hemisphere; nevertheless, President Roosevelt ordered the occupation of Iceland in July 1941.

70. Consider, for example, the following provision (deleted by the SSCI) of S. 1721 as introduced, referring to intelligence activities in general:

Such activities shall ordinarily be conducted pursuant to consultations between the President, or his representatives, and the intelligence committees, prior to the implementation of such activities.

(Proposed amended Section 501(a) of the National Security Act of 1947.) This seems to be an attempt to incorporate in legislation a situation that Deputy DCI Robert Gates says already exists: "The CIA today finds itself in a remarkable position, involuntarily poised nearly equidistant between the executive and legislative branches." "A CIA Insider Looks at the Battle over Intelligence," *Washington Post*, November 29, 1987, p. L1.

71. "Intelligence Oversight Act of 1988," Select Committee on Intelligence. U.S. Senate Report, 100-276, 100th Congress, 2nd session.

72. Ibid., p. 24. The extent to which the proponents of congressional oversight seem to be inevitably driven to an "advisory council" model may be seen in the Church Committee's view of the events leading to the 1976 Clark Amendment banning expenditure of funds for any covert action in Angola:

The dispute over Angola illustrates the dilemma Congress faces with respect to covert operations. The Hughes-Ryan amendment guaranteed information about covert action in Angola, but not any control over this controversial instrument of foreign policy. Congress had to resort to the power of the purse to express its judgment and will. *Final Report*, Book I, p. 152.

73. U.S. Constitution, Art. I, sec. 9.

74. The power "to make all laws which shall be necessary and proper for carrying into execution the foregoing powers, and all other powers vested by this Constitution in the government of the United States, or in any department or officer thereof." Art. I, sec. 8.

75. James W. Ceaser, "In Defense of Separation of Powers," in Goldwin and Kaufman, eds., *Separation of Powers*, p. 172.

76. See "Central America: The Dilemma," *Washington Post*, March 4, 1982, p. A1; Alexander M. Haig, Jr., *Caveat* (New York: Macmillan, 1984), pp. 128-29; and Malcolm Wallop, "U.S. Covert Action: Policy Tool or Policy Hedge?" *Strategic Review* (Summer 1984), p. 10.

77. In this regard, one should consider the fate of the recommendations of the National Bipartisan Commission on Central America chaired by Henry Kissinger. The commission's hope for establishment of such a consensus should be juxtaposed with the behavior of Congress toward Central America, and, in particular, Congress's passage of more than half a dozen vacillating and distinct versions of legislation affecting contra aid since 1982.

78. Gideon Rose, "When Presidents Break the Law," *National Interest* (Fall 1987), pp. 50 ff. See also Walter Berns, "Public Trial by Public Fury," *Wall Street Journal*, July 24, 1987.

6

The Impact of Limiting Legislation on the Quality of Defense Personnel

Stephen P. Rosen

*In republics, public employments are attestations of virtue, deposi-
tions with which a citizen is intrusted by his country, for whose sake
alone he ought to live, to act, and to think; consequently, he cannot
refuse public employment.*

MONTESQUIEU, *The Spirit of Laws*

*Government service or employment is a public trust requiring DOD
personnel to place loyalty to country, ethical principles, and the law
above private gain and other interests.*

DEPARTMENT OF DEFENSE DIRECTIVE

Federal legislation has adversely affected the competence of the Department of Defense bureaucracy. In particular, there are unintended
consequences of conflict-of-interest legislation on the ability of the
Department of Defense to hire and retain people with the kinds of
technical and managerial skills needed to prevent "waste, fraud, and
mismanagement." The question of what draws talented men and
women into the federal bureaucracy and keeps them there strikes
many people, including senior government officials, as less important
than the resolution of the issues of the day, which appear to be
handled by people whose pay grade is usually above that of even
senior bureaucrats. The assumption has been that average wages,
plus job security, plus public spirit would be enough to draw high-
quality employees into government service. This attitude would strike
many managers of law firms, business corporations, or management
consulting firms as odd. All of these private sector organizations
compete actively and spend money trying to attract the most qualified

employees at all levels, on the reasonable assumption that no company will make money if it is filled with lackluster recruits who have no other alternatives and are simply seeking security. Nonetheless, the reform of civil-service regulations and hiring practices is almost guaranteed to elicit general indifference.

A "Quiet Crisis"

Previous efforts to shake up the general indifference to federal personnel issues have not met with major public success. Very few efforts have been publicly made to challenge the wisdom of the current application of the conflict-of-interest laws. In 1986 the Brookings Institution and the American Enterprise Institute jointly sponsored a conference on the state of personnel in the federal government bureaucracy, referring to it as the "quiet crisis." In his December 1987 Boyer Lecture to the American Enterprise Institute, former Federal Reserve Board Chairman Paul Volcker referred to the same problem and made a powerful case for reforms that would make it possible to attract and keep higher quality people in the federal service. Constance Horner, director of the Office of Personnel Management, has spoken in similar terms about the difficulties that exist in cultivating an improved federal work force and has proposed legislation that would make it easier for the federal government to attract and financially reward merit and talent. The Center for Excellence in Government, a group of former federal officials now in the private sector, has for several years sponsored work on ways to improve the quality of the federal work force. Yet the "quiet crisis" has remained quiet, and independent observers believe that Horner's legislation will not succeed. Former Secretary of the Navy John Lehman and former Under Secretary of Defense for Research and Engineering Donald Hicks both spoke out after their retirement about the undesirable effects of the current conflict-of-interest legislation, again without noticeable effect.

Interviews with former Defense Department officials provide anecdotes that suggest the nature of the problem. According to a retired air force major general, the Strategic Defense Initiative Office (SDIO), a Defense Department component created in response to a personal presidential policy initiative strongly supported in private and in public, was unable for several years to hire an adequate technical staff. One deputy director of the SDIO, briefed in 1987 by the Office of the General Counsel of the Department of Defense about newly enacted conflict-of-interest laws, chose to resign his position. Officials from the general counsel's office also report that when they routinely brief men and women about to join the Defense Department from the private sector about the newly legislated restrictions on postgovernment employment, roughly 20 percent change their minds and refuse to enter federal service. Members of the Defense Science Board, a highly respected group of very senior technology experts in the private sector assembled to provide the government with advice on military problems, have resigned from the board because of the fear that they might be in violation of the new conflict-of-interest laws.

The uniform testimony of former defense officials, military and civilian, is that the quality of the middle-level staff in the offices responsible for technological development in the Defense Department, those agencies responsible for the military systems that in the past gave us a qualitative advantage over the numerically larger forces of the Soviet Union, has declined steadily since the late 1960s. The concern is not restricted to one political party. One individual who worked with Secretary of Defense Harold Brown to recruit highly competent managers for the Office of the Secretary of Defense after the election of Jimmy Carter tells of being turned down repeatedly by people in private industry. Subsequently, this same man worked with the U.S. Navy to recruit plant managers from private industry to manage several large quasi-industrial organizations. He employed professional headhunters to find and hire talented executives, but was turned down by all of them.

The abstract problem of civil-service reform is also a matter of concern for those interested in American national security and strategic planning. It is possible that American military policy making will be hampered not only by Soviet actions and ideological divisions within the United States about the proper role of the United States in the world, but also by the inability of the Defense Department to competently execute strategies of any administration, regardless of its political character.

This chapter cannot present a quantitative portrait of the decline in the quality of Defense Department personnel holding middle-management positions. The right of government employees to privacy prohibits the use of official government personnel files. Even if such files were available, in many cases the relevant facts would not show up in the personnel files at all, but only in the histories of people who decided not to work for the government. Instead, I rely on interviews with senior government officials now in the private sector to present a picture of the structure of incentives created largely, though by no means entirely, by congressional legislation affecting government employment. I draw tentative conclusions about the kinds of people most likely to be drawn into the government by that incentive structure and the kinds of people who will avoid government service. Proposed legislation is reviewed to consider its potential impact.

Love of Country Not Enough

It appears that legislation intended to prevent waste, fraud, and mismanagement has created a situation in which there may or may not be less fraud, but in which the people who are best able to end waste and mismanagement are systematically discouraged from accepting government employment. Congress has legislated on the assumption that love of country, "for whose sake alone he ought to live, to act, and to think" would be enough to continuously draw into government service talented people, regardless of the calls of "private gain." That assumption, in peacetime, in a wealthy nation in which talented people had many opportunities to better their condition, was not totally warranted, and the government has suffered in consequence.

In World War II, the defense mobilization of the United States was greatly facilitated by the use of experienced private sector senior- and middle-management personnel in the government. The famous "dollar-a-year men" usually remained on the payroll of their old companies so that they could do the nation's business but not have to accept the lower government salaries. No one, quite rightly, questioned their patriotism because they wanted to continue to draw their private sector wages. Reasonable conflict-of-interest problems were handled by barring these men by law from doing business in their official capacity with their old employer or from becoming involved in contract negotiations.

While the number of dollar-a-year men declined after the war, the incentives facing men and women considering work in the Defense Department in the 1960s continued to incline them toward government service. In the 1960s the government, in effect, did have the ability to compel young men from Ivy League schools to take jobs with the Defense Department. It was called the draft, which could be avoided only by enrolling in graduate and professional school and subsequently by serving as a civilian or a reserve military officer. This should by no means be taken as a veiled slur on the "whiz-kids" who went to work for the McNamara Defense Department. Given the choice of serving either in the regular military or in a management position in the Defense Department, some of these men decided that both the government and they themselves would be better off if they went to work in the Pentagon. In addition, they were not being called upon to make either short- or long-term financial sacrifices by doing so.

In the decades after the 1960s, according to Paul Volcker, government salaries have lagged behind inflation by 40 percent. This change in the salary structure, which is set by Congress in a civil-service salary schedule tied to the top salaries of members of Congress, can be seen in the changes in the salary paid to entry-level Pentagon employees. In the mid-1960s, according to one official who entered government service at the time, his fellow graduates of the Woodrow Wilson School of Public Policy at Princeton could earn roughly as much at the starting government salary as they could as an entry-level employee of an investment bank. Today, starting government salaries are roughly half of their private sector alternatives.

Conflict-of-Interest Laws

To be sure, everyone understood that one could go on to make considerably more money in the private sector while government salaries would grow more slowly and reach a much lower peak. But even in the longer term, salary prospects were less bleak than they are today because movement between the private sector and the Pentagon was much easier. The analysts in the McNamara Pentagon could, and in some cases did, leave government service to build successful and well-paid careers in companies that did business with the Pentagon. Men could go to work for the government without making a permanent commitment to a civil-service career, providing the government with needed skills at entry-level rates while gaining valuable experience, and then leave to pursue another career. In addition to these lower-level officials, men from senior positions in private industry could and did go to work for the Pentagon for salaries far below those they were already earning. The government obtained their skills at bargain prices, the officials received the satisfaction of serving their government as well as a higher market value for themselves upon their return to their private sector jobs.

There were conflict-of-interest laws, of course, in the 1960s. Sections 201–218 of Title 18 of the U.S. criminal code applied to all U.S. citizens and to all federal employees. These laws prohibited offering anything of value to a federal employee with the intent of influencing an official decision and likewise prohibited a federal employee from soliciting or receiving anything of value in return for an official act. Former government officials were enjoined forever from representing a client in an appearance before the government or by oral or written communication with the federal government in any matter "in which he participated personally and substantially as an officer or employee through decision, approval, disapproval, recommendation, the rendering of advice, investigation or otherwise, while so employed."

The provisions of the law against offering, soliciting, or receiving bribes are unexceptionable. There are, however, two perspectives on the other sections of the legislation that ban contacts between ex-government officials and their former agencies. The first, most often adopted by ex-government officials themselves, is that these sections of the law define such contacts as wrong even when the ex-official and his client approach the government with ethical and honest intentions—that is, with the desire to show the merits of their case as clearly and knowledgeably as possible. To assume that all such contacts are efforts to take advantage of a "buddy-system" of former colleagues still in government is unwarranted and unjust. The section against bribery is unexceptionable because the exchange of valuable goods has nothing to do with the merits of a case before the government. The sections on personal contacts and counseling a client, however, prohibit the exchange of information, which may or may not have anything to do with the merits of a case before the government. If the contacts play upon improper preferences, then they should be prosecuted, but a blanket prohibition on all contacts and counseling is unreasonable.

Proponents of the opposite point of view would plead that such blanket prohibitions were necessary because of the difficulty in proving that in any particular case the arguments made by a former official to his old friends in government (or those made by people using his knowledge of his old friends) played an improper role. Given the potential for abuse, it was better simply to ban the whole category of activities.

These theoretical arguments aside, did the old law create any difficulties in practice? To some extent it did, and changes to the code were enacted in 1962. A category of special government employees was created to allow the government to recruit people whose skills were needed and later allow them to return to their "real" jobs. These jobs were reserved almost exclusively for scientists, but lawmakers recognized that conflict-of-interest legislation might not always be in the interest of the government if it prevented the government from hiring the people it needed. Agency heads were also given the right to waive the statutes in exceptional cases for people with needed scientific and technical skills. Beyond this, in the judgment of men who were in a position to evaluate the quality of Defense Department personnel, the old laws in effect for decades do not seem to have created any severe problems attracting talented people into government. The changes in the quality of new government personnel from the late 1960s to the late 1970s appear to be the result of three other factors: the effective end of draft calls in 1972; the negative impact of the war in Vietnam on the social acceptability of Pentagon service, particularly for university professors; and the failure of the government pay scale to keep up with inflation. Other social and political decisions appear to have been more important than conflict-of-interest laws for the observed changes in the quality of government personnel in this period.

Restrictions on Employment. The rules of the game changed subtly during the late 1970s and early 1980s. In addition to the old permanent ban on contacts with the government in matters having to do with issues in which ex-officials had been personally and substantially involved, an amendment to Title 18, section 207 of the U.S. criminal code barred government officials leaving the government after July 1, 1979, from acting as agents or otherwise giving advice, assistance, counsel, or aid to another party doing business with the government in any matter pending in the area of responsibility of the former official during his final year of government service, whether he participated personally and substantially in that matter or not. This ban is in effect for two years after an employee leaves the government. Amendments introduced into the criminal code by way of the 1986 Defense Authorization Act, section 2397, extended the notion of blanket prohibitions on the actions of ex-government employees to prohibit the employment of ex-officials by any major defense contractor, defined as a company having sales of $10 million or more a year to the Defense Department. By this criterion, Pepsi-Cola and Quaker Oats, for example, are major defense contractors. Specifically, "certain former DOD officers and employees shall not receive compensation from a major defense contractor for a two-year period, beginning on the date" of separation from DOD. This restriction would apply to DOD officials who had spent the majority of their days handling procurement functions on-site with a contractor, who had worked anywhere on the procurement of a major defense system, or who had acted as the primary government representative in the negotiation of a major defense contract. It is important to note that these restrictions do not simply forbid a government employee from going to work for a particular company whose contract he had supervised, but forbade his employment by *any* major defense contractor. Finally, the 1978 Ethics in Government Act required that senior government and military officials disclose annually their financial holdings and make arrangements to avoid conflicts of interest.

The impact of the new laws has been severe, in the opinion of DOD officials. Laws intended to regulate postgovernment employment and to prevent government employees from feathering post-government nests for themselves have become one of the biggest barriers to the entry of experienced private sector personnel into the Defense Department. Consider the position of a manager working for a defense contractor. He may be needed to reform government arsenals, or to help NASA reform its operations. He makes far more money than he would in any government position, but still might be willing to work for the government for several years if he knew he could go back to his old job or to a comparable one in the defense industry. The new legislation creates formidable additional penalties on government service.

Requirements for Financial Disclosure. First, if the job is a middle- to high-level management position, the Ethics in Government Act will require the employee to disclose all of his financial assets. As it has been applied in recent years, he will be forced to handle possible conflicts of interest caused by ownership of stock in major defense contractors. This conflict of interest will arise very often because of the number of firms with sales of at least $10 million a year to the Department of Defense. Paradoxically, if his holdings are large, his problem may be easier because he can place his assets in a blind trust to be managed without his direct control. This option is attractive to wealthier people because the management costs of a blind trust will be smaller than the income produced by the assets. An employee with more modest holdings may not be able to afford a blind trust and will have to sell the offending stock. He will then have to pay capital gains taxes on the proceeds of that sale, even though it is mandated by the government. He therefore begins his government career with a big drop in salary and a hefty addition to his tax bill.

Restrictions on Hiring. What happens to federal employees when they wish to leave the government to return to their original careers? The new legislation makes such men and women unemployable by any defense contractor for two years after they leave the government. The new legislation even makes it difficult for them to find interim employment as consultants during those two years because of the prohibition against giving advice on issues that were pending during their last year in government. Even in a small office, it is by no means an easy task to keep track of all the pending decisions in which one is not personally involved, but for which one bears formal responsibility. No consulting company will want to risk breaking the law by hiring such people, and few ex-officials will find it easy to provide comprehensive lists of what was or what was not pending during their last year of employment. In summary, managers from defense industries must now give up their current salaries, pay tax penalties, and then face the prospect of having no job for two years after leaving the government. Not surprisingly, fewer and fewer of them are doing so, if the interviews with former defense officials are any indication.

Interpreting the Laws

The way in which almost all corporations are structured to handle legal problems exacerbates the effect of the law. A government official leaving office can now obtain a ruling from the general counsel's office enumerating those issues in which he had a major role and on which he may not lobby the government. But the law is more general than that. No one can be employed in marketing in an area that was "pending" during his last year in government service. The law prohibits employment by any defense contractors of former government officials who spent the majority of their days in "procurement functions." At what point in his or her career does a test pilot, a military analyst, or a test engineer become involved in procurement functions that make him subject to this law? Typically, an ambiguous case will be turned over to the legal department of the corporation. That department knows that if it recommends hiring an individual and the government subsequently decides that the individual in question was involved in a newly defined procurement function, the corporation will pay a large fine, and the legal department will have to explain where it went wrong. If, however, the individual is hired and is a big success, the legal department will receive no particular credit, because it did not find or hire him. The incentives presented to the legal department of any defense contractor are such as to incline them to resolve ambiguous cases by being cautious. In cases reported by the former officials, military men leaving their service have been rejected for employment for fears of conflicts of interest until the president of the hiring company personally intervened. Similar efforts by the legal staffs of consulting firms doing work for defense contractors has led some of them to adopt a rule that they will not hire anyone who could not be hired directly by a defense contractor, further restricting the employment opportunities of ex-Pentagon employees.

Just as the legal staff of a corporation is inclined to be conservative in interpreting the laws, the legal staff of the government must read the laws with an eye toward interpretations that might cause future difficulty. An issue currently causing some concern is the problem of pension funds. Although a man may leave a private company for government employment with no major financial holdings other than his house, he still may have rights to benefits from the pension fund of the corporation for which he worked. Because decisions he might make as a Defense Department official could affect the market value of the portfolio owned by his private employer's pension fund, such decisions could constitute a conflict of interest. The pressures on legal staffs within the government may be to err on the side of caution and to require the sale or conversion of those pension benefits.

The Future of Public Service

Needless to say, the Defense Department continues to find people who are willing to accept employment with it. A few generalizations are possible about the people who are not deterred by the new regulations facing prospective Defense Department employees. First, they tend to be younger or older than the average. Young men and women without previous private sector employment do not have assets or command the salaries earned in the private sector, nor do they have the financial burdens of many middle-aged men and women with families. Government service as a first job offers the opportunity to gain experience. But those young people are, by and large, not those with attractive career prospects in the private sector. As Paul Volcker has pointed out, only 16 percent of those who received master's degrees in public policy at the Kennedy School of Government at Harvard over the past ten years are now in federal service. Older business people nearing the end of their careers with no desire or need to return to the world of private defense contractors are less affected by the new legislation governing postgovernment employment.

Second, they tend to come from professions that are, in one way or another, exempt from the conflict-of-interest legislation. Law firms, for example, do not ordinarily do contract business with the Defense Department or the U.S. government, which has its own lawyers, and are therefore not major defense contractors. Lawyers can leave and return to their firms without conflict of interest. An extraordinarily large number of middle- and senior-management posts in the Defense Department are now held by lawyers. The last secretary of defense, the current and last deputy secretary of defense, the secretary of the army, and one of the under secretaries of the air force are all lawyers. Some Defense Department personnel come from the staff of senators and congressmen, to which they can return with no conflict-of-interest problems. Recent secretaries of the navy and under secretaries of the air force, for example, have Capitol Hill backgrounds. Finally, the declining job prospects for graduate students in the social sciences in the 1970s, plus the relative attractiveness of government salaries as compared with the salaries of social science academics, have led many young Ph.D. recipients into the Pentagon during the 1970s and 1980s.

Young people, experienced older business people, lawyers, congressional staffers, and academics may be valuable employees, and no effort should be made to exclude them from the Department of Defense. It is odd, however, that the incentives and disincentives that have been legislated over the past ten years have systematically tilted the balance against men and women in the prime of their professional lives (ages 40–60) who have experience in managing large industrial units in a competitive environment. It is equally odd that it is more and more likely that the people making policy choices controlling the research, development, and procurement of major Defense Department systems will have no experience in the private sector with analogous management problems.

Needless to say, there are many personnel issues in the Defense Department to which legislated restrictions are irrelevant. Individual services have adopted policies that make it difficult for their officers to obtain the kinds of advanced scientific degrees that may be useful in managing research and development at the leading edges of technology. On the brighter side, others have begun to create career paths so that officers can specialize in management and procurement. Neither of these policies was mandated or prohibited by legislation. Nonetheless, Congress has created an environment in which both the reality and the perception of reality are that legal obstacles make service in the Defense Department more unattractive to business people now than it has been in this century.

Changing that reality will not be easy. Conflicts of interest do exist and do, from time to time, create visible and politically costly scandals. Congressional legislation reflects that political fact and can do little to change it. Efforts to enable Defense Department officials to retain their wealth, however much they have earned it, or to go back to the high-paying jobs, no matter how much they deserve them, are never likely to be causes that will spawn popular enthusiasm. The tendency, instead, is for Congress to go even further in legislating tighter conflict-of-interest laws. Senators Carl Levin, Howard Metzenbaum, and Strom Thurmond introduced a substitute to S. 237 to amend the current conflict-of-interest laws. It divides government officials into tiers according to salary. Among other things, the highest officials would be prohibited, after leaving government, from communicating with the executive branch of the government of the United

93

States for one year. The idea of a "cooling off" period after government service to prevent the abuse of personal contacts may be carried to the point where their basic First Amendment freedoms are called into question. This kind of legislation will always have a constituency, and public calls to relax controls on the well-to-do who are in a position to serve the government will never be popular. Whether this is a problem caused by legislative excess that can be reversed or is the result of more basic factors is a question outside the bounds of this chapter.

7

Dangerous Constraints on the President's War Powers

Caspar W. Weinberger

It is vital to recognize the ever-increasing involvement of Congress in all aspects of executive branch affairs. The consequences of this involvement are nowhere more significant than those raised by the War Powers Act.

No one will be very surprised to hear that I believe the War Powers Act is unconstitutional. Every president who has ever been subjected to it believed it to be unconstitutional, and I do not think that any president could support it and feel able to carry out his oath of office. A law that has passed the Congress, even one passed over a veto, must be enforced until it is held to be unconstitutional. Although we have problems in establishing the kind of case that can make such a determination under our legal system, since we do not have advisory opinions, none of this should preclude presidents—and indeed none of them have been precluded—from arguing publicly that the law is in fact unconstitutional. This view now has some support even in Congress, with some members indicating their basic dissatisfaction with the law.

One senator, however, Sam Nunn, has proposed a typical congressional compromise: he would not require the president to withdraw the troops, but Congress would have to vote very quickly on whether any money would be allocated to the deployment. This proposal, of course, which enables congressmen to be on all sides of a controversial question, is thus a typical congressional response. The problem is that one just cannot conduct foreign policy—one cannot do what the Constitution directs the president to do—if there is a legislative veto with such serious consequences hanging over the executive.

The War Powers Act, as we know, was inspired by the Vietnam experience and is based primarily on the conviction that executive authority should be limited and that there should be no way for a president to move decisively without congressional action. The problem is, of course, that technically the act did not even achieve its purpose. The resulting practice, which we frowned on heavily at the Federal Trade Commission when it was applied to consumers, is the negative option. That is, a company sends some unordered merchandise, and if the consumer does not return it, it is his, and he has to pay for it.

The War Powers Act says that if Congress does not affirmatively authorize the presence of troops in certain situations, when hostilities are "imminent," then the president must take the troops out on the ninetieth day. From the point of view of the military, the ninetieth day may very well be an unsafe day for withdrawal, particularly if hostilities have occurred. Withdrawal may have to take place not as a result of a congressional vote but of a congressional nonvote. And there are, as everybody knows, a great many situations in which Congress may not be able to act within ninety days or, indeed, in the case of the budget, at all. During my tenure as secretary of health, education, and welfare we had more than two years of continuing resolutions rather than a budget because Congress could not agree on what should be done about abortion. Many things can block a resolution: Congress might adjourn, or the ninetieth day might be a holiday, for instance.

Yet one way or another, according to the War Powers Act, the troops would have to come out on the ninetieth day, no matter where they were, no matter what the situation was—and this by a *nonaction* of the Congress, a legislative veto, over which the president has no authority to act. Merely declaring the War Powers Act a bad law that can be cured by requiring a quick vote on whether to give money to the president to fund the military action is not much of a cure.

Interestingly, in few situations has the executive branch sought a declaration of war. In our history, whereas more than 200 events have involved our troops abroad, we have had only six declarations of war. Increasingly, the country will face circumstances in which the line between hostilities, war, declarations of war, and events that require the participation of American forces is more and more blurred. We certainly will have many cases in which the president, as commander in chief, will have to deploy America's armed forces to defend our interests.

The assumption in the War Powers Act that the power to make war always belonged to the legislative branch and was simply being regained after being usurped by the president is plainly wrong, as the debates of the Founding Fathers show very clearly. With good reason Presidents Nixon, Ford, Carter, and Reagan have all believed that the War Powers Act is unconstitutional and incompatible with the ability of a strong president to carry on his duties as required.

None of these arguments deny Congress a role in foreign policy; clearly it has a role. It has the power to declare war. The Senate has the power to confirm appointments and advise and consent on treaties. Congress is also briefed regularly and holds its own hearings. Congress has the absolute and indisputable leverage on all of these matters because it has the power of the purse. No actions can be carried on without the necessary funding.

With this in mind, one must recognize that the history of the country shows without any doubt that the primary responsibility for international affairs and foreign policy lies with the president. The founders placed this responsibility with the president because they had a far different view of presidential power than did the legislators who enacted the War Powers Act. Hamilton, of course, argued in *The Federalist* that the prime characteristic of the presidency is energy. By that, of course, he meant the capacity for prompt, unambiguous, and decisive action.

In the conduct of foreign affairs, among the greatest errors that can be made are indecision, delay, or frequent shifts in policy. These weaknesses quickly dispirit our allies. They send a signal of weakness that encourages our foes and invites aggression. A body whose principal strength is debate, working out compromises, or forming or determining consensus and that is under constant pressure for favorable political support will necessarily lack an ability—or even a willingness—to act decisively in a way that may be thought unpopular. This is not to say that public opinion should be flouted, but some situations require quick action, where debate and deliberation, which are the strengths of the Congress, cannot occur without potentially serious consequences to the nation's very ability to survive.

Jefferson joined Hamilton in this view of the power of the presidency. Jefferson, perceived as the archrival of the Federalists with their advocacy of a powerful presidency as their principal hallmark, was well known for great concern over executive powers, and *The Federalist* is filled with debates on the subject. Jefferson assumed without any question or debate, however, that the president had supremacy in international affairs. He said that the transaction of business with foreign nations is "executive altogether" in a letter to Washington in 1790. He said that executive powers belonged to the head of the executive department, except such portions as may be specifically submitted to the Senate, exceptions that he said had to be

97

construed very strictly. These exceptions were obviously such things as confirmations and ratification of treaties.

This was a good position for Jefferson to take, because he did not have to change it when he became president a decade later. He did not hesitate to use the full executive powers, whether to authorize the Louisiana Purchase or to dispatch U.S. naval forces to defend against the Barbary pirates that were preying on commercial vessels in the Mediterranean.

Another of Jefferson's actions was of great interest to me when I was at the Office of Management and Budget. He refused to spend funds that Congress had authorized to purchase a gunboat for use in the Indian wars. When the Indian wars ended, Jefferson believed the gunboat was unnecessary and did not buy one. That action prevailed, and the view held that a president could impound funds—until 1974 when unfortunately a president signed a bill that took that power away.

An interesting and disturbing example of what can happen when Congress intervenes or attempts to direct international affairs occurred last year. The United States was requested to protect international shipping in the Persian Gulf by keeping international waters free and open for nonbelligerent navigation and commerce of an extremely important nature, the flow of oil. We were asked to do this and concluded that we should. When we sent American naval vessels to the gulf, the opposition was loud and strident. Some even called for impeachment of the president for this terrible "violation" of the Constitution. While some senators supported the president, most called the action a violation of the War Powers Act and demanded that the act be invoked. Others sought some way to exert control over the president's action in the gulf without resorting to the act.

In the end after considerable debate, the Senate produced a resolution that was rather Delphic, not in its wisdom but in its ambiguity. The Senate passed a resolution that might or might not support the president's course of action in the gulf. The Senate voted twice: the resolution was defeated forty-seven to fifty-one, but within hours it was passed fifty-four to forty-four. And the resolution still, of course, has to pass the House and be signed by the president, which remains one of the less likely events of the year. The House held up the resolution because of a pending lawsuit brought by many congressmen alleging that the War Powers Act should have been invoked. The president will thus have the opportunity in that lawsuit to raise the unconstitutionality defense.

This Senate resolution directed that the president submit a report on the Persian Gulf within thirty days after enactment. It then put the

Senate on a quick schedule, so-called expedited procedures, so that another vote must take place thirty days after that. And that vote, what would that be on? That vote would be on a resolution that has yet to be drafted. Nobody really knows what it would contain because the resolution simply said that Congress was to vote on a resolution within this period of time. It did not acknowledge anything to guide a drafter of that resolution. It could be for almost anything: a declaration of war; removal of all forces from the gulf; or any permutation or combination of the two. So what the Senate did not pass, but then did pass, is a resolution that called for a resolution of some kind to be voted on within thirty days. It sounds confusing—because it is.

Indeed, even the Senate found itself in a quandary. Senator Dale Bumpers said that the resolution that finally won approval was carefully designed to do nothing. I have not always agreed with the senator, but I do on that. And Senator Lowell Weicker, with whom I have also had substantial disagreement, was very disappointed. He said that even though the resolution was too weak, nevertheless he would vote for it because it is better to do something than nothing. Senator David Pryor summed it up as well as anybody with words to the effect that, in the final analysis, we do not know what we have done.

Worse than the confusion is the signal it sends of a lack of American resolve. I am not sure that that is the signal we want to send to the Ayatollah, the Soviet Union, NATO, or any of our other allies. In the collegial chambers of the Senate and House, exercises in foreign policy making makes for rousing debate. But when the time comes to act, all too frequently the debate ends in indecision, contradiction, or inconclusiveness.

As a footnote to all this, we have had some fifteen years of debate about whether we should deploy a modern missile in response to the SS-18s the Soviets deployed. The Minuteman has been in the ground now since the 1960s, and we finally got permission to deploy some of the MX missiles. During that period of debate and indecision, the Soviets deployed four new and very deadly and accurate missile systems. They are working on a fifth. We do not want to emulate the Soviet system, but we must recognize that indecision, inability to bring debate to a conclusion, and unwillingness to vote on unpopular or difficult issues can put us at a serious security disadvantage.

The controversy over the War Powers Act and the debate about the gulf matter epitomize the problems that arise from applying congressional deliberation to events that require quick resolution. What would follow a determination that the War Powers Act is constitutional? Because it had not voted affirmatively, after the notification period Congress would not permit our naval forces to be in the gulf. Congress would presumably continue to debate the whole gulf policy, perhaps become enmeshed in a number of things, and might very well adjourn.

When I once made a vigorous argument on this matter to a House committee, a prominent member asked what I was worried about. He said that the House might pass a resolution that I would like. It is that "might" that worries me: the House *might* of course, but it might not take any action at all, or it might pass an unfavorable resolution, at which point all the ships would have to come home. The convoys would then have been notified—indeed, we would have notified the world—that they were unprotected.

We have longstanding interests in the Persian Gulf, where our naval forces have been since the 1940s. I believe that it will be necessary for those forces to be there more or less permanently. We cannot defend the United States, we cannot defend freedom, we cannot preserve peace, by staying within our own borders. We must be a global presence—with our troops deployed as close as possible to areas where they might be involved. The Persian Gulf is clearly an area of immense importance to us and our allies, some of whom have no oil at all. All need the free flow of commerce in this area. The gulf effort has been a substantial success. We have had many convoys pass through the gulf uneventfully under American naval escort. Our allies have weighed in very heavily, too; in fact, there are more allied ships than U.S. ships now protecting commerce in the area.

Moreover, we have successfully excluded the Soviets from a larger presence and role in the gulf, which they have sought for a long time and which would be against our interest. We have enhanced our credibility with the moderate states of the gulf and with our allies. Perhaps the greatest accomplishment is that we have moved this entire operation off the front page and it is now accepted as a routine and necessary continuing action.

The policy was initiated by the president. It was important that it be done and be done quickly and decisively. It is also important to note that the executive branch has regularly given briefings to members of Congress, committees, and individuals in the leadership on this matter. We even went so far as telling them when a convoy was scheduled to start, within two or three days, a fact that duly found its way within hours, of course, to the front pages. It is important, however, that a president have the ability to take this kind of action. It is important that Congress be informed about it; it is important that the funding be provided by the people's representatives. It is also important, though, that no president face a situation like the one in the gulf in which those ships might have to be pulled out because of congressional inaction or one in which any American forces engaged in a vital action would have to be disengaged regardless of the military consequences.

Although we should be concerned about the constitutionality of the War Powers Act, we should be equally concerned about the safety of our forces and about the necessity of deploying our forces in many parts of the world quickly and decisively. Of course, the president is responsible to the people and to Congress, and it is vital to consult with the Congress, as he does. But many in Congress seem to want something beyond consultation: they really want to run foreign policy. Yet Congress is not a body designed to deal with rapidly moving day-to-day events that are the hallmark of foreign policy and national security.

It is an inherent and perfectly proper part of our system for lengthy debate to be held and consensus reached on all kinds of domestic policy. It is perfectly proper for the president to have to report to the Congress and to the American people. It is also proper, nevertheless, as the founders directed, that the president have the responsibility for the conduct of foreign affairs and that he not be fettered in a way that prevents him from fulfilling this duty.

This issue can almost make one a warm admirer of the parliamentary system. Winning an election in a parliamentary government usually ensures the majority necessary to carry out the program presented to the people and approved through the ballot. When I mentioned this once to Prime Minister Margaret Thatcher, she said, "Oh, but you ought to see some of my backbenchers." So there are probably problems even there. What it comes down to, then—and it is very difficult to explain to foreign leaders—is that there are two American governments. In this kind of world, that can be a very difficult arrangement.

The constitutional status of the War Powers Act must be determined, or Congress must become sufficiently aware of the problems so that it will not unconstitutionally and dangerously fetter the presidency. Our responsibilities and capabilities as a superpower are fundamental to the powers of the presidency but are now being challenged in an impractical, risky, and unconstitutional way. Unless this issue is resolved, our presidents will not be able to fulfill their intended role. Consequently the United States will not be able to take the actions that can keep our freedom and our peace.

8
Commentaries and Exchanges on Military and Defense Policy

Commentary by Richard N. Perle

Executive authority means the discretion to exercise judgment in the face of uncertainty; and if this discretion means anything, it must include the discretion to make mistakes. And mistakes have surely been made—a succession of mistakes extending over a number of administrations. The Congress has responded with legislation that has contained the power of the executive to what seems, to most officials in the executive branch, a dangerous degree.

It is now virtually impossible in the defense and security area to make any decision of consequence without reference to batteries of lawyers who, in turn, have to consult an enormous volume of often confusing, sometimes contradictory, regulations. One is very much at the mercy of departmental lawyers. It is Department of Defense policy that all legal counsel to officials in the department must come from the Office of the General Counsel. Thus senior Defense Department officials are denied the opportunity to hire their own lawyers. Hiring one's own lawyer is highly desirable if one is in government, because government lawyers do not necessarily consider that the policy makers for whom they work are, in fact, their clients. They have a great many other constituencies to serve and a great many other interests to which they inevitably look. One cannot count on the sort of help that in the private sector, for example, one expects from one's lawyer.

The thicket of regulations with which one has to contend is expressed in one crude measure by the number of pages of the authorizing legislation. The last time I looked at the volume that contained the regulations affecting our foreign assistance program, it was well on the way to 2,000 pages. This is a set of rules, regulations, and directives that, when William Fulbright was chairman of the Foreign Relations Committee and Jack Kennedy was president, covered about a dozen pages.

At the time, Chairman Fulbright argued the following view of the proper relationship of the Congress to the executive with respect to foreign assistance: it is up to the Congress to decide whether there should be a foreign assistance program; once having made that decision, it is up to the executive to decide who should be assisted and to what extent and under what circumstances. That was a philosophy that Chairman Fulbright modified dramatically as he presided over the enactment of at least half those 2,000 pages during a period when the Foreign Relations Committee was hostile to the position of the executive during the Vietnam War. This has led me to be suspicious of broad, philosophical generalizations about the proper balance of authority between the legislative and the executive branch because that proper balance invariably depends on the substance of the issues involved.

Another problem is that as a government official one cannot make commitments on behalf of the United States when dealing with foreign powers. The ability to make commitments is so substantially circumscribed that other countries in their dealings with us often refuse to believe that the powers of the executive representatives could be as limited as they in fact are. I had occasion to negotiate access to American military facilities abroad, for example. It was a simple, straightforward proposition. We wanted access to real estate in other countries' territory while they wanted assistance of one kind or another. One quickly finds oneself explaining that the executive authority of the United States has no competence to commit the government of the United States to any program of assistance. We can promise to make an effort to persuade Congress to support assistance to the country in question, and frequently do, but we can make no firm commitment with any confidence at all that we will be permitted by Congress to carry out those commitments.

This has made it enormously difficult for us to negotiate our facilities around the world. It has created a great turbulence in our relations with a number of countries, including a number of friendly countries. It is difficult to explain—not only to government officials with long experience in dealing with the United States but more broadly to the press and the public and frequently the parliaments in those countries—that while they are expected to make firm commitments, we cannot be counted on to do so.

Moreover, in addition to the limits imposed by lawyers and by the requirement for congressional consent year after year, yet another problem makes it difficult for executive authority to be exercised in any consistent or coherent manner: congressional influence on the executive branch itself, especially on the bureaucracy. Several years ago, for example, a decision was made in the Department of Defense to proceed with the research and development of a tactical nuclear missile that would follow a missile deployed in Europe now nearing the end of its operational life, the Lance missile. To have a successor in place in a timely fashion, we had to begin the research and development. The army then was instructed to embark on a program.

There was some opposition to this program in Congress. Unfortunately, in this case opposition came from the chairman of the Armed Services Committee, Senator Sam Nunn, who preferred that the army not proceed with the program. An amendment was therefore adopted in an authorization bill that prevented the army from going forward with research and development. This amendment was, strictly speaking, passed by Congress as a whole, by both houses. In fact, it was an amendment on an issue—small, technical, unimportant to most members—that was the product of three or four senators at most and accepted in conference. It was never subject to serious debate.

The army looked at its options in the aftermath of this legislation and was instructed to proceed with long-range planning with a view to eventually persuading Senator Nunn that he should permit this program to go forward. The army lawyers, however, held it to be a violation of the law even to consider how we might proceed if eventually we were given the authority to act. That is, no funds could be expended for the purpose of this program, and that included thinking about assigning officers to think about what they might do if they were able to bring about a change through the normal political process.

A quite extraordinary argument occurred between the Office of the Secretary of Defense and the Office of the General Counsel of the United States Army, with the result that absolutely nothing happened until it was possible to persuade the Senate, as we eventually did, that it was wrong to have imposed that restriction. Three years later— three years having been lost in the meantime—we are now looking at a successor to a missile that will probably cease to be effective before we have a replacement ready.

One could hardly find a more obvious example of the difficulty the executive branch has in carrying out a coherent policy than the rollercoaster on which assistance to the contras in Nicaragua has proceeded these past several years. There were five Boland amendments, each one different from the one that preceded it and each one inhibiting to one degree or another the freedom and flexibility of the administration. None of them, however, was clear and categorical in adopting a policy fundamentally different from that of the administration. The result was to obscure authority and responsibility for whatever failures might occur with respect to that policy.

Another conflict between parts of the executive branch and Congress that will have profound consequences is the dispute over how to interpret the Antiballistic Missile Treaty of 1972. To reduce this controversy and its lesson to their essence, three years ago the executive branch read the treaty and the negotiating record and concluded that it permitted certain testing activities in space. The administration sought to alter the interpretation of previous administrations along lines it found valid. The administration was effectively prevented from doing so by action in the Congress—assisted by a lack of resolve within the executive branch, to be sure—with the result that a new constitutional doctrine has begun to emerge.

The new doctrine is that when the Senate of the United States ratifies a treaty, as it did in 1972, that treaty is to be interpreted from that moment onward as meaning what executive branch officials said it meant at the time, whether those officials were right or wrong, and independent of subsequent events. What this means, in essence, is that from the moment of ratification of any treaty the United States will be bound forever to the interpretation put on that treaty at the time of ratification, even if the other party to the treaty disputes that interpretation and, on the basis of their differing view, implements the treaty differently and in a way that gives it greater rights than the United States reserves for itself. In short, if a treaty is interpreted to inhibit the United States and if the other signatory says it does not wish to be inhibited in that manner because it interprets the treaty differently, then the United States will face greater inhibitions than the other party. If one accepts the view asserted by Senator Nunn and included as a rider to the INF Treaty, which President Reagan rejected only after ratification, we will be bound forever by that treaty interpretation unless the Senate is prepared, through some mechanism not yet defined by the Senator and his supporters, to approve a change in interpretation of that treaty.

This encroachment on executive authority is truly breathtaking, apart from being a very foolish waste of opportunity for the United States to negotiate agreements in which the rights and obligations of all the parties to the agreement are the same. If this doctrine prevails, our negotiating partners will understand that they can protect for themselves rights denied us by remaining vague on the terms of treaties and by permitting the executive branch of the United States, which alone has to discuss treaty interpretation in public, to commit itself to constraints that our negotiating partners may not be prepared to accept.

Commentary by Morton Halperin

Our discussion of the congressional role in foreign policy reminds me of discussions about the weather: we would love a system in which the sun shone all the time and it was hot, but not too hot, except that rain fell on each of our gardens and on the farms that grow our food. We would all agree that this would be the best situation, and we can spend a lot of time talking about how wonderful that would be. But as with the gardens, nobody knows how to bring about this world in which the executive branch is full of wise and sensible people and the Congress wisely allows the president to do what is in the national interest. That will not happen and cannot happen, given the reality that the people involved care about power, principle, and procedure. To proceed as if that ideal state will happen produces unfortunate and ineffective policies.

Mr. Perle told us that the Boland amendments were not very clear. What is true about the Boland amendments is that they are not wholly consistent with each other or with a clear policy position. If we ask ourselves why we would choose to fight one way but then tie our hands in a variety of complicated other ways, we could not deduce any policy reason to do so.

The answer, of course, is that the executive branch was confronted with public opposition, as shown by the polls, to the president's view that we needed to overthrow the Sandinista government and with Congress's unwillingness to support an attempt to overthrow that government. Instead of reading that information and deciding that until it could persuade the public and therefore Congress that the United States should not engage in a half-hearted war, the executive branch engaged each year in an effort to get as much authority to aid the contras as it could. Congress, where a majority at least in the House believed we should not be supporting the contras at all, resisted and fought back by giving additional tidbits of authority to the president to keep a majority of the vote against his position.

That is why our policy makes no sense and makes us look foolish in the world. The alternative to that approach cannot be to tell the Congress to go away: the alternative is for the executive branch to recognize that it cannot take such actions without public and congressional support and that such support is necessary to start those actions, rather than complaining later that what Congress did was inconsistent or imprecise.

Similarly, some argue that the requirement for prior notice of covert operations might be unconstitutional. That argument can be made. I think it is wrong, but it is certainly debatable. What is the alternative, though, to accepting Congress's power to require prior notice? The alternative is for Congress to refuse to allow the executive branch to spend money for a covert operation unless it is included in the annual authorization for the intelligence community. The reason the president can begin a covert operation without congressional authorization is that Congress appropriates money to the CIA and allows that money to go into a contingency fund, which it says the president can draw on to initiate a covert operation.

If Congress voted no money for the contingency fund and prohibited any money from being used for covert operations except for those approved in the secret annex to this authority, that would be constitutional in everybody's view. That is where the executive branch will drive the Congress, if the president vetoes this legislation and insists that no prior notice is constitutional. What is our alternative? Our alternative lies in accepting the legitimacy of Congress's role, or if that is distasteful, the inevitability of Congress's role.

It is time to stop wishing for a weather pattern that does not exist, to accept the reality of the situation, and to listen to the words of a great American, Senator Vandenberg, who explained to Harry Truman and Dean Acheson many years ago one of the fundamental principles of the American constitutional system. What he said was, "If you want us [the Senate and the House] in on the landings, you have to have us in on the takeoffs." What he meant was that the Congress would not support the president in his foreign policy ventures in the end, as they became increasingly unpopular at home, unless the lawmakers were involved in designing the policy and in sharing responsibility for the initiation of the policy. He was right then; I believe he is right now. Not only is that view consistent with the Constitution, but also it is the only approach that will produce sensible and sustainable policies supported by the consensus that makes them effective in the world.

We should turn the process around, so that when the executive branch concludes that a group engaged in military or paramilitary operations is one we should support or encourage, the process ought to begin with consultation with the Congress and with a congressional resolution committing the United States to the political movement engaging in such activity and authorizing the executive branch to support that movement effectively.

We ought to debate that resolution openly. The president ought to describe why we should support these people and why it is in our interest to do so and not pretend that he cannot discuss the situation because it is secret. Then if that resolution passes the Congress, Congress will be in on the takeoff and in on the landing both. We will have a credible and effective policy. And if that resolution cannot get through the Congress, we ought not to start the paramilitary operation.

Finally, I suggest we need to do the same thing on the War Powers Resolution. Senator Sam Nunn has proposed that we start over by having Congress create a small committee of people that it trusts on the issue and it ought to tell the president, "Stop reading the fine print of every law; stop getting your lawyers to figure out why you don't have to consult on this, because it fits right between the War Powers Resolution and covert operations." And tell the president that when he is thinking about sending American forces anywhere in the world where a conflict is going on, he must talk to these members of Congress before he takes action and must decide with them what the appropriate involvement of the Congress is in the process before he sends the troops.

Commentary by Carnes Lord

I want to exceed the framework of the discussion to address the role of the National Security Council and the NSC staff as instruments of executive power.

The Iran-contra affair proves little about how the NSC has been or should be used by the president. The Tower Commission Report made clear that the arms-for-hostages diplomatic activity and the off-the-books covert operation to fund the contras were not typical of the Reagan NSC staff. Contrary to what many seem to believe, the NSC has been an inherently and fundamentally weak institution within the executive branch. With the partial exception of the Nixon-Kissinger period, no president has attempted to operate a genuinely top-down national security policy-making process with the NSC as its prime instrument. Beginning with Kissinger, the NSC's involvement in operations has been largely an expression of this basic weakness. A decision was made at the outset of the Reagan administration to restore cabinet government at the expense of the White House staff, especially the NSC. Except for a relatively brief period during the tenure of Bill Clark, who sought to expand the NSC staff role in response to what he saw as a lack of agency responsiveness to presidential direction, the NSC advisers had a clearly subordinate place in the administration's councils.

What is the basic function of the national security adviser and his staff? According to the conventional wisdom, the NSC can either coordinate policy or make it, and the coordinating role is the more suitable, given the problems that necessarily arise if the adviser and the secretary of state are always fighting for control of policy. Further, that the NSC should have no operational or implementing functions tends to be taken for granted, especially in the wake of the recent scandal.

This view rests on two basic errors: that the genuine coordination or integration of policy can occur at the national level without an overall strategic approach that exceeds the competence—in both senses of that term—of any single government agency and that implementation of presidential policy can be safely left to the bureaucracy.

The single greatest flaw in the design and operation of our national security apparatus is the lack of an integrating strategy or strategic approach. This state of things, of course, has something to do with the executive-congressional relationship, but even Congress has increasingly recognized the problems caused for the government as a whole by bureaucratic fragmentation and myopia within the executive branch. And in 1986, Congress required the president to prepare an annual report on national strategy. Needless to say, preparing a report is not the same as having a strategy.

So the question of the institutional mechanisms for developing national strategy is fundamental because it bears directly on the nature of the presidency itself. As chief diplomat and chief intelligence officer of the United States, as well as commander in chief of the armed forces, the president is uniquely positioned to develop a perspective on the nation's security needs and a comprehensive strategy for meeting them.

Unfortunately, presidents have often been slow to appreciate the role that they can and should play in this area. Particularly, they have been slow to recognize the need for supporting an institutional mechanism that goes beyond the loose, personalized, and transitory arrangements characteristic of White House staff operations. Then there is the largely unrecognized problem of implementation. Most observers fail to understand the difficulties any president faces in implementing his national security policies because they fail to grasp the inevitable difference in perspective separating the president and the national security agencies. They also underestimate the weakness of the presidential office and the steady decay in recent years of bureaucratic discipline.

The president needs a staff with acknowledged authority to oversee policy implementation by the line agencies and to impose clear penalties for failure. He also needs to retain a staff capability to undertake certain operational functions of particular sensitivity or importance.

Since this latter point so directly conflicts with the conventional wisdom after Irangate, I want to avoid unnecessary misunderstandings. There are obvious reasons for minimizing NSC staff involvement in covert diplomacy and covert operations. Such activities are a distraction from the NSC's central mission and always involve a risk of crossing wires with the bureaucracy, not to mention the problems caused by bringing such activity into close proximity to the president. It is not clear, however, that it would be prudent to deny the president this option. One can imagine a number of circumstances in which the president might legitimately hesitate to entrust an operation of great sensitivity to the bureaucracy.

On balance, it is apt to be better for the president to take whatever steps are necessary to see that such an operation is properly performed by those who should bear the responsibility for it. Yet this by no means exhausts the subject of the NSC's operational responsibilities. An excellent case could be made for a greatly strengthened NSC role in all of the following areas:

- Intelligence support and information management. This includes highly sensitive areas such as the management of compartmented intelligence information of presidential interest, briefing of the president on current and long-range intelligence issues, and the computerized management of data from all sources bearing on national decision making.
- Crisis management. NSC authority in this important area has been widely recognized, at least since the Cuban missile crisis. Early in the Reagan administration, a major effort was made to improve technical capabilities within the White House and agreed procedures for crisis management. But this momentum has unfortunately been lost.
- Speech writing. NSC and White House speech writers should have full control of the mechanics of preparing presidential speeches, which are a prime instrument and expression of national strategy. They should have authority to review major speeches by agency officials as well.
- Support for the president's diplomatic role. The NSC should have

full authority to manage the president's relations with key foreign leaders. The NSC, not the State Department as is now the case, should have responsibility for summit preparations, particularly with the Soviet leadership.

• Support for the president's military role. This key point has been neglected in most discussions of the NSC role and also of the president's foreign policy or national security prerogatives. The president, as commander in chief of the armed forces, has some critical operational responsibilities. The NSC needs to serve him better than it has in the past as a staff for these functions. The NSC should have a major oversight responsibility, above all, for presidential command and control of U.S. nuclear forces and related communications. It should be centrally involved in governmentwide planning for ensuring the continuity of government functions and national preparedness in emergencies and war and should be ready to serve as an essentially civilian wartime staff to the president.

Finally, there is a widespread perception, stemming from the bureaucratic wars of the 1970s between the NSC and the State Department, that the NSC's basic sphere of activity is foreign policy. True as this may have been at particular times, I think it obscures the much wider field on which the NSC can and should play. The NSC can and should become more deeply involved in the military and intelligence communities and less involved in day-to-day foreign policy decisions. In all three cases, the NSC should serve not merely a coordinating role but also a checking and balancing function, forcing the different agencies to address critical strategic and longer-term issues. In the case of the intelligence community, for example, the NSC needs to be more active in shaping intelligence requirements, in designing and coordinating assessments of U.S. and foreign military and other capabilities, and in ensuring the effective use of intelligence by the policy agencies.

A reorientation of the NSC along these lines would face many obstacles, but it would be less than a complete revolution. Part of the problem is that presidents themselves, who usually know little about military and intelligence matters, are overly impressed with the mystique of military and intelligence professionalism. For this reason any attempt at NSC reorganization must address the need for greater institutionalization of the NSC's role to make it an instrument of genuine civilian control of the national security bureaucracy.

ABRAM SHULSKY: Morton Halperin's example of Senator Vandenberg is very interesting. When Senator Vandenberg rejected isolationism and supported NATO, that action meant something. And it did not just mean Vandenberg's vote. It did not mean that some other Republican would go off on his own. Senator Vandenberg took a substantial block of the party with him, and that was that. If you don't have a senator with substantial influence to serve as an interlocutor with the administration, then it is very hard for the Senate to be in on the takeoff; each senator goes his own way and is free to jump ship whenever the policy runs into trouble.

QUESTION: Mr. Perle, would you comment on Morton Halperin's question? If the administration were unable, as it was, to get congressional support for involvement in Nicaragua, should the United States have stayed out?

RICHARD PERLE: I believe that had the administration forced the issue in a way it chose not to, the support for the limitations enacted in the several Boland amendments would have been insufficient. The opposition in Congress would have collapsed. That is, the president had the option of saying, "We will do this my way or we will do it your way, but I will not put forward a policy of assisting the contras in containing the Sandinistas in Nicaragua and then have that policy nibbled to death by restrictions and inhibitions and diminished funding. So we pull out and let history take its course, unless we get support." I think under those circumstances, particularly when the president was at the height of his powers, he would have defeated the opponents in the House and could have had a coherent policy. He chose not to do that. The tragedy of the incoherence of our policy toward Central America is a shared responsibility between the president, who lacked the courage of his convictions, and the Congress, which lacked the courage of its convictions.

Despite what Mr. Halperin says, the various Boland amendments always left open enough ways in which assistance could be given to the contras so that the Congress would not have to face up to the responsibilities of a disastrous, calamitous defeat of the contras. The floor debate on various Boland amendments shows that those who pushed for more absolute, clear, and definitive prohibitions on assistance to the contras were defeated. That is, various members of Congress argued on a number of occasions for going beyond the language of the amendment that was then before the House, because they pointed out that it left many loopholes that the executive could exploit to continue assistance to the contras. It was a conscious and deliberate decision by the Democrats in the House to leave those loopholes.

113

Then when the president actually exploited those loopholes, forgetting that they were co-conspirators in the deal, House Democrats launched the Iran-contra recriminations in a manner that obscured their participation in permitting that sort of activity to go forward—and in particular on the issue of whether the National Security Council was an intelligence agency. Anyone reading the floor debate that led up to that particular Boland amendment would conclude that the Congress shied away from listing the National Security Council with the prohibited institutions.

MORTON HALPERIN: I agree with two-thirds of what Mr. Perle just said. First, I agree with his prediction of the outcome. The way to make all members of Congress responsible is to make them vote. If the president had said a halfway measure would do no good, that we must either do it all or do nothing and recognize that we are accepting a permanent Sandinista regime, my guess is that the Congress would have agreed to do what the president wanted.

Second, I did not say the Boland amendment was totally comprehensive but that it was clear about what it did and did not prohibit. Some things in each case were allowed to stand because Congress did not have the votes to make it absolute. What I do not agree with concerns the National Security Council. There are very clear letters that people have been indicted for and may go to jail for sending. In them they said to the Congress: "The NSC is covered by the Boland amendment. We recognize that it is covered, and we are obeying the spirit and the letter of the law." If the administration thought that the NSC was not covered, it should have said publicly that the loophole was deliberate and that the NSC would work on this issue. Colonel North should have done what he did openly. That would have put it to the Congress either to tighten the provision or to allow him to do it. Instead, what brought on Iran-contra was that the administration assured Congress that the law covered the NSC and then secretly violated those assurances.

RICHARD PERLE: We are talking here about the Congress and the executive as though these two parts of government had roughly comparable competence. It is worth remembering that these are two entirely different institutions. In the Congress are individuals whose responsibilities require them to exercise broad judgments on a great many issues every day. Typically, a senator will vote a thousand times or more in the course of a year on issues ranging from domestic policy to foreign policy to budgets and law and the like. The departments of the executive branch enjoy the luxury of employing people who have mastered the details of quite complicated subjects. It is unreasonable to expect individual members of Congress to possess, or for the institution to possess, the expertise and competence appropriate and necessary to the decision-making process.

For this reason alone, a certain deference to executive authority would seem justified to me recognizing that our political process permits the removal from power of executive authority at regular intervals when it no longer commands the support of the American public. But Congress frequently intervenes in issues on which its ignorance is considerable and understandable, given the responsibilities of its individual members.

QUESTION: If the Senate is not supposed to ratify a treaty based on what the officials of the executive branch say the treaty means, what should be the basis of treaty ratification?

RICHARD PERLE: We should be clear about one thing: executive branches do not speak; individuals do. Individuals speak with differing competence, expertise, and comprehensiveness. The particular case that triggered the current debate is a treaty passed in 1972 containing an obscure provision on the development and testing of systems that did not then exist. There was very little debate about this treaty in 1972, virtually none. The treaty was passed with only two votes in opposition. I remember this debate well because I participated in it as a member of the Senate staff. No senator paid the slightest attention to the provision in question because it was not relevant to anything the United States was doing at the time.

To the degree that the issue in question was discussed, it was misunderstood by the senators and frequently misrepresented by executive branch officials, all of whom were middle- and low-level officials. The secretary of state never commented on this particular issue, the secretary of defense never commented on it, and those individuals who did comment were operating from briefing books prepared by GS-15 level officials. Fifteen years later, then, Senator Sam Nunn says that this issue was disposed of definitively by an act of the Senate of the United States and any change in the interpretation that was represented by those middle- and low-level officials operating from briefing books, provided by still lower-level officials, is permanent U.S. law and cannot be changed in any way.

Tens of thousands of words will be spoken about the INF Treaty by various administration witnesses, and still there will remain an enormous number of ambiguities in the interpretation of that treaty. What is the treaty to mean fifteen years from now when one has to confront the implications of one of those ambiguities that was never satisfactorily resolved because nobody in the Senate had the time or the inclination to delve deeply into the subject? This is, in fact, what is going on. I have testified now four times on this treaty, and the comprehension of the senators considering it, with respect to the details, is appallingly low. I doubt that a single senator has troubled himself to read the negotiating record, although it is available to him. I know that was true in 1972 as well.

The practical issue then, is this: On complex treaties, invariably containing ambiguous provisions about which no authoritative statement can be made at the time of ratification, is every word said by every official at all levels, contradictions and all, to be regarded as absolutely binding for all time on the executive branch? I think that is just nonsense.

PART TWO
Congress and the Administration

9
Budgetary Breakdown and the Vitiation of the Veto

Judith A. Best

The budgetary process has broken down because its source of disciplinary energy, the presidential veto, has been debilitated. Serious though this is, it may be a portent of far more serious damage to the presidency as an institution—an institution vital to the solar system of governmental power. Analysis of the current budget process and of the constitutional function and purpose of the veto leads to the conclusion that an item veto for the president might be the very repair necessary.

The Executive vs. the Legislature

All forms of government, as Aristotle pointed out, suffer from the vices that attend their virtues, and republics are no exception. In monarchies the king's person is sacred, but in republics the law is sacred, and the legislature is inclined to think that its will alone is the law. The result is that a republican legislature has an instinctive animus toward a powerful and independent executive. Tocqueville understood the legislature's inclination to "Whiggery"—that is, the doctrine that urges a weak, dependent executive:

> It is to be feared lest [the legislators] should gradually appropriate to themselves a portion of that authority which the Constitution had vested in his hands. This dependence of the executive power is one of the defects inherent in republican constitutions.[1]

The problem with Whiggery is that the law as a general rule may not be sufficiently flexible to meet pressing needs and swiftly changing circumstances and, further, that the legislature, because it is a legislature—a collective body—cannot satisfy the social and political need for leadership, for direction and discipline, or for discretion and dispatch. These characteristics are the contributions of a strong, independent executive. The only way to restrain the legislative animus and overcome the defect of republics is to give the executive a portion of the sacred law-making power. The executive is no match for a republican legislature whose law-making power is plenary.

The founders endeavored to do this in part by giving the executive a qualified veto, a veto that could be overridden by two-thirds vote of each chamber of the legislature. In so doing they gave the president one-sixth of the legislative power, one-sixth being the difference between an ordinary majority and a two-thirds majority. There was no real debate in the Constitutional Convention over whether there should be a veto power but only over the proper override percentage (some delegates, including Madison and Morris, thought it should be three-fourths) and whether the executive acting alone should employ it. There was no mention or discussion at any time of possible substantive limits to the veto power. The veto was to be as broad, as all-encompassing as the legislative power granted to the whole Congress.

The fear was not that the power would be too all-embracing but rather that the legislature would try to evade it. It occurred to Madison that "if the negative of the President was confined to bills, it would be evaded by acts under *the form and name* of Resolutions, votes, etc."[2] Acting on this concern, the convention added clause 3 to Article I, section 7: "Every Order, Resolution, or vote to which the Concurrence of the Senate and House of Representatives may be necessary (except on a question of Adjournment) shall be presented to the President" for his approval or veto.

Their fears were justified. Congress has endeavored to evade and has succeeded in eviscerating the veto power. Congress has been quite inventive and persistent in its Whiggery, and in recent times congressional attempts to finesse the veto power have reached new highs. Now Congress employs last minute omnibus appropriations bills packed with "pork" and carrying numerous legislative riders to make the president an offer he cannot refuse. Provisions vetoed or threatened with a veto earlier in the year are resurrected and placed in the omnibus bill. Congress offers all-or-nothing choices that are intimidating in themselves and then compounds the threat by presenting the president with these hydra-headed bills at the last minute. He either signs, or he bears the onus for shutting down the whole government.

In 1987, the omnibus appropriations bill was not passed and presented to the president until just before Christmas, with hours, not days or weeks, to go before the entire government would have to be shut down. All thirteen separate appropriations bills were combined into one lump sum of $600 billion in a voluminous (2,100-page) document that could not have been analyzed and digested in less than weeks. Even with over 200 budget examiners working for him, the president could not have been properly informed about such a document in such a short time. The members of Congress themselves do not know what such a bill contains until weeks after they have voted on it.

This omnibus bill provides proof positive that the congressional budget process rates nomination for the title of biggest national disgrace of the decade. Not only has the budget process become a congressional attempt to pull a fast one on the president, but it has now also deteriorated to the point where our representatives pull fast ones on each other. Ignorance and irresponsibility held sway as our representatives engaged in blind voting. Private vengeance was there to salt the pork and flavor the campaign contributor payoffs.

"It was a lousy $8 million," Representative Obey paradigmatically remarked, when asked how Senator Inouye obtained a grant to build a school for Sephardic Jews in France, a project the French government had refused to finance.[3] If each of the 535 members of Congress is to be indulged in a "lousy $8 million," the budget is increased by more than $4 billion. Some, however, get far more. In another paradigmatic statement, Representative Rogers explained how Senator Kennedy's rider, aimed at Kennedy critic and publisher, Rupert Murdoch, was included: "I did not understand that it took away the FCC's waiver powers. This took place over *a ten-second period of time*."[4] Is it politically possible for the president to veto and shut down the government because of a "lousy $8 million" or even $5 billion out of a $600 billion bill? Can he shut down the government because someone surreptitiously inserts a private interest or private vendetta rider, even if it were possible for him to discover it in time?

Accountability and Congress

Congress likes to vaunt its great accountability as a representative institution voting on the budget. Here is what actually happened in the 1987 budget process. In the last frantic days and hours, budget items and riders were swapped, slipped in, and even concealed with only two or three legislators present in multiple miniconferences, some held simultaneously although supposedly run by the same

121

person. No one at all—not a single senator, congressman, or staff member—knew what the whole bill contained. Everyone who voted for this bill in effect signed a blank check on the American people's checking account:

> In the wee hours of Dec. 22, all the conference results were stacked into a pile on the floor. "Members were told, you can look at it if you want, but don't mess it up," says one staffer. The House, for its part, had all of an hour to debate before voting. Most members had to rely on little more than blind faith. Two weeks later, congressional staffers say they're still trying to find out what's all in the bill.[5]

Here we have the very "haste, inadvertence, or design" that, in *Federalist* 73, Hamilton declared produce bad laws, characteristics, he added, that a vigorous veto power should prevent. If there were any way that the media could depict this debacle with the same immediate drama it can give to a presidential signing or vetoing of a bill, there would be 535 more people soon looking for a job.

This case is not an aberration. This was the second year in a row that Congress failed to comply with and therefore waived the law regarding the thirteen separate appropriations bills, in order to bundle them all together. In 1986, the omnibus bill totaled $576 billion. And, let us note, the situation is generally escalating despite the avoidance of a continuing resolution in 1988. In 1984, Congress actually managed to complete four of the thirteen appropriations bills before the fiscal year ended and only packaged nine of them in one bill of $470 billion. In 1985, Congress was considering an omnibus appropriations bill well into December and did not complete its work until March 1986, a mere seven months late.

Failure to comply with the law and its own rules has become a way of life in Congress. For over a decade Congress has been habitually late in passing the basic budget. Not only can it not meet a deadline, it chronically waives any existing rule that would produce direction and discipline, from rules of germaneness to rules that forbid appropriations that surpass its own budget target resolutions.

Why has the situation gotten so much worse in the past ten to twelve years? In part the answer is that in 1974 Congress passed the Budget and Impoundment Control Act, which not only does not work but also ended the long-standing presidential power of impounding funds, a power that, as Senator Sam Ervin recognized, worked as a de facto "item or line veto."[6] In the main, however, the answer is that the last minute omnibus appropriations bill is virtually vetoproof, and the veto is a mechanism for discipline and prudence.

In presenting the president with last minute omnibus appropriations bills, Congress is playing the deadly game of chicken; it risks a governmental crisis because it has good reason to believe the president will capitulate. Congress is not necessarily more courageous than the president, but rather it has less to lose. The president is more visible, more conspicuous and thus will appear more culpable when the checks do not go out and the government offices do not open. The press will not take a picture of the entire Congress or even of those responsible for such a bill, and if it did there would be so many faces that any given legislator would be lost in the crowd.

Congressional Encroachment on Foreign Policy

Perhaps the most egregious attempts to finesse a veto arise when Congress encroaches on the foreign policy-making powers of the president by placing provisions that would surely be vetoed in vital appropriations and authorization bills. As L. Gordon Crovitz has pointed out, all five Boland amendments (attempts to place restrictions on the president's constitutional foreign policy-making power) were inserted in defense or intelligence bills, and "most of them wound up as small details in massive continuing resolutions."[7] Not one of these amendments was vetoed by President Reagan, and Crovitz points out that "one reason was that, in the absence of a line-item veto, he could not do so without 'closing down' the entire federal government." The other reason was that "no one at the time thought that any of the Boland amendments represented a complete bar to support of the *contras* by the executive branch."[8]

If the president had anticipated the current revisionist interpretation and if he had recognized this as a use of appropriations bills to usurp the president's constitutional foreign policy-making power, what should he have done—veto, and shut down the government? Faced with similar subsequent congressional attempts to erode the constitutional powers of the executive, President Reagan has issued public declarations of unconstitutionality that are de facto line-item vetoes.

Included in the 1987 intelligence agencies' spending bill was a provision "requiring that the Attorney General file an annual report to Congress on cases in which Soviet-bloc diplomats are allowed to enter the U.S. over the objections of the FBI."[9] Though President Reagan signed the bill, he attached to it a statement that since the requirement for this report was an unconstitutional invasion of the authority of the president, he would instruct the attorney general not to provide the report. In the 1987 State Department authorization, Congress included a provision to require the president "to close the PLO office at the United Nations."[10] Again, Reagan signed the bill although he declared the provision to be an unconstitutional intrusion on the president's power over foreign relations.

Although he was charged with exercising a nonexistent line-item veto, both of these actions can be traced back to Franklin Roosevelt's response to a provision of the Lend-Lease Act of 1941. The story is reported by Justice Robert Jackson, who in 1941 was the attorney general of the United States.[11] The objectionable provision was sec. 3(c), and Roosevelt considered it unconstitutional as it permitted Congress to repeal the act before its termination date by mere concurrent resolution, without presentment to him for his approval or veto. This Roosevelt deemed to be a violation of his rights under Art. I, sec. 7, and a clear attempt to evade a veto. Nonetheless, he signed the bill into law because, with this exception, it was "an outstanding measure which sought to meet a momentous emergency of great magnitude in world affairs.[12] It is worth noting that the bill was entitled "An Act to Promote the Defense of the United States" and the president as commander in chief must be the preeminent defender. But he is also sworn to defend the Constitution, including the other constitutionally granted powers of his office such as the veto.

Here was a dilemma: damned if he did, damned if he didn't. An item veto would have solved the problem. Not having one, Roosevelt decided on a quasi-item veto. He gave his legal opinion on the unconstitutionality of the provision in the form of an official memorandum, dated April 7, 1941, to the attorney general. Although a legal opinion by the president may seem unusual, it surely lies within his powers. Despite the tendency to call the attorney general the chief law enforcement officer of the United States, the Constitution is clear that the title actually belongs to the president, for it is he who shall "take Care that the Laws be faithfully executed." Further, as every student of judicial review knows, nothing in the Constitution vests the judiciary with the exclusive power to interpret the Constitution. John Marshall's argument for the right of the judiciary to exercise this power was based on legal necessity, on the duty of the courts to decide cases and controversies. The president also has constitutionally assigned duties, the performance of which may also necessitate (as in Roosevelt's case) a declaration of unconstitutionality.

Such a declaration may look very much like a line-item veto. Roosevelt's statement was a declaration that presidential consent to the objectionable provision, though apparently formal, was not actual: "I felt constrained to sign the measure," he said, "in spite of the fact that it contained a provision which, in my opinion, is clearly unconstitutional."[13] Moreover, he wanted this fact on the record, because he did not wish his action "in approving the bill which includes this invalid clause, to be used as a precedent for any future legislation comprising provisions of a similar nature."[14]

Tocqueville rightly called the veto "a sort of appeal to the people."[15] Roosevelt's action was not a veto and definitely not an appeal to the people. It was an appeal to posterity and especially to jurisprudence. The memorandum was to be placed in the official files of the Department of Justice and, by Roosevelt's personal request in a separate note to the attorney general, eventually to be published as an official document. Robert Jackson complied in 1953.

Fearing to strengthen opponents of Lend-Lease and to embarrass supporters, Roosevelt did not go public with his objections at the time. Roosevelt may have acted prudently, but in my judgment he did not go far enough. Presidents must be willing to cry foul *publicly* when they are constrained by congressional strategies to sign bills containing provisions they deem unconstitutional. They may have to play the congressional game, but they should play under public not private protest. The veto is essential to the balance of power between the executive and the legislature and should not be debilitated without a real fight, without an appeal to the people. Nowhere were the founders more prescient than in their prediction of legislative assaults on the powers of the president. The Constitution declares that the president is to have a substantial share in the legislative power, but the Congress does not want to share, the Constitution notwithstanding.

There is no disputing the fact that the veto power has been debilitated. Even some opponents of a line-item veto have conceded the point that "the President's general veto power has been weakened to some extent by omnibus appropriations bills."[16] There is near universal agreement that the budget process is out of control. Congress cannot control itself, nor was it designed to control itself fully. Of the two primary constitutional controls on Congress, popular election is merely periodic; the veto is to be the permanent and ongoing control. In an era where congressional elections are verging on pro forma ritual (in the 1986 election 98.4 percent of all House incumbents seeking reelection were returned), a vigorous veto power is all the more indispensable.

Checks and Balances

The founders fully expected that the legislature would not be able to control itself and would attempt to prey upon the executive, for they understood the nature of republics and concluded that in republics the legislature is the most dangerous branch. This latter point cannot be overemphasized because it is the key that explains the inclusion of the checks and balances into the separation of powers and the *pivotal role* of the veto power in the balance of the whole governmental system. During one of the several discussions on the veto power in the Constitutional Convention, Madison spoke on the nature of republics:

> Experience in all the States had evinced a powerful tendency in the Legislature to absorb all power into its vortex. This was the real source of danger to the American Constitutions; and suggested the necessity of giving every defensive authority to the other departments that was consistent with republican principles.[17]

Later in *Federalist* 48, he reiterated the point, declaring that simple separation of powers is insufficient, mere "parchment barriers" to tyranny, because "the legislative department is everywhere extending the sphere of its activity and drawing all power into its impetuous vortex." He contended that the checks and balances are indispensable to the separation of powers so that "the more feeble" branches can defend themselves against "the more powerful." He asserted that while executive usurpation is the typical problem of monarchies, in republics the usurper is usually the legislature. In fact, he said, "It is against the enterprising ambition of this department that the people ought to indulge all their jealousy and exhaust all their precautions."

Federalist 51 contains Madison's famous formulation of the policy that informed the whole Constitution: the policy of "opposite and rival interests." He used two adjectives, not one. Mere separation, mere opposition does not suffice. The interests must also be rivals, competitors of equal or nearly equal power. The merely separated departments are not true rivals, however, for "in republican government, the legislative authority necessarily predominates." Since it is a natural fact that in a republic the legislature outweighs the other two departments, the policy will not work unless steps are taken to create a greater equilibrium.

The convention separated the executive from the legislature, excluded any legislator from simultaneously holding executive office, found a mode of presidential selection that made the president independent, and gave the president a fixed salary and a fixed term of office. These efforts, however, did not create a balance of power, because in a republic the law-making power is the sacred power. The founders, then, divided the legislature; they chose bicameralism because it is a device to prevent improvident and ill-advised laws. Because bicameralism decrees that the law-making process of committee consideration, hearings, reports, and floor votes must ordinarily be gone through twice, it is designed to prevent hasty action.

The veto, of course, reinforces bicameralism. Because the veto can be overridden, it institutionalizes a process of reconsideration. But this time the reconsideration must be done in light of the views of someone in a different situation, with different duties, and with a larger, broader constituency—a national constituency. Because of their mode of selection, the legislators speak for narrow, parochial, and even special interests. The president alone speaks with a clear and authorized voice for the national interest, for the whole that is greater than the sum of its parts. The legislature cannot match that kind of authorization with a mere majority in each chamber. To match it requires an extraordinary majority of each chamber. The veto institutionalizes reconsideration from a national perspective.

The reconsideration function of the veto is based on the lessons of common sense. In the important decisions of ordinary life, like medical or surgical treatment, we are always told to seek several opinions and to be deliberate. Acting on first thoughts or passions usually leads to trouble. This function of the veto is justified not by any claim of superior wisdom and virtue in the president, but rather by the advisability of looking at a problem from many perspectives, of listening to all objections, in a phrase, by the wisdom of reconsideration.

If reinforcing bicameralism were the only function of the veto, there would be less cause for alarm over the evisceration of that power. The veto has another and even more important function—to protect the executive office by creating a balance of power. Gouverneur Morris explained why bicameralism would not suffice to create a balance of power between the legislature and the executive:

> The check provided in the second branch was not meant as a check on legislative usurpations of power, but on the abuse of lawful powers, on the propensity of the first branch to legislate too much, to run into projects of paper-money and similar expedients. It is no check on legislative tyranny. On the contrary it may favor it; and if the first branch can be seduced, may find the means of success.[18]

Bicameralism might serve to some extent to mitigate "abuse of lawful powers," that is, imprudent or unwise laws such as tax or debt laws. Bicameralism, however, is no real barrier to "usurpations of power," to legislative attempts to take over and perform the functions that belong to the executive. The representatives in the two chambers are all legislators with a common interest in a weak and compliant executive.

Thus, after explaining bicameralism and declaring that "the weight of the legislative authority requires that it should be thus divided," Madison went on, in *Federalist* 51, to suggest that "the weakness of the executive may require, on the other hand, that it should be fortified" with a veto power. The veto power is the *essential device* to adjust an inherent disequilibrium between a republican legislature and the executive. Only a veto power can prevent legislative encroachment on the executive tasks, tasks the legislature by its very nature cannot perform or perform well. In fact, Madison, in his last speech on the veto power in the convention, gave primacy to its balancing function: "The object of the revisionary power is two-fold, —*first*, to defend the Executive rights; secondly, to prevent popular or factious injustice."[19]

Hamilton, analyzing the veto power in *Federalist* 73 and describing it as both a "shield to the executive" and "an additional security against the enaction of improper laws," declared the first to be the main object: "The primary inducement to conferring the power in question upon the executive is to enable him to defend himself; the secondary one is to increase the chances in favor of the community against the passing of bad laws."

In the convention Gouverneur Morris argued for the protection of the executive office: the executive office is the major contributor to the energy and stability of the government. In fact, energy in the executive is the sine qua non of the union itself. In what is perhaps the most remarkable speech delivered in the convention, Morris declared energy in the executive to be essential to good government, a theme Hamilton was to take up later in *Federalist* 70. Morris said:

> It has been a maxim in political science that republican government is not adapted to a large extent of country, because the energy of the executive magistracy cannot reach the extreme parts of it. Our country is an extensive one. We must either then renounce the blessings of the Union, or provide an Executive with sufficient vigor to pervade every part of it.[20]

This is a powerful argument, but there is more. Morris went on to declare that "the Executive magistrate should be the guardian of the people,"[21] and in a later speech, he asserted that it was the president, "who was the general guardian of the national interests."[22]

In the same vein, Madison said, "The executive magistrate would be considered as a national officer, acting for and equally sympathizing with every part of the United States."[23] On another occasion in the convention, Madison analyzed the executive office by drawing an analogy between the executive and the judicial departments. After pointing out their similarity of function, he said,

> The difference between them seemed to consist chiefly in two circumstances,—first, the collective interest and security were much more in the power belonging to the Executive, than to the Judiciary, department; secondly, in the administration of the former, much greater latitude is left to opinion and discretion, than in the administration of the latter.[24]

Discretion, freedom to make one's own judgments, to act as one sees fit, was contemplated as a characteristic of a republican executive. Moreover, "the collective interest" as well as security is to be the appropriate focus of the executive power. A republican executive and not merely or solely the legislature can be the voice of the people. Since the collective interest and security of the nation are more the tasks of the executive than of the judiciary, Madison finds that legislative dominance over the executive is far more dangerous than dominance over the judiciary. Statements like these of Morris and Madison repudiate the Whig theory of the president as a mere clerk who faithfully executes the will of the legislature.

Morris came to the convention convinced that to establish a more national, more energetic government, they had to find a way to liberate the executive power from subordination to the legislature in a republic. There he joined with Wilson and also with Madison, whose preconvention concern focused on the failings of the state legislatures. These three men, all master rhetoricians, led the fight in the convention—not just on the veto but on all provisions touching the executive—to create a powerful, independent president. Though they lost a few battles, they won the war for a liberated executive.[25]

A careful study of Madison's *Journal of the Federal Convention* reveals that the delegates gradually but continually moved to increase the powers and independence of the executive. Powers that were originally to be granted to the legislature, such as the appointments power (especially of the justices) and the treaty-making power (a law-making power) were taken away or modified to give the executive the initiative. Power to select the president, originally to be granted to the legislature, was taken away and given to the people acting through special electors. To read the *Journal of the Federal Convention* as an argument for Whiggism is to read it backward.

The delegates had learned from experience in their colonial and confederal legislatures what legislative usurpation of the executive

129

powers produces weak, vacillating, and irresponsible government. They wanted strong, decisive, responsible government. Throughout the convention there was a growing, if sometimes inchoate, awareness that the great advantage of the separation of powers was precisely that it could free the potential energy of the executive office. If properly defended by a veto power, the executive would not be subordinate to, dominated or overwhelmed by the legislature.

The veto, said Hamilton in *Federalist* 73, is the constitutional armor without which the executive "would be absolutely unable to defend himself." Tocqueville also singles out the veto as the indispensable bulwark of the executive: "The President, moreover, is armed with a suspensive veto, which allows him to oppose the passing of such laws as might destroy the portion of independence the Constitution awards him."[26]

Why Not an Absolute Veto?

This being true, the question is, Why didn't the founders give the president an absolute veto? As Madison said in *Federalist* 51, "An absolute negative on the legislature appears, at first view, to be the natural defense with which the executive magistrate should be armed." Bicameralism, after all, gives each legislative chamber an absolute veto over the other. The Senate has an absolute veto over presidential appointments and usually over treaties. Madison, however, rejected this remedy for the imbalance of power between the two departments on the grounds that it would neither be "safe nor sufficient." Here Madison succinctly described the reaction in the convention to Wilson's proposal for an absolute veto for the executive.

Recognizing that an absolute veto would appear odiously monarchical to their fellow republicans, Wilson, supported by Hamilton, argued that it would rarely be used, for a legislature inclined to trespass on the executive would anticipate the certain defeat of such measures: "Its silent operation would therefore preserve harmony and prevent mischief."[27] The proper check on an abuse of a presidential veto, Wilson suggested, was popular election of the president, not legislative override. But, they both contended, there really was little or no risk in an absolute veto, for as Hamilton pointed out, "The King of Great Britain had not exerted his negative since the Revolution."[28]

Opposition to an absolute veto came not only from those who thought it monarchical—too much power for a single man—but also from those who thought it would make the executive too weak. Madison agreed that an absolute veto would rarely be used and, implicitly suggesting that the veto ought to be more usable, spoke for a qualified veto on the grounds that the president would not "have firmness enough to resist the Legislature, unless backed by a certain part of the body itself."[29]

The argument that an absolute veto would rarely be used backfired. The delegates understood quite well why it would rarely be used and knew further that the "silent operation" of such a veto would be nullified. Silent operation is contingent upon anticipation by the legislature, but a republican legislature would not anticipate an absolute veto. Unless the legislature proposed a patent perfidy—an undisguised attack on the people—a republican executive would not dare to exercise an absolute veto, and the legislature would be well aware of that fact. Such a veto certainly could not be used for disagreements over the wisdom or expedience of a bill, because even those members of the legislature who might agree with the reasoning of the president would be incensed by the arbitrary character and implicit claim of superiority in a plenary negative by a single man. Yet, as Roger Sherman argued, "We ought to avail ourselves of his wisdom in revising the laws," though "not permit him to overrule the decided and cool opinions of the Legislature."[30]

The convention decisively rejected the proposal, for they recognized that in a republic an absolute veto would be a declaration of war between the executive and the legislature. It would be a true constitutional crisis that could be resolved only by the people rather than by compromise, negotiation, and adjustments between the departments themselves.

Hamilton, who analyzed the veto power and explained the convention's reasoning in *Federalist* 73, there described the absolute veto as "a power odious in appearance, useless in practice." Whether or not he was completely convinced by the arguments against the absolute veto in the convention, his explication here is faithful to their position, and he was a perceptive rhetorician. He could not have missed the fact that his "infrequent use" argument backfired in the convention.

The delegates wanted a veto power that could be used with some frequency; they did not want it to be a weapon of last resort, a weapon reserved for a constitutional crisis. They thought blatant treachery or bold invasions by the legislature would be uncommon. They predicted gradual intrusions not blitzkrieg. Gradual intrusion requires more frequent use of a veto power. On the other hand, they did anticipate fallibility, precipitancy, and the pernicious effects of parochial factionalism in the legislature. Defense against legislative tyranny, legislative usurpation of the executive powers, may have been the chief function of the veto, but it was not the only function. If it were to perform the second function of being a "security against the enaction of improper laws," it had to be quite usable; fallibility is common.

Having perceived this, Hamilton did a rhetorical about-face in *Federalist* 73, where he argued against the absolute veto on the grounds that it would be useless most of the time. He said, "There would oftener be room for a charge of timidity than of rashness in the exercise of it." Again noting the reluctance of the British king to employ an absolute veto lest he incur the wrath of his people, Hamilton asserted a republican president would be even more cautious. As a result, he warned, "There would be greater danger of his not using his power when necessary, than of his using it too often or too much." It could be used only in the rare case where there was "an immediate attack upon the constitutional rights of the executive, or in the case in which the public good was evidently and palpably sacrificed."

He then argued for the qualified veto on the grounds that it "is a power which would be more readily exercised than the other." He said that the convention chose a veto that would "both facilitate the exercise of the power . . . and make its efficacy to depend on the sense of a considerable part of the legislative body."

Hamilton did not exaggerate when he suggested frequency or ordinary use. Madison also spoke of ordinary use in *Federalist* 51, where he declared that an absolute veto is not the proper remedy for the disequilibrium between the legislature and the executive because "on ordinary occasions it might not be exerted with requisite firmness." Ordinary operation, as Hamilton pointed out, includes "silent operation." An effectual veto power works through anticipation as well as through its formal invocation and perhaps even more often. Hamilton explained this in *Federalist* 73:

> A power of this nature in the executive will often have a silent and unperceived, though forcible, operation. When men, engaged in unjustifiable pursuits, are aware that obstructions may come from a quarter which they cannot control, they will often be restrained by the bare apprehension of opposition from doing what they would with eagerness rush into if no such external impediments were to be feared.

Compromise and the Veto Power

There is no question that a great many compromises have been made in our history because of the "silent operation" of the veto. It must be emphasized here that "silent operation" rests upon anticipation, and a Congress that has good reason to believe that a veto cannot be used has little reason to compromise. Congress now has less reason than ever to anticipate a veto. Through the use of last minute omnibus appropriations bills, Congress has transformed the qualified veto into something that approaches an absolute veto—a device that cannot be used "on ordinary occasions" either to defend the constitutional powers of the president or to serve as "an additional security" against bad laws.[31] A president with the "right stuff" might, if faced with a particularly intolerable omnibus bill, call Congress's bluff and shut down the government. But how often will he? How often can he do so? Can he do it every year? Congress can produce a last minute omnibus appropriations bill filled with pork, riders, and even open attacks on the president's constitutional powers every year.

In fact, as Stephen Glazier recently pointed out, "Each Congress, which sits for two years, could determine that all its actions for that period would, on the last day, be bunched together into one huge bill."[32] And the president would be faced with a take-all-or-nothing choice of unthinkable proportions. The veto would then be extinct. This worst-case scenario is highly improbable and even politically impossible, but, like all caricatures, it serves to make us aware of a real problem. The problem is that with its last-minute omnibus appropriations bills, Congress is playing the very "form and name" game that Madison and the convention anticipated and tried to forestall when they inserted clause 3 into Art. I, sec. 7. Glazier argues that "if the clause means anything, it means that the President can unbunch such bills by vetoing line-items and riders." Simply, he claims, the president already has a line-item veto.

This is an interesting argument and surely deserves serious consideration not only because the purpose of clause 3 is very clear but also because of at least three Supreme Court decisions relating to the powers of the executive, the separation of powers, or both. In *Myers v. United States,* the Court held that a congressional limitation on the president's power to remove officers of the executive branch was unconstitutional because the removal power "is an incident of the power to appoint them" and was included in "the natural meaning of the term 'executive power.' "[33] On the basis of this case and clause 3, it may be argued that the power to uncouple omnibus bills and consider separately provisions that could stand on their own as individual bills is "an incident of" and "part of the natural meaning of" the veto power. For just as a president cannot effectively exercise the executive power and "take Care that the Laws be faithfully executed" unless he can control subordinates through the possibility of removal, so the president cannot effectively exercise the veto power unless he can prevent Congress from playing the "form and name game."

In *Nixon* v. *Fitzgerald*, the Supreme Court held that the president is entitled to absolute immunity from civil damages liability arising from his official acts because such immunity is a "functionally mandated incidence of the President's unique office."[34] Speaking of "the singular importance" of his duties, duties involving matters likely to arouse "intense feelings," the Court declared that it is precisely in such cases that the public interest in the president's fearless performance of his assigned duties is greatest. The president is entrusted with a unique and essential power, the power to veto, to check the Congress. The Court's power to check Congress, judicial review, extends only to congressional acts that are unlawful—that violate the Constitution. The president was granted a broader power, the power to check congressional acts that he believes are unwise and not in the national interest, as well as those he considers to be unconstitutional. It could be argued on the basis of this case that an item veto may be a "functionally mandated incidence" of the president's veto power, particularly when Congress attempts to finesse that power with a last-minute omnibus bill.

In *Nixon* v. *Administrator of General Services*, the Court stated that in determining whether the Nixon papers law violated the separation of powers, the issue turned on whether the law "prevents the Executive Branch from accomplishing its constitutionally assigned functions."[35] And, if so, the Court must "determine whether the impact is justified by an overriding need to promote objectives within the constitutional authority of Congress." The impact of last-minute omnibus appropriations bills is surely to disrupt and deter the exercise of the veto power, a constitutionally assigned function of the executive. It is difficult to imagine any objective within the constitutional authority of Congress that could possibly outweigh the need for a viable veto power. These three cases are compatible with clause 3 of Art. I, sec. 7, and together suggest that the last-minute omnibus appropriations bill device may be unconstitutional and the president may indeed already possess an item veto.

The people are overwhelmingly in favor of an item veto—polls indicate that nearly 70 percent of the people support it. Almost all presidents since the Civil War have wanted one. The U.S. Conference of Mayors has endorsed the proposal. The governors of forty-three states have an item veto. Even some members of Congress have come to support some form of item veto. In 1985, forty-seven senators cosponsored a proposal for a legislatively created two-year item veto for appropriations bills. The proposal fell to a filibuster, although its supporters came very close to invoking cloture.

Since the failure of this proposal, Congress has continued to subvert the veto with its last-minute omnibus bills. Congress will not voluntarily abandon this practice—a practice of very questionable constitutionality. Congress is equally unlikely to pass a constitutional amendment for a line-item veto and send it to the states. The wisdom of calling a convention to propose such an amendment is highly debatable. Glazier may be right—the president may have little to lose by simply exercising a line-item veto. Congress has not fared well in the courts of late in its various attempts to usurp the executive power. It lost on the legislative veto; it lost on Gramm-Rudman-Hollings when it attempted to present revenue bills to the controller general instead of to the president.

This latter attempt to exclude the president from exerting any real control over the budget not only illustrates the instinctive legislative animus against the executive (it would rather vest authority in an unelected what's-his-name than allow the president to have a real say over budget priorities), but also reveals the deepest reason behind opposition to an item veto: Whiggery, excessive fear of executive power, the defect of republics.

Although all kinds of arguments have been advanced against the item veto, the base line argument is that it would violate the separation of powers by changing the balance of powers between the legislature and the executive. The fact, however, is that the balance of power has already been violated by congressional encroachment on the crucial veto power, and something must be done to *restore* that balance.

Congress likes the separation of powers but only when it misinterprets it. Many in Congress appear to believe, erroneously, that the Constitution gives the whole of the legislative power to Congress. It does not. Yet many in Congress continue to believe that the president's proper role in the budget process should be merely advisory. He should send Congress a set of recommendations (which of late are usually characterized as dead on arrival), and after that his role is to be only that of interested spectator. His priorities are to be ignored.

To the extent that the veto has been debilitated, Congress does not have to negotiate and compromise with the president. Congress can pack all kinds of things that would be vetoed on their own merits into the last minute omnibus bill. A line-item veto, congressmen cry, would allow the president to frustrate, to thwart, to check the Congress. But that is the very purpose of the constitutionally created veto. The word *veto* comes from the Latin, meaning I forbid. It is the power to say no. This is what angers and arouses Congress, for as Hamilton said in *Federalist* 71,

The representatives of the people, in a popular assembly, seem sometimes to fancy that they are the people themselves, and betray strong symptoms of impatience and disgust at the least sign of opposition from any other quarter; as if the exercise of its rights, by either the executive or the judiciary, were a breach of their privilege and an outrage to their dignity.

Hamilton understood republican legislatures.

Congressional budgetary practices have eroded the veto power. The veto is essential to the energetic presidency. It must be revitalized. In a government of laws and not of men, the highest morality is, as the great constitutional scholar Alexander Bickel said, "the morality of process." Men who cannot and do not agree on substantive issues such as abortion or school prayer or even on the prudence of various appropriations must agree on the process by which such decisions are made. According to our Constitution, the qualified veto is part of the correct process. Any legislative practices that finesse, subvert, or eviscerate the veto violate the morality of process.

Notes

1. Alexis de Tocqueville, *Democracy in America*, vol. 1 (New York: Random House, 1945), p. 126.

2. James Madison, *Journal of the Federal Convention* (Chicago: Scott Foresman, 1898), p. 537. Emphasis added.

3. "The Budget's Hidden Horrors," *Time*, Jan. 18, 1988, p. 19.

4. Ibid. Emphasis added.

5. Paul A. Gigot, "Budget Process: Big Happy Family, 'Lousy' Millions," *Wall Street Journal*, January 8, 1988.

6. "The Abbott-and-Costello Veto," *Wall Street Journal*, Feb. 2, 1986.

7. L. Gordon Crovitz, "Crime, the Constitution and the Iran-Contra Affair," *Commentary* (October 1987), p. 23.

8. Ibid.

9. "Testing the Waters," *Wall Street Journal*, Dec. 22, 1987.

10. "Toward a Line-Item," *Wall Street Journal*, Dec. 28, 1987.

11. Robert H. Jackson, "A Presidential Legal Opinion," *Harvard Law Review*, vol. 66, no. 8 (June 1953), pp. 1353–61.

12. Ibid., p. 1357.

13. Ibid.

14. Ibid., p. 1358.

15. Tocqueville, *Democracy in America*, p. 126.

16. Louis Fisher and Neal Devins, "How Successfully Can the States' Item Veto Be Transferred to the President?" *Georgetown Law Journal*, vol. 75, no. 1 (October 1986), p. 192.

17. Madison, *Journal of the Federal Convention*, pp. 399–400.

18. Ibid., p. 383.
19. Ibid., p. 716. Emphasis added.
20. Ibid., p. 382.
21. Ibid., p. 383.
22. Ibid., p. 682.
23. Ibid., p. 406.
24. Ibid., pp. 371–72.
25. For a full treatment of this subject, see Judith A. Best, "Legislative Tyranny and the Liberation of the Executive: A View from the Founding," *Presidential Studies Quarterly* (Fall 1987), pp. 697–709.
26. Tocqueville, *Democracy in America*, p. 126.
27. Madison, *Journal of the Federal Convention*, p. 104.
28. Ibid., p. 102.
29. Ibid., p. 103.
30. Ibid.
31. For additional analysis of the subversion of the veto power, see Judith A. Best, "The Item Veto: Would the Founders Approve?" *Presidential Studies Quarterly* (Spring 1984), pp. 183–88.
32. "Reagan Already Has Line-Item Veto," *Wall Street Journal*, Dec. 4, 1987.
33. 242 U.S. 52 (1926).
34. 457 U.S. 731, 753–754 (1982).
35. 433 U.S. 425, 442–443 (1977).

10
Micromanagement by Congress: Reality and Mythology

Louis Fisher

Micromanagement is a relatively new word to express a very old complaint: intervention by Congress in administrative details. The problem is a real one, but telling Congress to "stay out" has never been very effective. Congress oversteps at times; on other occasions the executive branch conducts itself in a manner that invites, if not compels, Congress to intervene.

We cannot hope to provoke significant changes in the behavior of either branch. We can, however, encourage a deeper understanding of why Congress is involved in administration. Avoiding slogans about micromanagement is one step in appreciating the complexity of executive-legislative relations. I make two assumptions: it is easier to tolerate what one understands; understanding can improve the performance of government.

The Framers' Design

The framers were no doubt concerned about congressional involvement in executive details. They were familiar with the inefficiencies of the Continental Congress from 1774 to 1787 and hoped to devise a constitutional system that would ensure energy and accountability in the executive. It is helpful to recall the major developments over this period.

From 1774 to 1787 the Continental Congress experimented with various techniques for discharging the duties of government. Until a permanent executive was installed in 1789, Congress had to handle all three functions: legislative, executive, and judicial. During this interval Congress first delegated managerial responsibilities to a number of

---

The views expressed in this chapter are those solely of the author.

committees. This system failed to work, as did the later system of boards staffed by men recruited from outside Congress. When departments run by single executives were eventually created in 1781, it was not until delays and makeshift arrangements had imperiled the war efforts. "It is positively pathetic," wrote one scholar, "to follow Congress through its aimless wanderings in search of a system for the satisfactory management of its executive departments."[1]

On the eve of the Philadelphia convention, George Washington wrote to General Henry Knox about the need for a system with greater energy than the Continental Congress, which not only was "slow, debilitated, and liable to be thwarted by every breath" but also lacked secrecy and was defective because it combined legislative, executive, and judicial functions in one body.[2] Shortly after the Constitution had established three branches for the national government, Washington explained that this separation of powers was neither derived from doctrine nor an expression of timidity toward power. Rather, it reflected the search for a more reliable and effective government. "It is unnecessary to be insisted upon," he wrote, "because it is well known, that the impotence of Congress under the former confederation, and the inexpediency of trusting more ample prerogatives to a single Body, gave birth to the different branches which constitute the present general government."[3]

Comments by Alexander Hamilton and Thomas Jefferson reinforce these observations by Washington. Hamilton criticized the committees of the Continental Congress, stating in 1780 that Congress had kept the power "too much into their own hands and have meddled too much with details of every sort. Congress is properly a deliberative corps and it forgets itself when it attempts to play the executive."[4]

Elected to the Continental Congress in 1783, Jefferson joined a body paralyzed by inattendance. In numerous letters he reported on the bleak prospect of attaining a quorum to do business.[5] He considered it "rational and necessary" to create independent executive and judicial branches and join them in a council of revision over legislation.[6] In 1786, while serving as minister to France, he expressed hope that the convention scheduled to meet in Philadelphia the following year would create a separate executive body "so that Congress itself should meddle only with what should be legislative."[7] After the Philadelphia convention was in session, he said that Congress had shown a propensity to wait until the "last extremities" before executing any of its powers. Drawing on his experience with the Continental Congress, he further pointed out:

Nothing is so embarrassing nor so mischievous in a great assembly as the details of execution. The smallest trifle of that kind occupies as long as the most important act of legislation, and takes place of every thing else. Let any man recollect, or look over the files of Congress, he will observe the most important propositions hanging over from week to week and month to month, till the occasions have past them, and the thing is never done.[8]

The outrage routinely directed at congressional meddling seems a little less than principled, however, when we recall how often the executive branch is chest-deep in legislative affairs. Some scholars give Hamilton credit for drafting the bill that created the Treasury Department in 1789.[9] Hamilton was an activist in the Washington administration. The journals of Senator William Maclay record the close contacts of Hamilton with legislative leaders. When his plan for a funding system was in jeopardy, Hamilton "was here early to wait on the Speaker, and I believe spent most of his time in running from place to place among the members." When the Senate considered the excise bill, Hamilton "sat close with the committee." He attended to each detail of the legislative process. After a Senate committee agreed that the power of excise inspectors should extend only to importations and distillations, Maclay remarked that Hamilton "will have even to modify this to his mind. Nothing is done without him." The loyalty of Federalist members of Congress provoked Maclay to remark: "It was, however, only for Ellsworth, King, or some of Hamilton's people to rise, and the thing was generally done."[10]

The Jefferson administration followed the same liaison methods that had been pioneered by Hamilton. Jefferson and his secretary of the Treasury, Albert Gallatin, took responsibility for initiating the main outlines of party measures. Gallatin, who had served as chairman of the House Ways and Means Committee, remained in close touch with his former colleagues and attended committee meetings in the same manner as Hamilton.[11]

It is one of the anomalies of constitutional law and separated powers that executive involvement in legislative affairs is considered acceptable (indeed highly desirable) while legislative involvement in executive affairs screams of encroachment and usurpation. That does not seem quite fair. Even the Supreme Court in recent years has adopted this one-way philosophy.

Supreme Court Doctrines

In the legislative veto case of 1983 and the Gramm-Rudman-Hollings decision of 1986, the Supreme Court adopted a highly formalistic model of the relationship between Congress and the president. The net effect is to instruct Congress that it has no business in executive affairs. Predictably, Congress has ignored the Court's preaching, as it should.

In declaring the legislative veto unconstitutional in all its forms, the Court held that future congressional efforts to alter "the legal rights, duties, and relations of persons" outside the legislative branch must follow the full lawmaking process: passage of a bill or joint resolution by both houses and presentment of that measure to the president for his signature or veto.[12] The Court lectured Congress that it could no longer rely on the legislative veto as "a convenient short-cut" to control executive agencies.[13] Instead, "legislation by the national Congress [must] be a step-by-step, deliberate and deliberative process."[14] According to the Court, the framers insisted that "the legislative power of the Federal Government be exercised in accord with a single, finely wrought and exhaustively considered, procedure."[15]

What legislature is the Court describing? Certainly not Congress, where even the most casual observer can watch proceedings that fall short of being finely wrought and exhaustively considered. There is nothing unconstitutional about Congress's passing bills that have never been sent to committee. Both houses regularly use shortcuts: suspending the rules in the House of Representatives, asking for unanimous consent in the Senate, and attaching legislative riders to appropriations bills. Not pretty, but not unconstitutional either.

The Court also indulged in a rewriting of what the framers intended by the separation of powers doctrine. The Court claimed that "it is crystal clear from the records of the Convention, contemporaneous writings and debates, that the Framers ranked other values higher than efficiency."[16] "Convenience and efficiency are not the primary objectives—or the hallmarks—of democratic government."[17] These assertions are not documented; indeed they could not be. The framers placed a high value on efficiency and wanted a government more effective and reliable than the Continental Congress.

By misrepresenting the framers and the theory of separated powers, the Court issued dicta that in no sense capture the subtleties and dynamics of executive-legislative relations. Both branches have entered into agreements and accommodations that are directly contrary to the Court's ruling. I shall give some choice examples, but first I need to comment on the Gramm-Rudman-Hollings case.

In *Bowsher* v. *Synar* (1986) the Court promoted an even more rigid model of separation of powers. The Constitution, said the Court, "does not contemplate an active role for Congress in the supervision of officers charged with the execution of the laws it enacts."[18] The fact is that the Constitution does not contemplate a number of things, including the president's ability to make law unilaterally by issuing executive orders and proclamations. The Court insists that if Congress wants to legislate it must sedulously follow each and every rule, including submission of a bill to the president, while the president can make law on his own without any congressional involvement. Again, not exactly even.

The Court also stated that the "structure of the Constitution does not permit Congress to execute the laws; it follows that Congress cannot grant to an officer under its control what it does not possess."[19] Although Congress cannot execute the laws, there are circumstances where it is reasonable for congressional committees to share in the execution of the laws. I shall give some examples. Moreover, congressional oversight of executive activities is a legitimate constitutional responsibility. The Court seems to forget what it has said in the past. In 1957 the Court noted that the power of Congress to conduct investigations "comprehends probes into departments of the Federal Government to expose corruption, inefficiency or waste."[20]

Grounding itself on the legislative veto case, the Court claims in *Bowsher* that "once Congress makes its choice in enacting legislation, its participation ends. Congress can thereafter control the execution of its enactment only indirectly—by passing new legislation."[21] That, of course, is nonsense. Congress controls the execution of laws through hearings, committee investigations, studies by the General Accounting Office, informal contacts between members of Congress and agency officials, and nonstatutory controls. Congress controls the execution of laws when each house invokes its contempt power and when committees issue subpoenas. These actions do not conform to the legislative veto ruling (passage of a bill by both houses and presentment to the president), and yet the Court has recognized the legitimacy of both congressional contempt citations and committee subpoenas.[22]

In seeking precedents to support the Gramm-Rudman-Hollings ruling, the Court reached back to a passage from *Humphrey's Executor v. United States* (1935). In that case the Court upheld the right of Congress to place limits on the president's removal of commissioners of the Federal Trade Commission. In the Gramm-Rudman-Hollings decision the Court quoted this language from Justice George Sutherland in the 1935 case:

> The fundamental necessity of maintaining each of the three general departments of government entirely free from the control or coercive influence, direct or indirect, of either of the others, has often been stressed and is hardly open to serious discussion. So much is implied in the very fact of the

143

separation of the powers of these departments by the Constitution; and in the rule which recognizes their essential coequality.[23]

What would we say if a student of American government, in a final examination, wrote that the separation of powers doctrine kept the three branches of government "entirely free from the control or coercive influence, direct or indirect, of either of the others"? Would we not wonder where that student had been throughout the semester? Had the student read nothing of Madison's essays in the *Federalist* Nos. 37, 47, 48, and 51, where Madison emphasizes again and again that branches will not stay separate unless they have some control over one another? Was the student absent or asleep when the class discussed checks and balances? Did the student ignore Hamilton's essay in *Federalist* No. 66, where he said that the separation maxim was "entirely compatible with a partial intermixture" and that this overlapping was, in fact, not only "proper, but necessary to the mutual defense of the several members of the government, against each other"? Hamilton drove home the same point in *Federalist* Nos. 71, 73, and 75.

To support its unsupportable interpretation of the separation of powers doctrine, the Court in *Bowsher* tried to corrupt the writings of James Madison and Justice Robert H. Jackson. Consider the following passage:

The declared purpose of separating and dividing the powers of government, of course, was to "diffus[e] power the better to secure liberty." *Youngstown Sheet & Tube Co. v. Sawyer*, 343 U.S. 579, 635, 72 S.Ct. 863, 870, 96 L.Ed. 1153 (1952) (Jackson, J., concurring). Justice Jackson's words echo the famous warning of Montesquieu, quoted by James Madison in the Federalist No. 47, that "'there can be no liberty where the legislative and executive powers are united in the same person, or body of magistrates.'"[24]

Anyone even vaguely familiar with Jackson's concurrence in *Youngstown* will recognize that the Court has irresponsibly distorted his position. His full statement, without question, endorsed powers as shared, not separate: "While the Constitution diffused power the better to secure liberty, it also contemplates that practice will integrate the dispersed powers into a workable government. It enjoins upon its branches separateness but interdependence, autonomy but reciprocity."[25]

The Court also garbled Madison's position. Although Madison quoted Montesquieu that there can be no liberty where the legislative and executive powers are united in the same person, immediately afterward he explained that the French philosopher did not mean that "these departments ought to have no *partial* agency in, or no *control* over, the acts of each other." The meaning of Montesquieu, said Madison, "can amount to no more than this, that where the *whole* power of one department is exercised by the same hands which possess the *whole* power of another department, the fundamental principles of a free constitution are subverted."[26] Gramm-Rudman-Hollings had many consitutional defects, and I identified several when I appeared before the House Committee on Governmental Affairs.[27] The deficit-reduction scheme, however, which delegated to the comptroller general a role in the sequestration process, was never an effort to place the whole of the executive power within the legislative branch. The writings of Madison give no support for the Court's decision in *Bowsher*.

The Constitution contemplates an overlapping, not a separation, of powers. At the time of the Philadelphia convention, a contemporary pamphleteer called the separation doctrine, in its pure form, a "hackneyed principle" and a "trite maxim."[28] Some of the states wanted to add a separation clause to the national bill of rights.[29] The proposed language, which Madison submitted to the House in 1789, read as follows:

> The powers delegated by this constitution are appropriated to the departments to which they are respectively distributed: so that the legislative department shall never exercise the powers vested in the executive or judicial [,] nor the executive exercise the powers vested in the legislative or judicial, nor the judicial exercise the powers vested in the legislative or executive departments.[30]

Here was a good opportunity to go on record against intervention, meddling, overreaching, and micromanagement. Congress rejected the proposal, as well as a substitute amendment to make the three departments "separate and distinct."[31]

The Supreme Court has not always been as doctrinaire on separation of powers as in the *Chadha* and *Bowsher* cases. In 1974 the Court rejected the claim of President Richard Nixon's counsel that the assertion of executive privilege was absolute because of the separation of powers. Under the counsel's theory the president is insulated from a judicial subpoena in a criminal prosecution.[32] The Court explained that under the system devised by the framers, allocating power among three branches, "the separate powers were not intended to operate with absolute independence."[33] The Court supports this point by quoting Justice Jackson in full from the steel seizure case, rather than in part as in *Bowsher*. Accepting Nixon's rigid argument, said the Court, "would upset the consitutional balance of 'a workable government' [quoting Jackson]."[34]

Three years later, in a case involving access to the Nixon tapes, the Court once again rejected a rigid doctrine of separated powers. Specifically, it examined the language of *Humphrey's Executor* that "each of the three general departments of government [must remain] entirely free from the control or coercive influence, direct or indirect, of either of the others."[35] Instead of following this wooden formulation, the Court opted for "the more pragmatic, flexible approach of Madison in the Federalist Papers and later of Mr. Justice Story."[36] It said that the proper inquiry is whether a statute "prevents the Executive Branch from accomplishing its constitutionally assigned functions" and a "potential for disruption" is present.[37]

More recently, on the same day that *Bowsher* was announced, the Court also adopted a pragmatic view of separated powers. A case was brought challenging the authority of the Commodity Futures Trading Commission to adjudicate certain matters. It was argued that adjudication by an executive agency violates the principle of separated powers. A 7–2 Court, with only Justices William J. Brennan and Thurgood Marshall dissenting, refused to adopt "formalistic and unbending rules" to decide the separation of powers issue.[38] Such rules might "unduly constrict Congress' ability to take needed and innovative action."[39] The Court weighed a number of factors "with an eye to the practical effect" that the congressional action would have on the structure and powers of government."[40]

The Legislative Veto

Probably no congressional action in recent years matches the reputation for intrusiveness and micromanagement so much as the legislative veto. This device was attached to hundreds of statutory provisions, allowing Congress or one house or its committees and subcommittees to control executive activities. All these devices had a common quality: none went to the president for his signature or veto. Some had the additional quality of requiring action by only one house. A well-known article in 1975, suggestively called "Congress Steps Out: A Look at Congressional Control of the Executive," concluded that the committee veto "should be considered per se invalid."[41] Moreover, this study said that the use of most simple (one-house) and concurrent (two-house) resolutions "should be considered invalid as inconsistent with the Framers' intentions and their views of the separation of powers."[42]

In *Chadha* the Court agreed with this assessment by striking down the legislative veto because it violated two constitutional principles: bicameralism and presentment of bills to the president. What the article in 1975 and the Court decision in 1983 never came to terms with is that the legislative veto was not a case of Congress's "stepping out." It was not a tool invented by legislators to invade the executive branch or dabble in micromanagement. It was a mechanism to further the interests of the *executive*. Unless you understand that, you cannot comprehend either why the legislative veto began or why it persists even to this day, despite the Court's pronouncement.

The legislative veto emerged in the 1930s primarily as a way to broaden executive authority. President Herbert Hoover wanted to reorganize the executive branch without having to pass a bill through Congress. He realized that Congress would never consent to delegating that authority without being able to check his actions with something short of passing a law. Thus a pact was born: Hoover could submit a reorganization plan that would become law within sixty days unless either house of Congress disapproved.[43]

This was the essence of the legislative veto: a simple quid pro quo that allowed the executive branch to make law without any legislative action but gave Congress the right to recapture control without having to pass another public law (and attract a two-thirds majority in each house to override a presidential veto). The legislative veto survives because, using Jackson's term, it helps make government "workable." It persists, notwithstanding *Chadha*, because it is better than the alternatives.

From the Court's decision on June 23, 1983, to the adjournment of the Ninety-ninth Congress in October 1986, Congress included an additional 102 legislative vetoes in bills and President Ronald Reagan signed them into law. A shocking case of Congress failing to comply with a high court edict? Another example of Congress willfully violating constitutional boundaries? Before we satisfy our moral appetite to issue condemnations, let us look at the record.

Most of the new legislative vetoes require agencies to obtain the approval of the Appropriations committees before taking certain actions. The agencies comply with this arrangement because it gives them a substantial amount of discretion to move funds around and initiate other managerial decisions. If they refused the quid pro quo, Congress would withhold the authority and force agencies to do what the Court in *Chadha* said is necessary: come to Congress and seek approval through the regular legislative process. Neither side wants to go through the entire legislative hoop—passage by both houses and presentment of a bill to the president—to make these midyear adjustments.

Take a look at what happens when these arrangements collapse. In 1984 Reagan received the housing appropriations bill and observed that it contained a number of committee vetoes. In his signing statement he asked Congress to stop adding provisions that the Court had held unconstitutional. He also said that the administration did not feel bound by the statutory requirements that agencies seek committee approval before implementing certain actions.[44] In short, he invited agencies merely to notify the committees and then to do whatever they wanted.

It did not take the genius of a Nostradamus to predict what would happen. The House Appropriations Committee reviewed an agreement it had reached with the National Aeronautics and Space Administration. The accommodation had placed dollar caps on various NASA programs, allowing the agency to exceed the caps if it first obtained the approval of the Appropriations committees. Because of Reagan's signing statement, the House Appropriations Committee said that it would remove the constitutional objection by repealing the committee veto. At the same time it would repeal NASA's authority to exceed the dollar caps. If NASA wanted to exceed those levels, they would have to comply with *Chadha*: get a public law.[45]

Here we leave the abstract world that neatly assigns "executive" and "legislative" powers to separate compartments and begin the search for workable solutions. The administrator of NASA, James M. Beggs, wrote to both Appropriations committees to suggest a new accommodation. Instead of putting dollar caps and committee vetoes in a public law, he proposed that the caps be placed in the conference report that accompanies the appropriations bill. He then promised that the agency would not exceed those caps "without the prior approval of the Committees."[46] What could not be done directly by statute would be done indirectly by informal agreement. *Chadha* does not affect these nonstatutory "legislative vetoes." They are not legal in effect. They are, however, in effect legal. If agencies violate agreements with their review committees, they can expect onerous sanctions and penalties. Is this micromanagement? You be the judge.

I will give another example of a committee veto that was challenged on constitutional grounds. After the fight was over and the dust cleared, it remains part of public law. For a number of years the following language has appeared in the appropriations bill for foreign assistance: "None of the funds made available by this Act may be obligated under an appropriation account to which they were not appropriated without the prior written approval of the Committees on Appropriations." For some reason the Reagan administration decided to challenge this procedure in 1987. James C. Miller III, director of the Office of Management and Budget (OMB), raised numerous objections to the foreign aid bill, including the provision for the committee veto. He said it "violates constitutional principles" established by the Court in *Chadha*.

The response from Congress was both predictable and bipartisan. David Obey, chairman of the Foreign Operations Subcommittee of the House Appropriations Committee, along with Mickey Edwards, the ranking minority member, told OMB it would delete *all* the language, removing not only the committee veto but the authority to obligate funds under a different account (transfer authority). Obey said that the OMB letter "means we don't have an accommodation any more, so the hell with it, spend the money like we appropriated it. It's just dumb on their part." Edwards added that OMB "has not had a history of being very thoughtful or for consulting people" and that the provision was an example of "the spirit of cooperation between the executive and legislative branches, which the administration is not very good at."[47] OMB backed down, realizing that it had shot itself in the foot. The language appears in the continuing resolution signed by Reagan on December 22, 1987 (P.L. 100-202). Another case of micromanagement? Judge for yourself.

Why Does Congress Intervene?

Instead of issuing broadsides about Congress's "meddling" or indulging in micromanagement, we need a better understanding of what Congress does and why it does it. Surely one of the deepest penetrations by Congress into administrative matters is the Iran-contra affair. For almost a year two select committees of Congress combed through hundreds of thousands of documents, many of them top secret. Confidential messages by National Security Council staff, after some redacting, were made available to the public. Committee staff took depositions of key officials. Many officers of cabinet rank, including Secretary of State George Shultz and Secretary of Defense Caspar Weinberger, testified in public about their participation in meetings involving national security. Even portions of President Reagan's diary were released to congressional investigators. Attorney General Edwin Meese asked the court to appoint an independent counsel to investigate possible criminal prosecutions. President Reagan said he gave this appointment his "full support and encouragement."[48]

In response to these developments, Vice President George Bush gave an address to the Federalist Society early in 1987. He objected that Congress had asserted "an increasingly influential role in the micro-management of foreign policy." He also said that the framers did not intend that "our foreign policy should be conducted and reviewed by grand juries."[49] Why did this level of congressional involvement occur? I suggest two reasons.

First, President Reagan failed to see that the laws were faithfully executed. During his "watch" it was his responsibility to ensure that subordinates were properly supervised and controlled. Either he knew of the operations and authorized them, or he was unaware of what was happening in his own administration. Presidents who fail to check abuse and criminal conduct within the executive branch cannot complain when Congress and grand juries step in.

Second, even when the scandal became public in November 1986, Reagan failed to respond adequately. The investigation by Attorney General Meese is a model of how inquiries should not be conducted. Meese assigned the task to Justice Department attorneys with known loyalties to the administration and with little experience in national security or with criminal investigation. Sufficient notice was given to Colonel Oliver North and his colleagues to give them time to destroy or doctor incriminating evidence. Instead of President Reagan's calling in John Poindexter, Robert McFarlane, North, William Casey, and others who were involved, discovering exactly what happened, and regaining control, that task was delegated to outside parties.

The report by the Tower commission was excellent, given the tight deadline it faced. One of the extraordinary findings is that it had to tell President Reagan what he had done: that he had traded arms for hostages. As President Reagan said in his address to the nation: "A few months ago I told the American people I did not trade arms for hostages. My heart and my best intentions still tell me that's true, but the facts and the evidence tell me it is not."[50] A president who wants to avoid congressional intrusion has to exercise better control than that.

Iran-contra involves congressional intervention at the highest level and for high stakes. Other examples of congressional intervention are less visible and less earthshaking. Nonetheless, they illustrate how Congress can be drawn into "micromanagement."

Consider the following language, which appears in section 626 of the agriculture appropriations bill, included in the continuing resolution signed by President Reagan on December 22, 1987:

> None of the funds provided in this Act may be used to reduce programs by establishing an end-of-year employment

ceiling on full-time equivalent staff years below the level set herein for the following agencies: Farmers Home Administration, 12,675; Agricultural Stabilization and Conservation Service, 2,550; Rural Electrification Administration, 550; and Soil Conservation Service, 14,177.

Why would Congress descend to that level of minutiae and circumscribe the flexibility of officials to manage their agencies? Every provision like this has a history. During the Nixon years, when the administration was impounding large amounts of appropriated funds, it was recognized that personnel ceilings were a more subtle form of impoundment. OMB could simply place a ceiling on the number of employees an agency could have, making it difficult for the agency to spend all its funds. Personnel ceilings could also be used by the administration to dictate priorities: give preferred programs full staffing and limit employees for programs out of favor. The Appropriations committees warned the administration, in committee reports, that continued use of personnel ceilings would result in statutory controls.[51]

The congressional concern became more pronounced when it was learned that personnel ceilings had led to waste and inefficiency. The "ceiling game" meant that thousands of employees would be separated from their agencies just before the end of the fiscal year and rehired when the new fiscal year began. Ceilings also forced agencies to use contractors for activities that could have been handled less expensively within the agency. Language in congressional reports became more specific, again raising the specter that these nonstatutory directives would be replaced by statutory controls unless the administration respected legislative priorities.[52] When it appeared that agencies would not make good-faith efforts to carry out the congressional will, Congress resorted to statutory controls. Personnel floors were established for a variety of agencies, and these floors remain in place today.[53]

These collisions between the branches and the failure to reach an acceptable accommodation leave behind a residue of statutory controls on what agencies can and cannot do. Agencies that maintain trust with their oversight committees can be expected to retain substantial discretion and relative freedom from legislative intervention. This takes integrity and honesty. A member of the House of Representatives once paid this tribute to William Jump, former budget official with the Department of Agriculture: "Members of Congress through long experience knew that they could trust Mr. Jump. They admired his vast knowledge and understanding of Departmental activities and finances, but over and above and beyond that they

151

respected his integrity in always giving them the full and true picture of Departmental activities."[54]

Compare that happy result with what happens when trust is broken. During hearings in 1973 Senator Edmund Muskie turned on William D. Ruckelshaus, administrator of the Environmental Protection Agency (EPA). Muskie reviewed the discretion and flexibility that Congress had given the EPA to carry out the clean water program, only to discover that the agency had cut in half (from $18 billion to $9 billion) the legislative commitment. Embittered legislators can be expected to respond with statutes that provide less discretion and less flexibility. Muskie told Ruckelshaus:

> Having in mind the devious motives that you pursued to undercut the purposes of Congress, I could now write better language and believe me, I will. Believe me, I will.
> The clear language and debate was what we were giving you, is what we understood to be legitimate administrative discretion to spend the money, not defeat the purposes. Then to have you twist it as you have, is a temptation to this Senator to really handcuff you the next time.[55]

The experience with EPA was repeated less than ten years later in the case of the Superfund scandal. Congressional committees had reason to believe that the major chemical companies were not paying their full share of the costs to clean up hazardous-waste sites. After initially agreeing to cooperate with the congressional investigation, the Reagan administration refused to turn over agency documents on the theory that the documents constituted internal, deliberative materials that contained the government's enforcement strategy. Had Congress accepted this theory, the congressional probe would have had to be put on the back burner for years until the administration completed its enforcement actions. The House of Representatives voted 259 to 105 to hold Anne Gorsuch, the EPA administrator, in contempt. Significantly, fifty-five Republicans joined 204 Democrats to build the lopsided majority. Under this pressure the documents were soon released to the congressional committees. Although only one EPA official, Rita Lavelle, was sentenced to prison as a result of this scandal, more than twenty top officials left the agency amid allegations of perjury, conflict of interest, and political manipulation of the agency.[56]

The Item Veto

Congress is criticized for inserting an increasing amount of detail into appropriations bills, forcing the president either to accept or to reject a bill as a whole. Many of these details, provisos, qualifications, and conditions give close guidance to agency activities. It is argued that these omnibus measures undermine the president's general veto authority. That argument is even more compelling when the president receives a giant continuing resolution in the closing days of a fiscal year, or perhaps even after the fiscal year has expired. Under these emergency conditions the president is under heavy pressure to sign the bill to prevent the government from closing down.

This is not the place for me to analyze the item veto in any detail. I have done that elsewhere.[57] Whatever merit the item-veto proposal has, however, should not be obscured by misconceptions regarding the framers' intent and the budgetary process.

First, it is not true that the framers expected Congress to provide funds by passing "separate appropriations bills for discrete programs or activities, rather than omnibus bills encompassing a variety of related and unrelated matters."[58] That position was advanced by Donald Regan in 1984, when he served as secretary of the Treasury. Regan claimed that "until about the time of the Civil War, Congressional practice was in accordance with this expectation. Presidents were thus able to sign or veto appropriations bills based upon the merits of the programs being funded and the need for the particular amounts."

There is no basis for these assertions. The first appropriations bill passed in 1789 was an omnibus measure, containing all funds for civilian and military programs. The same kind of bills passed in 1790 and 1791. Later congresses, as in 1814, passed three separate appropriations bills—for the army, the navy, and the civilian establishment —but it would be years before Congress settled into the practice of passing thirteen appropriations bills. Action has typically been through omnibus appropriations measures.

Second, it is asserted that the president, armed with an item veto, could eliminate wasteful "pork-barrel" projects. That is another misconception. Congress appropriates by lump-sum amounts, not by items. Individual projects and activities (so-called items) are generally placed in the conference report that accompanies the appropriations bill. The president has an opportunity to veto the bill, not the report.

Although this is a rather elementary point about the budgetary process, it completely escaped President Reagan when he delivered his State of the Union message in 1988. He claimed that with an item veto he could "reach into massive appropriations bills, pare away the waste, and enforce budget discipline." As examples of waste, he referred to "millions for items such as cranberry research, blueberry research, the study of crawfish, and the commercialization of wildflowers."

153

This seemed to me a strange list of projects to condemn in a presidential message, especially one on prime-time television. I had my doubts that the activities he mentioned would amount to "millions." Nevertheless, Reagan said that with an item veto he would "line them out." The simple fact is that he could not. The four projects were not in the continuing resolution he received. They were all in the conference report. Even if President Reagan had had the item veto when he received the continuing resolution, he would have been powerless to eliminate the four projects.

Here we need to take a detour and understand how Congress appropriates. The items he mentioned were funded under the agriculture part of the continuing resolution. They are part of an account called Cooperative State Research Service, totaling about $304 million. With an item veto, Reagan could have deleted the entire amount, eliminating good projects and bad projects alike. He might have gone somewhat deeper. The account includes what are called earmarkings: smaller amounts set aside for more specific areas. For example, the account includes $31 million "for contracts and grants for agricultural research." Whether this would be subject to an item veto is a disputed point. It could be considered an "item within an item" and therefore beyond the grasp of an item veto.

Even if Reagan could get at earmarked amounts, he still could not reach the cranberries, blueberries, crawfish, and wildflowers. They are mentioned only in the conference report, which explains the allocation of the $31 million for contracts and grants for agricultural research. This amount is subdivided among sixty programs, including $92,000 for blueberry shoestring virus in Michigan, $260,000 for cranberry/blueberry disease and breeding in New Jersey, and $50,000 for native wildflowers in New Mexico. No mention of the poor crawfish. After flipping back and forth the pages of the conference report, I came upon $200,000 for "research in Louisiana." Might it be? Could it be? I called the appropriations subcommittee and learned that this amount was indeed set aside for the crawfish. Add up the four items and you get the grand total of $602,000. Not much of a head start on a budget deficit that will run in the neighborhood of $170 billion. Even more to the point, the items were never subject to an item veto.

Of course, the budget process can be changed to permit the president to get at these items. Merely take all the detail in the conference report and include it in the appropriations bill. Instead of a single sum of $31 million for special research grants, identify the sixty programs.

There are two drawbacks. First, President Reagan complained about the size of the continuing resolution. He said it weighed fourteen pounds. Add all the detail from the conference report and it would probably weigh more than thirty pounds. Perhaps the opportunity to exercise a veto over these items might offset this disadvantage. The more serious drawback is that itemization of appropriations bills substantially reduces the discretion of agency officials. The present practice of appropriating in lump-sum amounts gives them latitude to move money around within a large account. In some cases they have to obtain approval from their oversight committees, but they are willing to do that because of the flexibility they get in return. Itemization would lock all the details in. If agency officials wanted to change any of the items, they would need to pass another public law. Neither branch wants that.

Conclusions

This has been a rather brisk tour of a very complicated subject. I have not meant to champion micromanagement. Neither do I denigrate it. If I am shown what is being micromanaged, I will be able to analyze the reasons and come to some kind of judgment. Obviously there are risks and costs to congressional intervention. If agencies want to minimize what we blithely call meddling, they can play the game straight. If they choose to sabotage statutory programs and decide to implement White House policy instead of public law, the light for congressional intervention turns green.

The larger question is what can be done to foster a climate of good faith and trust that permits agencies to carry out laws with minimal congressional interference. When trust is broken and promises are not kept, Congress is stimulated to acquire new staff and impose new statutory restrictions. To regain control of the programs it has authorized and appropriated, Congress creates a rival bureaucracy. It is not the best of all worlds. We can all agree to that. The more difficult issue is how to make it better. Constructive steps can be taken. Decrying micromanagement by Congress is not one of them.

Notes

1. Jay Caesar Guggenheimer, "The Development of the Executive Departments, 1775–1789," in J. Franklin Jameson, ed., *Essays in the Constitutional History of the United States* (Boston: Houghton Mifflin, 1889), p. 148.
2. George Washington, *Writings of George Washington*, John C. Fitzpatrick, ed. (Washington, D.C., 1931–1944), vol. 29, p. 153.
3. Ibid., vol. 30, pp. 300–301.
4. Alexander Hamilton, *Papers of Alexander Hamilton*, Harold C. Syrett, ed. (New York: Columbia University Press, 1961–   ), vol. 2, pp. 404–5.

5. Thomas Jefferson, *Papers of Thomas Jefferson*, Julian P. Boyd, ed. (Princeton, N.J.: Princeton University Press, 1950–   ), vol. 6, pp. 388, 419, 432, 437, 469, 569.

6. Ibid., vol. 7, p. 293.

7. Ibid., vol. 10, p. 603.

8. Ibid., vol. 11, p. 679.

9. Leonard D. White, *The Federalists* (New York: Macmillan, 1948), p. 118n.

10. William Maclay, *Sketches of the First Senate of the United States* (New York: Frederick Ungar, 1965), pp. 185, 373, 374, 376, 399. For Hamilton's other efforts to influence Congress, see pp. 377, 397–98.

11. John Quincy Adams, *Memoirs of John Quincy Adams*, Charles Francis Adams, ed. (Philadelphia, Pa.: J. B. Lippincott, 1874–1877), vol. 1, p. 447.

12. INS v. Chadha, 462 U.S. 919, 952 (1983).

13. Id. at 958.

14. Id. at 959.

15. Id. at 951.

16. Id. at 959.

17. Id. at 944.

18. 106 S. Ct. 3181, 3187 (1986).

19. Id. at 3188.

20. Watkins v. United States, 354 U.S. 178, 187 (1957).

21. 106 S. Ct. at 3192.

22. Anderson v. Dunn, 6 Wheat. 204 (1821) (contempt power); Eastland v. United States Servicemen's Fund, 421 U.S. 491, 505 (1975) (subpoena power).

23. 106 S. Ct. at 3188, quoting from Humphrey's Executor v. United States, 295 U.S. 602, 629-30 (1935).

24. 106 S. Ct. at 3186.

25. Youngstown Co. v. Sawyer, 343 U.S. 579, 635 (1952).

26. *The Federalist*, Benjamin F. Wright, ed. (Cambridge, Mass.: Harvard University Press, 1961), p. 338.

27. U.S. Congress, House of Representatives, Committee on Government Operations, *The Balanced Budget and Emergency Deficit Control Act of 1985*, 99th Cong., 1st sess. (1985), pp. 197–232.

28. M. J. C. Vile, *Constitutionalism and the Separation of Powers* (London: Oxford University Press, 1967), p. 153.

29. J. Elliot, ed., *Debates in the Several State Conventions on the Adoption of the Federal Constitution* (Washington, D.C., 1836–1845), vol. 3, p. 280 (Virginia); ibid., vol. 4, pp. 116, 121 (North Carolina); and John Bach McMaster and Frederick D. Stone, eds., *Pennsylvania and the Federal Constitution* (Lancaster, Pa.: Historical Society of Pennsylvania, 1888), pp. 475–77 (Pennsylvania).

30. Edward Dumbauld, *The Bill of Rights and What It Means Today* (Norman: University of Oklahoma Press, 1957), pp. 174–75, 183, 199.

31. *Annals of Congress*, 1st Cong., June 8, 1789, pp. 453–54, August 18, 1789, pp. 789–90; and U.S. Congress, Senate, *Journal* (1820), pp. 64, 73–74.

32. United States v. Nixon, 418 U.S. 683, 706 (1974).

33. Id. at 707.

34. Id.

35. Nixon v. Administrator of General Services, 433 U.S. 425, 441–42 (1977), quoting Humphrey's Executor v. United States, 295 U.S. 602, 629 (1935).

36. Id. at 442.

37. Id. at 443.

38. Commodity Futures Trading Commission v. Schor, 106 S. Ct. 3245, 3258 (1986).

39. Id.

40. Id.

41. H. Lee Watson, "Congress Steps Out: A Look at Congressional Control of the Executive," *California Law Review*, vol. 63 (1975), pp. 983, 1088.

42. Ibid.

43. Louis Fisher, *Constitutional Conflicts between Congress and the President* (Princeton, N.J.: Princeton University Press, 1985), pp. 162–72.

44. *Weekly Compilation of Presidential Documents*, vol. 20 (July 20, 1984), p. 1040 .

45. *House Report No. 916*, 98th Cong., 2d sess. (1984), p. 48.

46. The full text of the letter is reprinted in Louis Fisher, "Judicial Misjudgments about the Lawmaking Process: The Legislative Veto Case," *Public Administration Review*, vol. 45 (Special Issue November 1985), pp. 705, 707.

47. *Washington Post*, August 13, 1987, p. A 13.

48. *Weekly Compilation of Presidential Documents*, vol. 22 (December 2, 1986), p. 1620.

49. *Washington Post*, January 31, 1987, p. A 16.

50. *Weekly Compilation of Presidential Documents*, vol. 23 (March 4, 1987), p. 220.

51. Louis Fisher, "Effect of the Budget Act of 1974 on Agency Operations," in Rudolph G. Penner, ed., *The Congressional Budget Process after Five Years* (Washington, D.C.: American Enterprise Institute, 1981), pp. 159–60.

52. Ibid., pp. 160–62.

53. Ibid., p. 162.

54. Clifford G. Hope, "Legislative-Executive Relationships in the Formulation of Public Policy as Viewed by the Legislator," in O. B. Conaway, Jr., ed., *Legislative-Executive Relationships* (Washington, D.C.: Graduate School of the U.S. Department of Agriculture, 1954), p. 16.

55. U.S. Congress, Senate, Committees on Government Operations and the Judiciary, *Impoundment of Funds by the President*, 93d Cong., 1st sess. (1973), p. 411.

56. Fisher, *Constitutional Conflicts*, pp. 211–13.

57. Louis Fisher and Neal Devins, "How Successfully Can the States' Item Veto Be Transferred to the President?," *Georgetown Law Journal*, vol. 75 (1986), p. 159. I also helped prepare a committee print, *Item Veto: State Experience and Its Application to the Federal Situation*, House Committee on Rules, 99th Cong., 2d sess. (December 1986).

58. U.S. Congress, Senate, Committee on the Judiciary, *Hearings on the Line-Item Veto*, 98th Cong., 2d sess. (1984), p. 173.

11
Administration: An Idea Whose Time May Have Passed

Loren A. Smith

> *For forms of government let fools contest.*
> *That which is best administered is best.*
> —ALEXANDER POPE

Does the constitutional theory set out by the framers of our Constitution have any relevance to the current operation of the executive branch of government? That question can be divided into two components, one empirical and one normative. On the empirical level I provide some illustrative examples of how the operation of some aspects of executive government conforms to separation of powers theory. On the normative level I explore whether the framers' vision is still good or whether there are better approaches.

The Theory and the Practice

How does the executive branch work? The question is a little like asking how the universe works. A snappy answer to such a question would be, "Any way you like." Or perhaps, "From 9 to 5 with a long lunch break." A more serious answer, however, might be to describe briefly the broad characteristics of the "classic" separation-of-powers model that has become a stock figure in our public political philosophy and then test it against some recent governmental phenomena that appear to deviate from that model. Then the apparent deviations should be compared with the structure of the federal government to determine whether they are statistically or quantitatively significant.

A few examples of apparent deviations from the separation-of-

159

powers model are the budget and appropriations process, the regulatory system, and the role of judicial review in the administrative process. I focus here on the budget and appropriations process. It is important to note that these processes are only "possibles," or in a high-risk group; that is, they are at a high risk of being inconsistent with our traditional constitutional model of separation of powers.

First we may set out the classic model, after which we can analyze one of the possible deviations in its light. In *Federalist* No. 47, James Madison articulated the model in response to objections that the Constitution did not strictly adhere to it. He observed:

No political truth is certainly of greater intrinsic value, or is stamped with the authority of more enlightened patrons of liberty than that on which the objection is founded. The accumulation of all powers, legislative, executive, and judiciary, in the same hands, whether hereditary, self-appointed, or elective, may justly be pronounced the very definition of tyranny.

This model involves several fundamental concepts. First is the idea that liberty is safe only when governmental power is broken into several distinct components. The components, it is assumed, are the fundamental elements of governmental power, much in the same way that electrons, protons, and neutrons are the fundamental elements of atoms. (We will for the moment leave aside the analogy to quarks, neutrinos, mesons, pions, and all the other "fundamental" particles that have disturbed this tidy physics scheme in the past forty years!) And like the fundamental atomic components of earlier physical theory it was assumed that all government functions could be defined in terms of one of the three components.

The idea of three separate functions or components dates explicitly from the Baron de Montesquieu and is rooted in much older ideas from the medieval English and European past. At the core of the idea are law-making, law-enforcing, and law-interpreting powers. A serious question deserving exploration is whether the preeminent law-making function is relevant to many of the activities of modern government—functions such as research, military procurement, intelligence gathering, standard setting, resource distribution, running parks and forests, providing medical care, building or paying for roads—literally a list that would equal this chapter's length a hundredfold.

Although the money to pay for these activities comes from taxation (a traditional legal action), and the government undertakes these programs by formal statute, they are not actions of law. If performed by private entity, the actions would not be legal. For example, biological research conducted by a private corporation differs from that conducted by the government only in the method by which funds are raised to pay for it. Yet we generally assume that scientific research is an executive or law-enforcing function rather than a legislative or law-making function. Neither categorization is entirely logical or intellectually satisfying. On a visit with the Egyptian judiciary I was struck by a different sort of classification problem. The Egyptian judges were surprised that I was concerned about their practice of having the prosecutors sit with the judges in trials. They pointed out that, of course, prosecution was a judicial not an executive function!

A second fundamental idea of separation of powers is that it is a rational way to organize government—that is, that the attributes and structures needed for good judging are different from those needed for good law making or good execution. This notion is related to Aristotle's concept of the three kinds of government: democracy, monarchy, and aristocracy. The democratic structure, the legislature, is best at making the laws, and the monarchical structure, the executive, is best at carrying them out, while the aristocratic structure, the judiciary, is best at judgment. This idea had a large place in the framers' vision of government.

Further, today it is an implicit assumption of most governmental management theory. It underlies our distinctions between single administrators and collegial bodies as well as our theory of advisory commissions. It is at the heart of our structuring of the regulatory commissions, at least in theory. The idea has shaped the structure of cabinet departments, congressional committees, and governmental corporations as well. It can be found at the heart of at least the theory behind, if not the motivation for, the plethora of new and varied government agencies that have sprung up continuously since the New Deal. The winds of fashion may have blown back and forth between perceived needs for a strong executive in these bodies and a more legislative-like collegial head, but the underlying theory has remained the same.

It should be noted at this point that my translation of the Aristotelian idea into modern terms was a bit simplistic. It still serves, however, as an adequate genealogy of the concept, with one amendment. Although the modern legislature is seen as a relatively conscious and active player in the governmental process, the ancient, medieval, and eighteenth-century parliaments were largely not this type of entity. They were checks on the active prince or ruler who embodied the sovereignty. Through possession of the consent to be taxed they, at least in theory, kept the ruler from doing too much

161

damage to the various other orders of society. They were bodies with a powerful veto and a judicial-like role. The ruler was, however, the organ of the body politic for positive government.

A third fundamental idea in our model is that values other than efficiency are served by our system. Both critics and defenders of a strict adherence to separation of powers have contended that democratic choice, minority rights, pluralism, consensus, tradition, institutional inertia, and localism are all furthered by separation of powers. At the heart of this idea is a basic distrust of power, which is ultimately grounded in the Judeo-Christian belief in the fallibility of human nature. In the American context the idea is closely allied with a related concept: federalism. Just as tyranny comes from the functional centralization of power in the combining of the three functions, it can also occur by geographic or constituency centralization of power. The president, Senate, House of Representatives, and courts represent different constitutional and political constituencies. Each is entitled to a voice in the nation's affairs.

A fourth characteristic of the model is that it is self-consciously legalistic. It was created by lawyers, is entrusted to lawyers, and requires lawyers for its operation. As noted earlier, power is achieved by legal means—whether it is law making, executing, or interpreting. In fact, power and law are almost synonymous in our constitutional system.

A fifth and final characteristic of the system is that it relies on political parties to make it work. This is akin to purposely designing a house with no doors or windows on the assumption that some entry would be found to make the dwelling usable. This characteristic has important implications for relations between the president and the Congress. It is not supposed to have any relevance to the interaction of the judiciary with the other two branches, and only limited significance to the internal operations of the executive branch. While the model accords significance to the role parties play in intralegislative branch operations, it has never been characterized by a coherent code of behavior to guide parties in the legislative branch.

This model or norm under which our political system operates allows us to observe how contemporary political events relate to it. Do they violate its tenets? Or is the model irrelevant? Of course, the model itself may be either wrong or too crudely explicated to analyze government activities in detail. I have laid out a model of a government where the protection of liberty hinges on the separation of powers into three components, each with a separate institution. Each institution performs certain tasks best, and each institution represents (in the broadest sense of that term) a different interest of the body politic in a legal system where political parties play a legitimate and necessary role.

The budget and appropriations process is the central legislative task. The toughest intragovernmental battles are fought over it. More legislative time is consumed by it than any other legislative activity. It has become the primary means by which the Congress attempts to control the executive function. In fact, the budget reconciliation process has become one of the central vehicles for every type of legislation. Short of impeachment and criminal sanctions, only the budget and appropriations process allows Congress to effectively manage government programs. This is a reflection of the fact that most political battles between the Congress and the president are battles over how to manage government programs, not what government should or should not do.

Many hundreds of appropriations amendments each year mandate what money may be spent for and what money may not be spent for. These range from giving military personnel the "right" to have a wig paid for by the government if they have lost their hair, to forbidding agencies from buying coal from specific geographic regions. They even prohibit agencies from implementing certain management policies that seemingly require no funds, on the theory that the agency head's salary is being misappropriated if the restriction is violated.

In addition to the use of the appropriations process for specific management of the administrative apparatus of government, the Congress through the general allocation of money in the budget sets national policy by deciding on the size of the deficit, the amount of resources allotted to various governmental activities, and the relative mix of governmental functions, whether national defense, subsidies, welfare payments, regulatory programs, or grants and infrastructure expenditures. This function is the more important of the two on the national scale, though it generally has less effect on the day-to-day operation of the government. Of course, the two processes really merge, with budgeting describing the general allocation and the appropriations process implementing the budget.

How does this process compare with our model? At first glance it appears to conform to the model. The Congress seems to have the adversarial guardian-of-the-purse function the theory of separation of powers requires. It also is consistent with the functional division between the executive who manages and directs the spending of the money and the legislature that exercises a review and policy guideline function on the priorities of the government. On closer inspection, however, this congruence breaks down.

While in theory the executive directs the spending of the funds appropriated, the reality is often quite different. Specific amendments and general management statutes direct much of government spending into relatively narrow management options. The principal tool of private management is thus denied the federal executive for many of the most basic functions. Further, the increasing difficulty of passing virtually any piece of legislation without a significant internal or external congressional constituency has in effect locked into law the accumulated political pressures of the previous years. An agency or program must either be very unpopular or have virtually no interest group friend to be subject to radical exeutive branch budget reduction or restructuring.

Finally, the theory of the Congress as a budgetary watchdog and agency overseer against potential abuses by the president is undercut in large part by the fiefdoms created by congressional committees and even by the 535 individual members of Congress of the many bureaus, programs, agencies, and administrative units. Just as the powers of the great empires of antiquity declined with distance from the center of the empire, allowing imperial functionaries to become virtual local overlords and in many cases actual princes, the power of the president over the executive branch has waned as the size of the executive branch has outstripped the ability of any one president or political team to control even a majority of it. Herbert Kaufman commented on this process in *The Administrative Behavior of Federal Bureau Chiefs*:

> At the center of the pattern of relationships for all the [executive branch bureau] chiefs was Congress—its members, collectively and individually, its committees, its staffs, its evaluative arms (the General Accounting Office in particular). This set of congressional and congressionally related workers in the machinery of government seemed rarely to be out of the administrators' consciousness. The chiefs were constantly looking over their shoulders, as it were, at the elements of the legislative establishment relevant to their agencies—taking stock of moods and attitudes, estimating reactions to contemplated decisions and actions, trying to prevent misunderstandings and avoidable conflicts, and planning responses when storm warnings appeared on the horizon. Not that cues and signals from Capitol Hill had to be ferreted out; the denizens of the Hill were not shy about issuing suggestions, requests, demands, directives, and pronouncements.[1]

The other effect of this phenomenon of congressional suzerainty has been the disappearance of the oversight function. When Congress manages significant parts of the executive branch it cannot logically also exercise real oversight. Often what passes for oversight is a congressional attempt to thwart the executive's attempt to reestablish control over territories he has lost. Another type of oversight is in reality a cooperative effort with the nominally executive agency to promote a new policy or program, sometimes in opposition to, sometimes in cooperation with, the executive. Of the traditional model of congressional oversight—congressional review of what the executive is doing with the appropriations—there is surprisingly little.

This brings me to the title of this essay: "Administration: An Idea Whose Time May Have Passed." The concept of the president as the head or manager of the executive branch does not square either with the reality of government operations or with what we commonly mean by the terms "head" or "manager." In fact, the concept of administration, by which we mean a hierarchical group of people directed by some central structure, does not really describe the federal government. Rather, the government is a vast group of civil servants and a much smaller number of political appointees, organized into a mass of groups and confederations and subject to competing authority centers. They derive power, money, direction, and authority from different sources in different proportions that vary with time.

Central management structures like the Office of Management and Budget, the Department of Justice, the cabinet, and to a lesser degree the Office of Personnel Management and the General Services Administration do provide vehicles for some general presidential direction. In some instances executive orders also provide significant presidential control. But none of these devices gives a president general management authority. Central to such authority would be the power to implement a general budget and set operating procedures for specific agencies. U.S. presidents have not had such authority for some time. Given that this problem affects most of the operations of the federal government, it is a significant deviation in quantitative and statistical terms from the separation-of-powers model under which our political system operates.

The Validity of the Theory

We thus come to my second point of inquiry, the normative. If our governmental structure does not conform to the separation-of-powers model, does it or the model need to be corrected? This is not a question of constitutional law, but one of political theory. Although the budget and appropriations process may need a constitutional "fix," that is not the focus of this paper. This work focuses on whether we correct our concept of what separation of powers means or our concept of whether the federal government is functioning properly.

There are at least two reasons for taking the position that the current governmental structure needs to be corrected rather than our or the framers' theory of separation of powers. First, the federal management system has provided relatively objective clues to a serious dysfunction recognized by virtually all political factions. It cannot cope with the problem of deficit spending or even rational budgeting within a fixed time period. It has become increasingly rigid and immune to major reform regardless of the outcomes of elections. The system is increasingly seen by qualified professionals of all political stripes as an undesirable place for a permanent career. Over the past twenty years, at least, the public has increasingly come to view it, at best, as ineffective in dealing with the nation's major problems, and, at worst, as the cause of some of those problems.

While different factions blame different players in the process, it is almost undisputed that the process is not working. One reason may be that some of the players are incompetent or ill-intentioned, or that government the size of the current federal system is inherently unworkable; but it may also be that the structure of the federal system needs to be changed to again conform to the framers' model. Thus, at the very least there are some symptoms of illness in the way government is functioning, which is out of sync with the theoretical model of the relationship between the three branches.

A second reason, even more subject to debate, is that the model created by the Constitution, and made a part of our basic political culture by *The Federalist* and more than two centuries of political actions and pronouncements, has no effective political rebuttal. As early as Madison's writings in *The Federalist* the model was taken as axiomatic, and it agrees with much of our public political philosophy and our culture's insights into human nature. In this sense, the model of separation of powers is not so much an abstract theory, but a set of values akin to our belief in popular government, human freedom, and equality of opportunity. We believe in them not because they seem to work, but because we believe in them. Our faith is much the same as the faith we have in our most deeply held religious beliefs. In fact, we would probably not be impressed with the moral character of the individual who stated that he only believed in God as long as God did something for him.

My conclusion can be put rather succinctly. The system of separation of powers established by the framers in their constitutional scheme is not being followed in significant areas of operation of the

executive branch. In the author's view this is not desirable and requires a new approach to the operation of the federal government, not
a radical rethinking of the concept of separation as set forth by basic
constitutional theory.

Note

1. Herbert Kaufman, *The Administrative Behavior of Federal Bureau Chiefs*
(Washington, D.C.: Brookings Institution, 1981).

12

Out of Control: Congress and the Legal Services Corporation

Michael B. Wallace

The Legal Services Corporation (LSC) deserves a prominent place in any discussion of an enfeebled presidency. The Legal Services Corporation Act was the last legislation signed by the most enfeebled president in our nation's history, Richard M. Nixon. The architects of the Legal Services Corporation plainly intended to enfeeble not only the president of the United States but also the corporation itself. They wanted to free local providers of legal services to the poor, and especially the national lobbying groups that claimed to act on their behalf, from any effective central oversight and control, and, despite the best efforts of President Reagan and the occasional efforts of Congress, they have been largely successful.

Their success derives mainly from the structure of the corporation itself. Despite its appropriation of $305 million a year, the corporation is not a federal agency but a nonprofit District of Columbia corporation. Although the eleven members of its board are appointed by the president of the United States and subject to confirmation by the Senate, the act specifically provides that they are not officers of the United States. In theory, then, the corporation might be considered even more independent than the traditional independent agencies like the Interstate Commerce Commission and the Federal Trade Commission. In practice, the corporation has very few powers in the first place, and its ability to exercise those is severely restricted by each successive appropriations measure.

The Origins of the LSC

To understand this strange structure, we must review the history of federal involvement in the provision of legal services to the poor.

Local legal aid societies have existed in this country throughout the twentieth century. It was Lyndon Johnson's poverty wizard, Sargent Shriver, who first directed federal dollars to legal aid societies through the Office of Economic Opportunity (OEO). While some of the federal dollars went to established societies around the country, many more went to new, nonprofit local corporations organized specifically for the purpose of receiving those funds. Thus the actual providers of federal legal aid to the poor were not federal employees but local contractors. The federal government had only limited rights of oversight and control from the outset.

The early proponents of federal legal services were quite emphatic in their rejection of the traditional function of serving particular needs of particular poor clients. Rather, they were interested primarily in law reform, using litigation, lobbying, and community organizing to reshape society in a fashion they thought would benefit the "client community." Their efforts in such fields as integration, abortion, and union organizing naturally led to substantial political controversies. The most notable was probably the fight between Governor Ronald Reagan of California and California Rural Legal Assistance (CRLA). Congress had given governors limited veto rights over the expenditure of federal legal services funds within the boundaries of their states, and Governor Reagan was irate over CRLA's organizing activities on behalf of agricultural unions. After a lengthy bureaucratic wrangle, the federal legal services program won the right to operate in California and the continuing enmity of Ronald Reagan.

Such political friction endured throughout the Nixon administration. Most members of Congress were sympathetic to the plight of widows and orphans evicted from their homes in midwinter but did not want to fund the law reformers who would interfere in politics. The battle for a nonpolitical legal services program, like so many battles in Washington, became a struggle for the control of the vocabulary. To the man on the street, as well as the man in the congressional cloakroom, a nonpolitical legal services program was one that stayed out of politics and confined itself to the collection of child support and the resolution of consumer disputes. To the programs in the field and their allies on key congressional committees, a nonpolitical legal services corporation is one in which the president, the governors, and other elected politicians let local programs alone to get on with the business of law reform.

Each side achieved some victories in the Legal Services Corporation Act of 1974. Conservatives concentrated on placing particular restrictions on offensive behavior by legal services programs. The act restricts community organizing, the promotion of abortion, union organizing, lobbying, and busing litigation. The act also contains, however, a general restriction forbidding the interference with the legal services attorney's exercise of his professional responsibilities to his client. A dedicated law reformer who considers himself ethically bound to usher in the new Jerusalem can drive a tank through that loophole. Thus the restrictions in the act are of value only if those charged with executing the act have the authority to enforce them.

That is where the liberals won their battles in the compromise that became the Legal Services Corporation Act. The local programs remained independent contractors, not federal employees. More important, the act created a system of presumptive refunding. Existing programs cannot be terminated without an administrative hearing and a right of appeal to the federal courts. Since the act authorized local programs to set their own priorities, they could not be terminated simply for concentrating on, for instance, redistricting cases instead of domestic disputes. As a practical matter, the local contractors were given guaranteed funding unless central authorities could prove illegal behavior.

This supposed system of local control might have reduced political involvement if the federal authorities had continued to fund the traditional legal aid societies. In fact, as the program expanded to cover the entire nation during the Carter administration, corporation officials intentionally disregarded established providers of assistance. A revealing story in this regard is told by Congressman Bill McCollum of Florida, who was then president of the Orange County Bar Association. For many years, the local bar had run an active and successful pro bono project to provide services to the local poor. When the Legal Services Corporation refused to fund the project, Mr. McCollum went to the regional office in Atlanta to ask why. He was told that the county bar was not radical enough; the money went instead to the usual gang of law reformers and poverty activists.

Two other disputes over local programs were successfully fudged by their protectors in Congress. The programs funded by the OEO were almost exclusively staffed programs, made up of attorneys who devoted full time to the program and had no other practice. There were many advocates in Congress of the traditional pro bono programs sponsored by bar associations and charitable organizations around the country. Moreover, there were other advocates of judicare systems, whereby private practitioners agreed to be paid a reduced sum to devote some of their time to the needs of the poor. Instead of resolving this dispute, the act instructed the corporation to conduct a delivery system study over a period of several years, years that the corporation spent busily establishing staff programs all over the country. When the study finally came out, it proved inconclusive. It had a little something to please everybody but nothing to disturb the status quo of staff systems that the corporation had by that time successfully imposed across the nation.

Second, conservatives wished to give local officials some voice in the control of the programs. The architects of the act were well aware of the dangers of real local control over the programs, as opposed to the phony local control residing in the hands of the contractors carefully selected by the corporation staff. Accordingly, they agreed only to the creation of state advisory councils, appointed by the governor from nominees presented by local bar associations. The advisory councils were given no power at all, and, fourteen years later, not a single one exists.

Even with their substantial statutory independence, local programs could be significantly inhibited by vigorous federal oversight and law enforcement. The structure of the Legal Services Corporation itself was designed to make sure that that would never happen. Perhaps the most important decision was to establish the federal oversight authority as a District of Columbia corporation instead of as a traditional federal agency. As a corporation, LSC and its grantees are exempt from such usual statutory controls as the Hatch Act, the False Claims Act, the Anti-Deficiency Act, and various provisions of the federal criminal code. These basic safeguards on the handling of federal funds simply do not apply to the Legal Services Corporation and its grantees.

One of the major battles came over the president's authority to appoint the corporation's board of directors. Early versions of the act restricted the president's authority to appoint the board much as the authority of governors to appoint advisory boards had been restricted. The president could not appoint directors of his choosing but could choose a majority only from lists submitted by the American Bar Association, the National Legal Aid and Defender Association, and other favored organizations. President Nixon, insisting upon the president's right to appoint federal officers, vetoed the first version of the act.

The final version of the act, which Nixon accepted on his way to the helicopter in 1974, granted the president somewhat more authority. The act provided that no more than six of the eleven directors could be members of the same political party, a fairly standard provision common to many of the independent agencies. The act also provided, however, that at least two of the directors must qualify as eligible clients. Directors would serve fixed terms and could neither be fired by the president nor removed by Congress through impeachment. Since all directors would be subject to Senate confirmation, no president would have an easy time making his will felt in the affairs of the corporation.

The Veil of Ignorance

As a practical matter, it is no easier for the board to control the corporation than for the president to control the board. While boards have traditionally exceeded the four meetings a year required by the act, directors all have their own pursuits in the real world and cannot devote more than a fraction of their time to oversight of the corporation. The architects of the act undoubtedly expected that only the great and the good, along with poverty activists, would be able to afford to serve on the board. Indeed, until the advent of the Reagan administration, the board was dominated by the sort of prosperous liberals who generally serve on foundation boards and committees of the American Bar Association. The hope that the board would not interfere in the activities of the corporation staff, much less in the conduct of local programs, was largely realized.

The board's only real authority is to hire the president of the corporation. Early presidents and their staffs were veterans of the law reform wars of the Johnson and Nixon administrations—hardly the sort of people to clamp down on political activities by local programs in the so-called national and state support centers, which existed for the chief purpose of lobbying legislatures and administrative agencies. Had any board wished to establish a truly nonpolitical legal services program, its first obstacle would have been its own staff.

A more effective program for impeding executive control of a federal program could hardly have been devised. No program can be controlled without good information, and information is exactly what the Legal Services Corporation Act keeps far from executive hands. Most information relating to the conduct of the program is in the hands of those who operate the local grantees and the so-called support centers; as the experience of the Reagan board has proved, those programs resist every effort to disclose what they do with the taxpayers' money. The next most knowledgeable people are friendly members of Congress and their staffs. The authorizing and appropriations committees have an institutional experience that no board and no president can share. Moreover, their friends in the field programs feed them the information they need to resist administration initiatives. The staff of the corporation itself has access to some information. At least they work full-time at their jobs and have some opportunity to try to pry information out of the field programs. Whether they pass that information on to the board of directors is another matter. The board generally has no more than ten meetings a year at which it is exposed to such information as the staff and the field programs want to supply. Directors have little contact with the field programs and almost none with Congress. Finally, at the apex of this pyramid of ignorance, sits the president of the United States, with no involvement and no authority other than to appoint almost equally ignorant directors, by and with the advice and consent of the Senate. The system was designed to preclude effective control of the recipients of federal legal services funds, and it has worked brilliantly.

The Reagan Administration's Failure

All this provides the necessary historical background to President Reagan's well-publicized failure to gain effective control over the Legal Services Corporation. After failing to persuade Congress to abolish the corporation, he made several recess appointments on New Year's Eve 1981. The efforts of the first board to restrict political litigation by grantees were largely overturned by the courts, thanks to the supposed local autonomy built into the act. Nor was the Senate prepared to confirm the president's nominees for full terms on the board. By confirming the liberals and rejecting the conservatives, the program's protectors in the Senate could thwart the execution of the president's policies by the board. Faced with such a prospect, the president withdrew all eleven nominees, and governed through recess boards until after the 1984 election. Having picked up forty-nine states and a new Senate majority leader, President Reagan was in a stronger political position at the outset of the Ninety-ninth Congress. His eleven nominees, who had been reported from committee but had not been called up for floor action in 1984, were all confirmed in 1985.

Even so, the president's ultimate success in securing the confirmation of a board was largely due to his own efforts to meet congressional demands for balance. The board on which I have served since receiving a recess appointment shortly after the 1984 election is hardly a collection of unreconstructed right-wingers. Long-time conservative Republicans are counterbalanced by liberal Republicans and moderate Democrats. While conservatives generally enjoy control of the board, if not of the program, many important votes, most notably those on the budget, are routinely decided by a margin of six to five.

Although the board's battles to control the program have been similar in many ways to the battles faced by other federal executives during the Reagan administration, ours have been complicated by the strange structure of the corporation. Like many federal agencies, we face reprogramming requirements in our annual appropriations act, requiring us to clear new regulations and new expenditures of funds with the appropriations committees. Theoretically, after a fifteen-day notice period, the corporation is free to proceed. As a practical matter, execution of the laws without prior consent of committee staff leads to open warfare, as three examples will demonstrate.

The first is a complicated dispute involving computers, time keeping, and functional accounting. The fight arose from two separate but related decisions made by the board in its first few months in office. First, we recognized that access to computers was absolutely essential to modern law office management. Our offices needed computers for word processing, legal research, and accounting functions. Accordingly, we designated several hundred thousand dollars to purchase computers for our local grantees.

The board also immediately recognized that the corporation lacked any real information on the activities of local programs. While programs claimed that an overwhelming percentage of their cases involved such matters as domestic relations and consumer rights, available evidence indicated many of those cases involved only brief advice, while much more time and effort were poured into relatively fewer welfare rights cases and lobbying activities. Without requiring lawyers to keep time, then, as almost all law firms do, the board could not know what its programs were really doing. At the same time, the board wished to install functional accounting, as the General Accounting Office (GAO) had recommended. It is not sufficient for management purposes to know how much money is being spent on desks, pencils, and personnel. The real question is how much money is being spent on particular activities by each grantee. New accounting rules were devised in an effort to learn how much money was being spent on particular types of cases by our recipients. Obviously, the new computers would be extremely helpful for time-keeping and accounting purposes.

Although the grantees were delighted to get the new computers, they were appalled at the notion of having to account accurately for their time and money. The program had survived for a decade in Congress on the representation that it devoted the bulk of its effort not to law reform but to assisting ordinary poor people with ordinary problems. If the board were to discover that not to be the case, the proverbial jig would be up. The grantees went to work on Capitol Hill to kill the board's efforts.

Their advocates in Washington cleverly seized the computers themselves as a stick with which to beat the board. The corporation staff had concluded, properly in my opinion, that the decision to buy the computers was not one that needed to be submitted to the appropriations committees for reprogramming. The chairman of the Senate Appropriations Subcommittee, Warren Rudman, took jurisdictional umbrage at that failure, but what really annoyed him was that the corporation had bought Japanese computers. Representing thousands of electronics workers in the New Hampshire suburbs of Boston, Senator Rudman took action. Having been told by the grantees that the sole purpose of the computers was to implement the hated time-keeping and functional accounting programs, Senator Rudman instructed the corporation not to put those programs into place. Three years and two GAO reports later, that is where the matter continues to rest.

Unfortunately, the corporation's staff never tried to separate, much less did Senator Rudman succeed in separating, the computers from the issues of time keeping and functional accounting. Not until Director Pepe Mendez testified at the appropriations hearings in 1986 did Senator Rudman learn that the board had intended the computers primarily to improve the efficiency of the programs. Hearing Mendez's case, Rudman was hard put to disagree:

> I don't disagree with any of that. I don't disagree with anything you have said. But that is not why the computers were purchased, according to all the information this committee had up until this moment. We have had your President sitting with the chairman of the House committee and this committee. We have had interminable meetings. We have had all kinds of discussions.
>
> To my knowledge, and I will ask the staff if I am incorrect, this is the first time that anyone has told me that these computers were purchased for any reason other than to implement the timekeeping requirement.[1]

By that time, however, time keeping and accounting had been fatally linked with the Japanese computers. Senator Rudman was in no mood to retreat from his previous position, and the grantees got the best of all possible worlds: new computers but no reporting requirements.

The lack of information has impeded the board in its second major battle with Congress. In 1986, the board voted to propose the abolition of the so-called support centers and to concentrate available federal funds on programs at the local level. These specialized grantees focus on particular areas of law and supposedly serve to assist local programs that lack expertise in those areas. In fact, in a February 1, 1988, editorial entitled "Lyndon Johnson's Secret Weapon," the *Washington Post* has described the centers as "think tanks" which have "altered whole acres of the law." While those are words of warm praise from the *Post*, they confirm the board's major criticism of the centers.

For over three years, the board has been using its own limited resources to clean up the support centers, with generally successful, although occasionally perverse, results. The corporation won one court battle to defund one center and a second to reduce funding to another after proving that services adequate to justify the funds were not being performed. When auditors found that the executive director of a third center had misappropriated funds, however, the hearing officer refused to permit the defunding of the program, finding that the program's board of directors was somehow not responsible for the misconduct of its employees. The corporation succeeded, though, in a court battle to defund the National Clients Council for misuse of public funds, and the corporation reached an out-of-court settlement defunding a fellowship program for poverty lawyers.

Each of these battles took months and years to complete. As Congress has repeatedly cut back on funds for corporate administration to increase funds to grantees, the board simply lacks the resources and the time to prove its case in court against each center, one at a time. Nevertheless, the board has reached the reasonable conclusion that there is no good reason as a matter of policy to continue to fund admittedly liberal think tanks, many of which have already been proven guilty of waste, fraud, and abuse. Congress, however, has mandated continued funding for the programs through fiscal year 1989.

There is no doubt that the board has made significant tactical mistakes in the fight for congressional approval of the abolition of the support centers. Such mistakes are to be expected from eleven amateurs working part time. Moreover, we cannot satisfy congressional demands for detailed evidence to support our suspicions of centers that we have not yet taken to court. The congressional refusal to permit us to implement time keeping and functional accounting substantially inhibits the gathering of the very evidence that Congress demands. Our own deficiencies in the oversight of our staff, however, are substantially to blame. When the battle on the continuing resolution for 1988 went to the floor of the Senate, our staff had not completed a single monitoring report on the support centers despite three years of effort. Thus, we were hard pressed to supply our allies in the Senate with anecdotal evidence, much less hard statistics.

Nevertheless, there are signs of hope. In 1987, twenty-eight senators voted to abolish the support centers. No other proposed amendment to the continuing resolution gathered as many votes.

Had the status quo not been supported by the categorical imperative of adjourning for Christmas, no doubt more senators would have voted to repudiate the Appropriations Committee. In 1988, for the first time, President Reagan's budget message supported the board's position. Abandoning his position that the corporation should be abolished, the president agreed with his appointees that local services should be preserved, while Lyndon Johnson's secret weapon should be disarmed; Congress voted for continued funding in 1988 without major reforms.

Further Rounds

My own primary struggle with Congress has involved the implementation and enforcement of statutory restrictions on lobbying and other political activities by grantees. Not until the Reagan administration did the corporation make any effort to enforce the restrictions embodied in the 1974 act and subsequent amendments. In one notorious case, corporation officials under the Carter administration gave a special grant to a California recipient to organize efforts against a ballot initiative to restrict public spending. During President Reagan's first term, corporation officials attempted to defund the grantee, but the federal courts mandated continued funding. The court ruled that, although the political activity was illegal, the corporation could not punish the violation because its predecessors in the Carter administration had encouraged that activity.

Abuses of this sort led to the enactment of new restrictions on lobbying and other political activities as part of the appropriations measure enacted in 1983. The corporation adopted regulations implementing those restrictions in the summer of 1984, but the appropriations committees, which had resisted the 1983 legislation in the first place, denied a reprogramming request to implement those regulations. Even though the reprogramming denial could not invalidate regulations that the corporation had duly promulgated, our board agreed to review the regulations when it took office in December 1984. As chairman of the Operations and Regulations Committee, I was delegated primary responsibility for the task.

There were a few real problems with the regulation our predecessors had adopted. The record-keeping requirements were typically bureaucratic and more extensive than they needed to be. Moreover, the regulation did contain several ambiguities, although the program supporters were not necessarily any happier when we clarified some of those ambiguities to close potential loopholes in the regulation. The biggest loophole in the regulation, however, was the fact that it imposed few restrictions on the grantees' use of private funds. Our investigations disclosed that some grantees would use their federal funds for capital and overhead expenses while allocating private funds to pay the salaries of lawyers who were conducting lobbying and other political activities forbidden by law. From their point of view, a lawyer paid with private funds could use a taxpayer-funded desk, a taxpayer-funded telephone, a taxpayer-funded legal pad, in a taxpayer-funded office to conduct any political activities he chose. When the lawyer stopped his political activities, he went off the private payroll and back onto the federal payroll.

Our new regulation tried to bring this game to a stop. Rather than engage in endless accounting disputes, the board voted to apply the same restrictions to private funds as to taxpayer funds. Any grantee that wished to receive federal funds could do so only on the condition that it agreed not to use private funds to undermine the purposes of the act. Such indirect control of private funds by the use of federal funds is common in federal spending programs, most notably in the financing of presidential campaigns and in the new Grove City bill, the so-called Civil Rights Restoration Act.

The board adopted our new, clearer, and stronger regulation in January 1986, and the staff immediately submitted it to the appropriations committees for reprogramming prior to its final printing in the *Federal Register*. The fifteen days provided by law elapsed without comment from the committees. Still, the corporation staff waited in hope that the committees would agree to our putting the regulation into effect. The silence from the committees was not broken until I told the president of the corporation that I wanted the regulation put into effect unless we got a response in short order. We never did get a letter from Senator Rudman, but we did receive an unsigned memo from one of his staff raising several objections, especially to the new provisions on private funds.

At this point, the corporation was faced with a choice. The regulation had been considered for over a year and duly adopted pursuant to law. We could spend the balance of the Reagan administration letting congressional staff tell us what to do, or we could carry out our duty to run the corporation until Congress took that duty away from us. I told the president of the corporation to publish the regulation in the *Federal Register* and to proceed to enforce it.

Senator Rudman, who had maintained a discreet silence to that point, leaped to the defense of his staff and his prerogatives. At the subcommittee meeting the next month on the corporation's appropriations bill, he exclaimed:

> Their [the corporation's] lobbying regulation . . . came to us
> for reprogramming. We said we did not like it, we wanted to

179

change it. We want a good, strong regulation. We do not want them [the corporation] to be able to lobby without any limitation. They [the corporation] went ahead and published it anyway after hearing from us. They totally disregard this Committee.

The attitude of the Legal Services Corporation lately— maybe not Clark Durant, the chairman—but it seems to me of some of the membership there is that they are a quasi-private corporation. We give them money and they will decide how to use it. Well, nobody was elected there to do anything. We were elected. It is taxpayer money. We will decide how it is spent.[2]

No one has ever made a more eloquent argument against conduct of public policy through "a quasi-private corporation." Senator Rudman decided to put to rest the fiction of the corporation's independence by writing into the appropriations bill a withdrawal of the authority of the corporation to adopt any regulations in the area of "legislative and administrative advocacy."

The primary difference in modern public administration between appropriations bills and memos from congressional staff is that staff memos are not subject to amendment on the floor. By publishing the new lobbying regulation notwithstanding staff objections, the board moved the battle from the Appropriations Committee to the floor of the Senate. There, Senator Hatch, chairman of our authorizing committee, was prepared to move to strike Senator Rudman's language from the bill. As Congress hurried to adjourn for the 1986 elections, Chairman Hatch and Chairman Rudman reached a compromise. The corporation would not be permitted to enforce its 1986 regulation, but it would regain the authority to pursue a new regulation in 1987.

The board began 1987 in public negotiations with lawyers for our grantees. Many hours of hard work on both sides led to a compromise that all were willing to support. The new regulation withdrew some restrictions on the use of private funds, but it continued to restrict those funds far more than had the original 1984 regulation. As with all good compromises, there was unhappiness on all sides. The board nevertheless adopted it unanimously, and our recipients agreed to support it in Congress.

As in 1986, the 1987 reprogramming request languished in silence for months. In May, I testified at our Senate Appropriations Subcommittee hearing on behalf of the board. It is indicative of the difficulties of governing with part-time amateurs that after two and a half years of jousting over the lobbying regulation, Senator Rudman and I had never laid eyes on each other before. I briefly explained the practical problems we faced if programs could avoid the law simply by juggling the books. While Senator Rudman agreed with the logic of the regulation, he expressed concerns about the constitutionality of restricting the use of private funds. That ended the discussion.

Still, no final word came from the committees. Before the June board meeting, I told the new president of the corporation that I intended to ask the board to instruct him to publish the regulation without waiting any longer for word from the appropriations committees. He conveyed that position to committee staff, and, in the middle of our board meeting, he received a call from the staff informing us that the regulation would be approved.

The letters from the appropriations committees arrived shortly thereafter, and the corporation published the regulation in the *Federal Register* in July. By September, however, Senator Rudman's constitutional qualms got the better of him. There appeared without warning in the subcommittee's appropriations bill a clause forbidding the corporation from restricting the use of private funds, except where explicitly instructed to do so by the act itself. Having decided to concentrate on the issue of support centers for the 1987 floor battle, we made no direct attack on the subcommittee's language. The act does provide substantial authority for the regulation of private funds, so its effect on the scope of the regulation remains subject to dispute. While President Reagan's final budget proposed the removal of the restrictive language, for the time being the corporation and its grantees remain in substantial doubt over the scope of the regulation.

Conclusion—A Worthwhile Fight

For all its meager results, the four-year battle over lobbying has been well worth fighting. The enforceable portions of our new regulation are stronger than the regulation we inherited in 1984. Moreover, the board has served notice that its discharge of its duties can be regulated only by law, not by congressional committees and their staffs. At our appropriations hearing in 1987, Senator Rudman rebuked us for relying only on the statute, instead of committee reports:

> I think the bottom line is that whether it is legally binding or not, the Congress always has the option, if it gets report language that it thinks is important and that report language is not obeyed, then, the following year, the Congress will simply put it in the bill. . . .
> It seems to me that you ought to try to follow the report language, and if you have a problem come talk to the people who wrote it.[3]

"The people who wrote it," of course, are the hired hands of the committee staffs. By refusing to acquiesce to a staff memo, we forced the Appropriations Committee to put its wishes into the bill itself, where other senators would have a chance to amend it. On the lobbying regulations, at least, we achieved compromise on the Senate floor and compromise in the Code of Federal Regulations. Although that is hardly a famous victory, it was slightly better than the total defeat we had been offered.

The major significance of our congressional battles has not been the assertion of executive authority, but the protection of congressional authority against usurpation by its own committees. Chairmen and ranking members are perfectly happy with the current system of legislation through report language and subsequent amendment by reprogramming. Committee reports are not subject to amendment on the floor by dissident members, and reprogramming letters are never even seen. While committees can write any restrictions they like into their bills, members, at least in the House, do not enjoy similar rights on the floor. Indeed, the House rules have been amended in the past few years to make it practically impossible to restrain by floor amendment projects devised by committees and their agencies. The great virtue of the legislative veto, while it lasted, was not that it enabled Congress to control the executive, but that, through expedited procedures and modified rules, it gave the average member an opportunity to override "sweetheart" deals between the bureaucracy and committee staff. The board's willingness to carry its battles to the floor of both houses has given ordinary members a chance to be heard and has forced congressional leaders to cast their votes on the record. Our progress has been slow, but it has not been nonexistent.

The executive is most enfeebled when he refuses to fight. Only by public battles can public policy be changed. Our board is not so foolish as to think that the disputes over the Legal Services Corporation will be of decisive weight in any election to any office. But there are actual constituents who are hurt by the abuses of a Legal Services Corporation that was designed to be out of control. If senators and representatives want to continue to fund Lyndon Johnson's secret weapon, our board has given them an opportunity to explain themselves to their constituents. Sometimes that is all an enfeebled executive can do; it should never do less.

Notes

1. U.S. Congress, Senate, Committee on Appropriations, *Hearings on the Legal Services Corporation*, 99th Congress, 2d session, July 1986, p. 815.

2. U.S. Congress, Senate, Committee on Appropriations, Subcommittee on Commerce, Justice, State, the Judiciary, and Related Agencies, *Hearings on the Legal Services Corporation*, 99th Congress, 2d session, Aug. 12, 1986, p. 19.

3. Ibid., May 20, 1987, p. 28.

13
Commentaries and Exchanges on the Budget and Program Administration

Commentary by Louis Fisher

There is a tendency at this kind of symposium to go out after one branch—often Congress, sometimes the Court or the bureaucracy. If one of the branches steps outside the boundaries, it is fair game for criticism, but we have to keep government as a whole in context.

Despite the separation of powers, Congress continues to be involved in administrative details. Some people find that extremely offensive. They think that Congress should legislate and do nothing more, that it should not be involved at any stage of the administrative process. Why do we take a very strict view of the separation of powers when Congress is involved in administration but a very unstrict view when the executive branch is involved in legislation? No one thinks twice when executive officers visit Congress, even when they consult with conference committees and become very involved in the legislative process. That is how the government operates. It operates with a lot of overlapping that is totally consistent with what the framers expected as part of the system of checks and balances. We never adopted a pure separation of powers.

The Supreme Court in recent years has written some extremely rigid and formalistic decisions on the separation of powers. Both the key decisions—*Chadha* on the legislative veto in 1983 and the Gramm-Rudman-Hollings case, *Bowsher* v. *Synar*, in 1986—came up with the same message, that Congress is there to legislate. Once Congress legislates, it must keep its hands off and allow administration to be

185

performed entirely by the executive branch. It never worked that way before the *Chadha* and *Bowsher* decisions, it has not worked that way afterward, and it never will. The Court is championing a form of government that is wholly impractical.

I keep a list in my office of the legislative vetoes that have been enacted since *Chadha*. From *Chadha*, June 23, 1983, to the end of the Ninety-ninth Congress, October 1986, Congress enacted 102 legislative vetoes. This process continued in the One Hundredth Congress. The new legislative vetoes are more offensive than the one-house veto struck down by the Supreme Court in *Chadha*. They are usually vetoes given to the Appropriations committees. There is a reason for this.

One example of the pattern is the National Aeronautics and Space Administration (NASA) committee veto, contained in the housing appropriation bill enacted in 1984. The bill provided dollar caps on certain NASA programs; if the agency wanted to exceed the ceilings, it would have to get the approval of the Appropriations committees. President Ronald Reagan signed the bill but said the veto mechanisms were unconstitutional. He directed his agencies to ignore them, to notify Congress but not to get prior approval. The Appropriations committees said fine, we will have the supplemental appropriation bill repealed—since you do not like the committee veto—and we will at the same time repeal NASA's authority to go above the dollar caps without a new public law.

That was not what NASA wanted. So it entered into an agreement, with the cooperation of both branches, including officials at the Office of Management and Budget (OMB). As I understand it, the Appropriations committee staff was first approached by OMB. A letter went to Capitol Hill from James Beggs, the administrator of NASA, suggesting that the dollar caps be put not in public law but in the conference report; the agency would promise never to exceed the caps without prior approval from the committees. That is, of course, a legislative veto off to the side. It is a nonstatutory control. But it is a way to make government work better instead of having to pass laws for every little adjustment.

There are other examples. Sometimes they are not accurately presented. In President Reagan's State of the Union message, for example, he told the country that if he had a line-item veto, he would get rid of unnecessary pork-barrel appropriations and then cited special provisions for subsidizing development in blueberries, cranberries, crawfish, and the commercialization of wildflowers. I thought this was weird, because these were not big-ticket items. When I looked through the continuing budget resolution, I found that these things were not in there. I could find them only by forgetting about the bill that Reagan had before him and going through the conference report. In the agriculture report I found the cranberries, I found the blueberries, I found the commercialization of wildflowers—which all came to about $400,000. I could not find the crawfish, but I kept coming upon language that said, "Research, $200,000 for research in Louisiana." So I called the Appropriations Committee and they said, yes, that's the crawfish. It all came to $602,000, none of which would have been subject to an item veto, because the projects were not in the bill.

It could be argued that all these items ought to be in the bill in full detail, not merely in conference reports. Appropriation bills in state governments carry items as small as $2,000. But then President Reagan, instead of complaining about a continuing resolution weighing fourteen pounds, would have to cope with one weighing forty or fifty pounds. The bigger problem would be that, if all the details were taken out of the conference report and put into the bill to become public law, they would all be locked in, and the only way to get any adjustment would be to pass another law. No one in either branch wants to do that.

Such details are put in conference reports not to micromanage or meddle or get involved in administrative details but to give the agencies and the bureaus some discretion so that they do not have to get another public law for everything they do. Instead of making broad generalizations about micromanagement, then, we must understand the history of these matters. We will often find that behind some micromanagement, some offensive part of a bill, someone acted in bad faith, and Congress reacted to defend itself.

Commentary by Loren A. Smith

Many people say there is a duality in looking at the separation of powers or the proper arrangement of government. They say we have to find a balance between the evil of ineffective government and the evil of tyrannical government. I think that is a false duality. We used to think we could not have high inflation and high unemployment at the same time, and when we experienced them together, we coined a new term—stagflation. I think we may need a new term to cover the reality of ineffective tyrannies. Anyone who has traveled in the third world knows it is a reality—most tyrannies are ineffective, because tyranny is not an efficient system. Of course, that is no reason for praising tyranny or ineffectiveness.

The worst of all possibilities, in some ways, is a large government that is also ineffective. Some people who favor limited government feel that if we must have big, intrusive government, we should hobble it and make it ineffective. But that seems to me no real option. The separation of powers is misunderstood if it is viewed as a device for hobbling big government. It is supposed to ensure effective government, as well as safe government. Here I disagree somewhat with Louis Fisher.

Of course, there is a fundamentalist way of looking at the separation of powers that is an easy straw man to knock down. In this view, the judiciary should not do anything but judge, and the executive should not do anything but execute the laws, and the legislature should not do anything but enact laws. Clearly, if you take this view, you can show that even the framers were not for the separation of powers.

The framers' view is more sophisticated, but it is still meant to impose limitations on the way the government conducts its business. The true separation of powers theory is that each branch must have its functional integrity, must be able to perform its primary task. Other branches are given checks or controls, but these are mainly in the form of vetoes. Each branch is still intended to perform its principal responsibility on its own. The president's veto power is not a legislative power but merely a partial check on Congress, so that the president may protect executive concerns. Similarly, the power of the courts to strike down unconstitutional laws is not supposed to be a separate lawmaking power but simply a check resulting from the courts' obligation to enforce the legal requirements of the Constitution in particular cases or controversies. The same can be said about Congress. The power of the Senate to advise and consent to executive appointments is a check, but it is not meant to put Congress in charge of administration.

It is wrong to think that Congress is delegating power to the executive when it creates a program. Congress enacts law; that is its central constitutional function. But in constitutional theory the executive is not the agent of Congress. The president is an independent constitutional actor. His responsibility is to take what the legislative process has produced and manage a rational government on the basis of that power. He is the representative of one constituency, the national electorate. By looking at executive power as merely delegated by Congress, we have too often come to embrace a faulty perspective on the congressional appropriations power.

As a practical matter, much of what Congress has been doing has been an abdication of its primary responsibility. Congress does relatively little lawmaking, although this is supposed to be its core function. Instead, Congress does a lot of management. Casework is probably the biggest single activity of congressmen, because they view it as most important politically. They become involved in rule making by administrative agencies, they engage in resource allocation within programs, and so on. Perhaps Congress has abandoned its core function because interest group gridlock has made lawmaking an impossible task. Perhaps this is the ultimate fulfillment of Bismarck's remark that if people really knew how laws and sausages were made, they wouldn't touch either of them.

JUDITH A. BEST: I agree with Louis Fisher that flexibility and discretion are extremely important for the executive. The problem is that Congress allows flexibility and discretion only if it retains a subsequent form of control that is not subject to presidential veto. In practice this means it is not even Congress but a committee or subcommittee chairman that has the control. What Congress appears to be generously bestowing with one hand—flexibility and discretion—it is taking back with a much heavier hand. Congress is as much a victim of this situation as the executive. If we want to place blame, we can blame the executive for not jealously guarding its own powers in the budgetary process.

MICHAEL B. WALLACE: I agree that we should avoid Congress-bashing. I worked in Congress for three years, and I have great respect for the institution. I agree with Professor Best that the distinction is between Congress and congressional committees. What congressional committees say is not always what Congress would do if there were a free vote on the subject on the floor. I worked for the minority leadership in the House of Representatives, and our problem was not how to win votes on the floor so much as how to get issues onto the floor for any kind of vote. Committees would not report bills, and when they did, the Rules Committee would not let the bills be amended when they got to the floor. It was a remarkable process designed to keep issues from coming to the floor.

The problem with the NASA situation is exactly that—the deals that Beggs made with his committee might satisfy NASA, and they might satisfy the committee, but they might not have satisfied the majority of the members of the House of Representatives. The executive branch could force the committees to put such deals into their bills. It could give members of Congress a chance to do the job they were elected to do, which is to vote on public policy. They cannot amend a committee report or a reprogramming letter, or a telephone conversation between a civil servant and the committee staff. But they can amend a bill, and the president can veto a bill. One of the biggest problems in the Reagan administration was the willingness to do what Beggs did, which was to reach an agreement with congressional staff to avoid a confrontation. Having made those deals, it is silly to come back at the end of the administration and complain that Congress did not give them as good a deal as they would have liked.

The reason that everybody hates Congress and everybody reelects his or her congressman is that Congress has erected an elaborate system of secret deals that nobody is responsible for. Congressmen can go home and say, I didn't have anything to do with that; we didn't vote on that. They never get into trouble for a vote they did not cast on a committee report or a reprogramming letter. If we want to make the system work, we must require the people in Congress to do what they were elected to do—to make decisions in recorded votes.

MR. FISHER: Regarding Bismarck's comparison between lawmaking and sausage making, I think the reason Congress often looks bad is that we can see a lot more of what Congress does. It is not attractive, particularly the budget process. I am not a fan of the budget process in Congress. But if we saw how OMB puts together the budget we would not think quite so well of that either. If we saw how judges actually put their decisions together, we might get a bit nervous about that as well. In the 1950s, when conservatives were defending Congress and warning against executive power—saying the opposite of what we hear now from conservatives—Alfred DeGrazia formulated this point in a brilliant line. He said the president is Congress with a skin thrown over him. If we look at the executive branch and get past the skin, or beneath the veneer, we may find the executive does not operate very differently from the legislative branch in its resort to fragmentation and compromises and deals in the course of struggling along.

ABRAM N. SHULSKY: One of the oldest jokes in Washington is that the whole problem with the government is air conditioning: had it not been invented Congress would not stay around during the summer, the sessions would be shorter, and we would not have so many problems. It strikes me that Mr. Fisher's pragmatism in this area—endorsing whatever means come along that enable a congressional committee and an executive branch agency to reach a deal because it accommodates both sides—is another form of air conditioning. It allows Congress to make all sorts of small decisions in a convenient way and allows it to use its power of the purse in a much more detailed way than it otherwise could.

The claim is that if Congress cannot use the power of the purse in this way, with all sorts of legislative vetoes, committee vetoes, staff interference, and so on, Congress will withhold all discretion, and the executive can see whether it likes that any better. But that is not the issue. The issue is whether Congress would be willing to impose these constraints in law. It will have to ask whether the discretion involved is really important and whether the executive function is really important. If Congress thinks these executive programs are important—or thinks constituents will feel they are important—it will have to proceed in a constitutional way; it will have to pass an appropriation by law, just as the Constitution says. If Congress feels the program is not necessary, it can take responsibility openly and not pass the appropriation.

Of course, it may be more convenient for both congressional staffers and committees, on the one hand, and the agency representatives, on the other, to avoid all of this. But that does not mean that it is good for the rest of us or good for the country or good for the governmental process to proceed in this way. This kind of pragmatism says that any kind of arrangement that Congress can make is all right and in essence allows Congress to do whatever part of the executive branch function it wishes to do by simply saying that the alternative is no money at all. But that is not really true, or it will only be true, as Michael Wallace points out, if the executive branch does not stand up and fight.

Take the example of covert actions. If Congress wanted to cut off the contingency fund for covert action on the grounds that the president will not agree to prior notice, it could do it. But it would have to take the heat for that if, the following year, the president pointed to something he really should have done and explained to the country that he could not do it because Congress refused to give him a contingency fund. That is the issue here. The whole point of these constitutional requirements is to prevent Congress from taking over the rest of the government. One of the chief ways this is done is by forcing Congress to act by law, through relatively inflexible, permanent, general provisions. If Congress is not willing to act in that way, it should not be able to act. In the name of pragmatism we are destroying this scheme.

MR. FISHER: I would not argue for expediency or pragmatism as the only test of what is allowable. I do take very seriously the principles of executive energy and public accountability. Congress is willing to give up committee vetoes and take away from the executive branch the existing levels of discretion; Congress is willing to force the executive

191

branch to go through the whole appropriations process, to obtain a new public law for every kind of adjustment that is required during a fiscal year. But this is not practical. We have to find ways to protect the executive interest and the congressional interest without letting resources be allocated only by administrators.

QUESTION: Mr. Fisher protests the bashing of Congress, but he himself seems to be beatifying or canonizing it. What about the $8 million appropriated for Jewish schools in France in the 1988 budget resolution or Senator Edward Kennedy's midnight raid against Rupert Murdoch's conservative newspapers? Then he talks about how the executive branch misbehaves without mentioning that the administration's Nicaragua policy might have been out of control because of the Boland amendment, which forced it to act out of control to maintain its foreign policy.

MR. FISHER: No one is going to argue that everything Congress does is attractive or pretty. But the $8 million for the school in France was rescinded within a month. Congress does a lot of things that are regrettable. I am not here to defend such actions. The Boland amendment's language changing every year was in part a response to what the Reagan administration was doing, particularly in mining the harbors in Nicaragua. The language got tougher as a result of bad faith on the part of William Casey at the Central Intelligence Agency. What Congress did in the Boland amendments, changing the language as it discovered new evasions, was absolutely legitimate.

MR. WALLACE: What has been called the "morality of process" is important in any of these situations. I would be much happier with a bad result, a result we all felt was bad, where the process worked out correctly than with a good result where the process was destroyed along the way. The damage to the constitutional system is much worse when the process is destroyed, because that is permanent. Money can be wasted or a bad policy decision made or a stupid program set up. That is the nature of democracy. The only thing we have in permanence is the constitutional system.

QUESTION: There has been a lot of talk about a line-item veto for the president. I wonder if this is placing the emphasis on a secondary question we do not even need to reach. If line-item appropriations are quantified only in conference reports as part of the legislative history, I wonder if they are binding. Perhaps they are not law at all because they are not passed by both houses of Congress and presented to the president.

Ms. BEST: When Louis Fisher talked about the wildflowers and the blueberries and the crawfish, the point was that they were not in the bill that was sent to the president for his approval. If these expenditures are supposed to be mandatory—and Congress seems to think that they are—they must be presented to the president for his approval or veto. I do not see any way around that.

MR. FISHER: The administration is free to make the legal argument that the president is under no obligation to follow language in conference reports. This strategy is high risk. Upon reflection, I think the administration would back away from such a confrontation.

QUESTION: Mr. Fisher has counted 102 new legislative vetoes. I wonder if there are any other examples, such as the requirement that the Legal Services Corporation submit duly adopted regulations to the reprogramming process for Appropriations Committee approval. If there are other examples, do they offend the "morality of process"?

MR. FISHER: There are others. Reprogramming usually has to do with money or facilities, but it involves a lot of things in clearance procedures. It may be money or moving money around, but it may also be regulations. Whether this offends the morality of process depends on how pure a process we want. Alexander Bickel—who wrote a lot about the morality of process—said that a society totally devoted to pure, written principle could not survive. What level of abstraction do we want to deal with in considering morality and process? What give-and-take or what compromises do we allow?

If the executive branch wants to go to war on this to protect a prerogative, it can do so. It can try to strip all the committee vetoes and subcommittee vetoes. That will come at some cost, however, and the executive will have to decide whether the cost is worth it.

MR. SMITH: I agree that the executive could fight this. On the cabinet counsel I was an advocate for fighting some of these battles.

14

Wishing the Legislative Veto Back: A False Hope for Executive Flexibility

Barbara Hinkson Craig

In a 1981 *Washington Post* article, "Congress Can't Lose on Its Veto Power," Louis Fisher, a senior specialist in American national government at the Congressional Research Service, warned: "If the Supreme Court blocks its use the President is likely to be the one hurt."[1] When in 1983 the Supreme Court struck down the legislative veto in *INS v. Chadha*,[2] headlines in the *Post* read "Hill's Hard-won Gains of a Decade Wiped Out . . . Decision Alters Balance of Power in Government."[3] Now, five years after the Court's ruling, there seems to be some support for Fisher's position. But was it the executive branch that lost? Did the "grand realignment" forecast at the time of the decision really tip the balance of power in favor of the legislative branch?

One of the problems faced in weighing the pros and cons of the legislative veto is that it is one term used to describe many different procedural arrangements. Discussions about legislative vetoes quickly degenerate into comparisons of apples and oranges, with arguments about the success of one form used to rationalize the efficacy of an entirely different form. But there is no reason to assume, for example, that experience with vetoes over appropriation impoundments is generalizable to vetoes over safety regulations or that the results of vetoes over presidential exercise of foreign affairs power will be similar to the results of reprogramming vetoes.

Indeed, there is ample evidence that the legislative veto operated very differently, depending on (1) its form—one-house, two-house, or committee-level; (2) congressional motives for its enactment—to give Congress the ability to stop specific troublesome proposals, to ensure congressional participation in the design of proposals, or to permit delegation in the absence of consensus; (3) the policy arena over which it was applied—domestic or foreign policy, highly visible controversial issues or issues of low visibility and little salience to those not immediately concerned; (4) the intended target in the executive branch—president, agency head, or subagency head; and (5) the site of review in Congress—full house, committee, subcommittee, or congressional leadership.[4] Many questions must be answered before the effect of a legislative veto over a particular action by an executive branch or independent agency can be predicted. Yet few of these questions are ever asked by either the legislative veto's proponents or its detractors.

One argument in favor of the legislative veto is that with it executive agency heads could force control over their actions out of the hands of the subcommittee chairmen and staff (who often seem to expect to be, in effect, codirectors of their agencies) and onto the floor of the full House or Senate. There the problematic demands of the subcommittee might be overruled as wiser heads of the "average member" prevailed.

The Legislative Veto and the Legal Services Corporation

Michael Wallace, a director of the Legal Services Corporation (LSC), for example, describes elsewhere in this volume the congressional roadblocks faced by the directors of the LSC in their efforts to develop and implement regulations to gain managerial control over the programs and subordinate staff of their "independent, quasi-public agency." Faced with reprogramming requirements in the corporation's annual appropriations act, the board of directors had to clear new regulations and new expenditures of funds with the appropriations committees. "Theoretically, after a fifteen-day notice period, the corporation is free to proceed," Wallace notes. "As a practical matter," he continues, "execution of the laws without prior consent of committee staff leads to open warfare."[5]

Wallace then describes his efforts to fight such control and concludes that with the legislative veto the battle would have been more easily won. "The great virtue of the legislative veto, while it lasted," claims Wallace, "was not that it enabled Congress to control the executive but that, through expedited procedures and modified rules, it gave the average member an opportunity to override sweetheart deals between the bureaucracy and committee staff."[6] This conclusion reflects, I think, a major misreading or misunderstanding of actual legislative veto experience before *Chadha* and an unrealistic hope for its potential curative powers.

What if the Court had ruled differently in *Chadha*? If the legislative veto were alive and well, what sort of legislative veto would Congress have fashioned over the LSC? Wallace apparently assumes that it would be a one- or two-house veto that would enable the directors to go over the heads of their oversight subcommittees to get their action endorsed by the full House or Senate. In the time Wallace is describing (1984–1986) a two-house veto would probably have been necessary to accomplish his goal—so that if the Democratic House vetoed the directors' proposed changes (as they probably would have), the Republican-controlled Senate could save the day. Let us assume a provision that requires the LSC to submit any new or revised regulations to Congress with a review period of thirty days; if the regulation is not vetoed by both houses within that time, it can go into effect.

The scenario might proceed as follows. The board's regulation to enforce statutory restrictions on lobbying and other political activities by local recipients would be submitted to the House and Senate, where it would be directed to the appropriate subcommittees (normally the authorizing subcommittees with oversight responsibility, which might mean one, two, ten, or more subcommittees in each house). A subcommittee staffer would then review the regulation. (Members do not spend their time on such trivia.) At the same time the regulation would be published in the *Federal Register* with an explanation of the provision for congressional review and the date the rule would be effective if it were not vetoed.

Undoubtedly, local grantees would notice the published version (if career staff members in the LSC had not already alerted them to it). Members' phone lines would be buzzing, and their mail bags would be filled with complaints from local legal service offices. Pressure for a veto would mount. The expedited procedures would ensure a vote if the process went forward, and perhaps Wallace's prediction would be correct—that the "average" member would see the regulation as a fair implementation of the law and not veto it, although this was not the case when the members voted on an amendment to an omnibus continuing appropriations bill aimed at accomplishing the same end. Or perhaps the thirty-day time limit would make it difficult to get forces in both houses together to veto in time and, even with the expedited procedures, a few "friends" might be able to find a way to avoid a vote (by preventing a veto proposal from emerging from

197

committee or, as was done in the congressional effort to veto an air bag rule in 1977, by using parliamentary maneuvers to avoid a vote).[7]

Would the members in Congress who were concerned about the implementation of the law by the LSC under the Reagan administration have fashioned a two-house legislative veto over LSC regulations? I think not. The actions of local legal service providers, whether the issue concerns the quantity or quality of their services to the poor or the amount of time they spend in political lobbying, are not likely to be central concerns of many members of Congress. Those who will be concerned are the members and staffs of the oversight committees. The legal services programs define, at least in part, the oversight committees' power. LSC programs may be the sole responsibility of some staff members, their sole source of power. They have enormous incentives to find a way to have a say in what the agency is doing. The motive for congressional involvement is effective control over the implementation of the law by the subcommittee and its staff. The oversight subcommittees that want control are in charge of designing the controlling device in the first place. The fox is in charge of the henhouse and is not likely to build a fence that will keep him out.

If the legislative veto were still alive, directors of the LSC would most likely face a committee veto or, at the very least, a one-house veto that would be used by the subcommittee as a threat to force prior consultation. Although one might argue that such a provision could be successfully fought at the outset, little past evidence supports this hope. By the early 1980s (before the *Chadha* decision) legislative vetoes in all their varied forms were being appended to laws like boilerplate. Few were fought at all; fewer still were eliminated; many were not even noticed. Without the constitutional issue to focus the attention of the Justice Department and outside interest groups such as the Public Citizen Litigation Group, resistance to proposed veto provisions would be even less likely. A requirement for committee-level veto review of LSC rules would slip through unchallenged, probably unnoticed—particularly in light of the omnibus legislative packaging typical of the 1980s.

Of course, LSC directors could refuse to cooperate with their oversight subcommittees by issuing a rule despite objections by subcommittee staffs or members. As the first secretary of the newly formed Department of Education, Shirley M. Hufstedler tried this route by refusing to alter four minor regulations dealing with elementary and secondary education programs. Not only were the department's versions of the regulations vetoed (by both houses), but Secretary Hufstedler found herself in an impossible conflict with her congressional overseers. Within months she was forced to back down by altering the regulations to meet the committees' concerns. Within months the department staff were "consulting" regularly with the committee staffs on the content of proposed regulations to avert future vetoes.[8]

The relationship between agency and congressional committees is not a one-time affair. One skirmish may be won at a long-run cost that may simply be too high. With a two-house legislative veto provision, Wallace might have been able to "win" on his lobbying regulation (although, given the intensity of the disagreement between the agency and its oversight committee, that is not certain) but at the cost of antagonizing members and staff with whom he and his agency must do business for many tomorrows. The report-and-wait requirement of the reprogramming procedure at least holds out the possibility of ignoring the committee without legal ramifications, but the legislative veto, if it were constitutional, would create a *legal* shortcut to enable Congress to stop a regulation. The possibility of that shortcut (even if it were only occasionally used) would inevitably give Congress more power over the rule-making process. Because of the reality of congressional process, no matter what the form of the veto, increased power would be in the hands of those with a vested interest in paying attention to the agency—in other words, the subcommittee staff, chairman, and members (in that order). The overwhelming information and work overload in Congress prevents even the best intentioned from keeping sustained track of issues outside their bailiwick.

The problems with the legislative veto process do not appear to be significantly different, though, from the reality that Wallace faced in the absence of a veto provision. Subcommittee staff members made efforts to influence the content of agency rules before the fact. When the directors chose to publish a strong regulation anyway, the committee staff, backed up by the chairman, attached an amendment to an omnibus continuing resolution preventing the rule's implementation. The full membership voted in the committee's favor. The results look much the same: acquiesce in committee staff demands or make a stand and chance a "veto." Taking the second route in either case opens the agency to the possibility of future retribution by the committee in the form of more statutory controls and less flexibility. It is a route that must be cautiously traveled.

The level of disagreement between the LSC and its oversight committees is so high that with or without a legislative veto the struggle for control will be intense. The belief that the legislative veto would make it less contentious or would enable the agency to "win" more often is a will-o'-the-wisp.

199

The Legislative Veto and the Department of Transportation

If there is apparently little difference in process with or without the legislative veto, why should there be so much opposition to its use? The answer to this question can be found by assessing what a legislative veto would mean for the Department of Transportation if Secretary James Burnley's plaintive cry (chapter 17 in this volume) for its return were realized. Burnley cites several areas in which the department faced what seemed to him to be far more problematic congressional restraints—statutory deadlines and requirements for committee permission before action could be taken[9]—than it would have if the legislative veto were still available to Congress.

Take the case of the problems the department had with the sale of Conrail, the national freight railroad created by Congress in 1975 from the remnants of the bankrupt Penn Central and several other failing railroads, consisting of over 13,500 miles of routes in fourteen northeastern and midwestern states. When the newly elected Reagan administration announced that it was contemplating the sale of Conrail as part of its effort to get the government out of businesses that could be better run by the private sector, the response from Congress, especially from members from the Midwest and Northeast (Republicans and Democrats alike), was a resounding no—at least, not now. Among many other requirements and restrictions, the law Congress passed in 1981 to prevent an immediate sale of Conrail contained a two-house legislative veto over any future proposal of the department to sell the railroad.

After the Supreme Court ruling in *Chadha*, John D. Dingell (Democrat, Michigan), chairman of the House Energy and Commerce Committee, introduced a bill to require the passage of a law before the sale of Conrail could go through. Dingell was not taking a chance that the department might try to sell Conrail without the possibility of congressional influence. If Congress wanted to stop the sale after *Chadha*, it would have to pass a law to do so, which might mean having to get two-thirds in both houses to override a presidential veto. The quick response of the committee is a measure of the intensity of their concern about this issue. Not many of the more than 150 legislative vetoes on the statute books were addressed by Congress with this speed. In fact, five years after the Court decision many of these provisions remain on the books, presumably unenforceable but nevertheless untouched by any congressional efforts to refashion them into constitutional alternatives.

In a letter to Dingell, on August 3, 1983, Secretary of Transportation Elizabeth Hanford Dole said that "the requirement that a law be passed approving the sale would hamper DOT negotiations with potential buyers." She said, "The uncertainty would discourage potential purchasers from even expressing interest in the railroad."[10] Soon thereafter the department's counsel determined that a law would be required anyway because an attempt to sell without a law would undoubtedly cause a court challenge on the basis of severability. It would be difficult to prove from the legislative history of the 1981 act that Congress would have been willing to give the department the power to sell Conrail without retaining the power to prevent the sale by a two-house veto. Since the power to sell was not severable from the power to veto, the elimination of the veto by its unconstitutionality would cause the power to sell to fall as well. Dingell did not have to pursue his amendment to the law since the department was clearly going to follow his wishes.

Because the Conrail sale was a political "life or death" issue for members from the affected areas, they had much concern to express and much incentive to express it. The department had support for the sale from many members, but they did not feel strongly about the issue—it was not particularly salient to them. This "soft" support was not very helpful in deflecting the pressures on the department to compromise with those who did feel strongly, those who would be hurt. Burnley suggests that if the department had been able to work under the 1981 statutory scheme that allowed a sale proposed by the department to go through unless both houses vetoed it, the department's original proposal to sell the railroad to Norfolk Southern would have been successful. Inherent in this conclusion is the assumption that Secretary Dole would have been willing to confront Dingell and other congressional opponents, including a number of powerful senators from her own party. Perhaps she would. Perhaps the department would have won, and perhaps, if it had had the same numbers and kinds of legislative vetoes over its powers that existed in 1981, the fight would have been worthwhile. It is unlikely, however, that the department would have been in a position in 1986 that would have made these eventualities likely.

The Department of Transportation is very different from the LSC. It is an executive branch department with a single head. It is responsible for a wide array of programs—from airport safety to commercial space transportation, from highway and car safety to guarding the U.S. coastline. In theory at least, the department is responsible to higher-level presidential control. LSC is a quasi-public "independent," nonprofit "corporation," headed by an eleven-member board appointed by the president and confirmed by the Senate (although board members are not officially "officers of the United States"), with responsibility for a single program—legal services to the poor. LSC is not clearly responsible to the president or Congress or, indeed, to anyone. The policy arenas of these two bureaucracies could not possibly be more disparate, and, not surprisingly, the addition of legislative veto power over their actions would have very different results.

Before the *Chadha* decision, Congress had attached several veto provisions to specific delegations of power to the Department of Transportation. In 1974, for example, a two-house legislative veto provision was added over any future department effort to fashion a passive restraint rule.[11] In 1975 Congress added a one-house veto over any regulations concerning the discontinuation of routes or services by Amtrak,[12] and in 1977 a committee veto was added over any effort to collect higher fees and charges for a number of specified services.[13] There were a few other veto provisions, including the two-house veto added in 1981 over any future proposal to sell Conrail, but the department escaped the fate of a number of other agencies—a legislative veto applied to all agency regulations. The Department of Education and the Federal Trade Commission were subject to this sort of generic veto.

Across-the-Board Legislative Vetoes

If the constitutionality of the legislative veto had been upheld, the Department of Transportation, along with many, if not all, other executive branch and independent agencies, would not have been so fortunate. The many and controversial regulatory responsibilities of the department made it a prime target for an across-the-board legislative veto.

When the legislative veto is used sparingly by Congress for issues that are particularly controversial in Congress (such as a passive restraint rule), there may be some advantage for executive agencies. Occasionally, when agency heads decide to do what they believe is best in spite of the chance of a veto and the possibility of congressional retribution, they may win (as the Department of Transportation did in the 1977 congressional effort to veto its rule requiring air bags). When the veto is applied to every regulation of an agency, however, the potential for congressional involvement in the day-to-day operation of the agency is enormous. Under these circumstances the congressional comanagers are likely to be the committee and subcommittee staff and often personal staffers as well. It is not that such involvement never occurs without the legislative veto, it is just that the addition of this sort of broad veto power is an open invitation for as much involvement as committee and subcommittee chairs and their staffs choose to initiate.

Imagine the various subtle and not so subtle changes in the way the game could be played. With the ability to veto nearly every rule of the agency, congressional subcommittees could pick and choose which rules to threaten with veto. Highly visible and controversial rules that critical members or staff wanted to influence (on which they might conceivably lose in a veto attempt) could be held hostage by threats to veto other rules that were particularly problematic from a managerial perspective but that would attract little support from members at large in a veto fight.

The subagencies of a department might be able to undermine secretarial or presidential policy preferences by arguing that their version of a regulation is the only way to avoid a congressional veto. As Harold Seidman has pointed out, "Collusion between the legislative and executive bureaucracies to alter administrative policies is not an unknown phenomenon."[14]

Departments with broad areas of responsibility must deal with many congressional committees and subcommittees. The cross pressures from these congressional overlords, often in league with executive subagency bureaucrats, can cause difficulties for department heads under the best of circumstances. The potential power of the legislative veto would compound those difficulties many times, and it would matter which committees or subcommittees in Congress chose to pay attention. The Education Department found itself forced to respond most often to the House Committee on Education and Labor chaired by Representative Carl Perkins (Democrat, Kentucky); its Senate oversight committee payed much less attention to the details and made much less effort to influence day-to-day actions. Undoubtedly several committees and subcommittees would want to have a say in decisions of the Department of Transportation, and some of them would be willing to expend the staff time and energy to make the department aware of their desires. In the Conrail sale Chairman Dingell clearly would have used all means at his disposal to fight for the protections that concerned his district. Given the jurisdiction of his committee and the availability of a legislative veto over all the department's rules, he would have had ample means of exerting pressure.

In light of driving political forces of the 1980s, which have subjected nearly all policy making to fiscal constraints, heightened contentiousness among policy makers was inevitable. Added to this is the complication of divided party control of the executive and legislative branches and, for six years, divided party control in Congress. With or

203

without the legislative veto considerable confrontation and great frustration for all the participants were inevitable. Wishing the legislative veto back for the few circumstances in which it might be useful is not the answer. Moreover, irrespective of the constitutional questions, at least in the area of congressional-agency relations, the disadvantages of its return far outweigh the advantages.

The Legislative Veto in the Regulatory Arena

One of the major reasons for Congress's love affair with the veto in the late 1970s was the discovery of its utility in the regulatory arena. During the late 1960s and early 1970s Congress passed dozens of broad, often vague laws calling for clean air, clean water, safe workplaces, safe products, equal opportunities, and the like. By the mid-1970s executive branch and independent agencies responsible for implementing those laws were publishing new regulations by the hundreds to accomplish the laws' goals. Citizens and businesses affected by those regulations could now see exactly what the attainment of these glorious goals was going to cost them. Distressed by what they perceived as the unfairness (sometimes the stupidity) of the regulations, these citizens and business groups complained to their elected representatives. Elected members hoped to soften the effect, to fashion an exception, to get a postponement. The elected representatives found, however, that they could not do much to help short of passing new, more explicit laws—an alternative that was difficult, because it required achieving majority agreement in both houses, and distasteful, because of the internal conflict it caused and the political problems that might result from going on the record in opposition to "motherhood" and "apple pie" goals.

The old iron-triangle model of regulatory relationships, where the congressional committee, the agency, and the interests being regulated worked in cozy cooperation, no longer existed, especially not in the areas of new social regulation. Partly this was because these areas involved many more interests and many more groups inside and outside Congress (political scientists describe these new political arenas as "issue networks" or "whirlpools"), making it difficult for the informal agreements and accommodations typical of the iron-triangle relationships to be developed.

The members' inability to influence administrators' implementation of the law as much as they would like has to do more with the judicialization of the rule-making process. Pressed by both statutory requirements and court dictates, the administrative process had become much more formal—more open, more on the record, more bound by procedure, and, conversely, less receptive to the informal hints, suggestions, or demands of congressional members and staff. The old style was so much nicer, so much more convenient. If it required an ax to get back to the "cooperative" iron-triangle model, so be it. The legislative veto was an available and attractive ax.

The legislative veto is not really about "democratic control" and accountability, as its promoters have claimed. The elected members who are involved in legislative veto reviews in the regulatory arena often turn out to be unelected congressional bureaucrats. An elected member who is involved is usually a subcommittee chair or individual member out to protect some district interest, not to see that the agency follows the law. Congressional intent is debased to mean what the member or staffer at the other end of the phone line wants. Accountability is blurred because these informal contacts (made powerful by the potential of a legislative veto) are rarely recorded and can rarely be traced by citizens or reviewing courts (indeed, they can rarely be traced by other interested members).

The legislative veto is about mistrust but not really about a fear that the executive branch will not follow the law. When a majority in Congress can agree on what it wants done, it can and will put its wishes in the law. If Congress then mistrusts the executive, it has far more precise means of ensuring that the law will be followed—deadlines for issuing regulations, minimum requirements for content of regulations, requirements that specific funds be expended, and so on. (And if all this fails, the courts can almost always be relied on to enforce congressional intent when that intent is made clear.) Congress freely used these means before *Chadha* and has continued to do so after the veto was lost. But for this alternative to have legal force, members of Congress must agree sufficiently about substantive goals to get these kinds of requirements into the law. (Committees often put similar restrictions into committee reports—documents written by staff and rarely read by any members with the possible exception of committee or subcommittee chairs. These are powerful prods, and agencies often feel compelled to abide by them; but they do not have the force of law, and an agency that chooses to disregard them is not subject to suit for doing so.)

Congress is often unwilling, sometimes unable, to agree on legal language that would provide substantive guidance to the executive; yet it feels compelled to do something about pressing problems. Congress has to delegate, but what it is delegating is lawmaking, not executive, power. Since the courts have upheld these vast and vague delegations, Congress, unable to do otherwise, continues to give what is really its own power away. There are ways around this, of course. Congress could delegate the power to design a solution and then require the plan to be passed by Congress before becoming law. This was the threat held out by those who cautioned against the invalidation of the legislative veto—that agencies would become mere study commissions with all their actions, especially regulations, requiring confirmation by law before they could go into effect. But Congress finds this route just as difficult as making the hard decisions in the first place.

The motivation that prompted Congress to append vetoes to so many of its delegations was mistrust of its own law as much as anything else. The law, as Congress could or would fashion it, could not effectively direct agency actions. In the absence of an ability to reach agreement within Congress about what should be done, power could be delegated to the executive branch, with the promise held out that committees and even individual members could still influence the agency's implementation process. The agency could be "encouraged" to interpret the law to mean what a few members, one member, or even a single staffer wanted it to mean at any given moment and in any given context. Controversy could be postponed and, except for the highly visible and salient issues, could be resolved later out of sight of the press, constituents, and, indeed, most other members. With the primary focus of individual members and staff on district and reelection needs, it is not too difficult to see to what ends those pressures would work. In the event that they failed to "persuade" the executive, there was always the opportunity to go for an actual veto. Thus members could vote for vague laws, even vague laws that might adversely affect their districts. They could embrace the general glittering goals that the polls showed their constituents supported, like safe disposal of toxic waste, while retaining the power to protect the profitable toxic waste plants in their districts if need be. No wonder the legislative veto was attractive. These results, however, fly in the face of general notions of the rule of law. Used this way, the legislative veto is not likely to encourage Congress or its members to act more responsibly, to increase accountability of either congressional or executive branch actors, or to give executive branch actors more flexibility and discretion.

Many within Congress are well aware of their own shortcomings. Convoluted procedural designs like the Gramm-Rudman-Hollings deficit reduction process, the Sentencing Commission, and a special nine-member commission appointed to compile a list of military bases to close are evidence of congressional mistrust of itself, the president, the executive branch—indeed, all the accountable components of a democracy.

There is little evidence that Congress would have learned to use the legislative veto with restraint if the Court had not intervened. More and deeper intrusions into agency decision making were inevitable. The legislative veto provision over the Department of Education is instructive:

> The standards, rules, regulations, and requirements of general applicability to which the new procedure has reference should be understood to mean any administrative document of general applicability. . . . If an agency piece of paper is intended to be binding on the public, it should be issued under the [legislative veto] procedures set forth in the new subsection.[15]

By the time of the Conrail sale proposal, there seems little doubt that the Department of Transportation would have been subject to an all-encompassing legislative veto.

If the legislative veto had just been about giving Congress the ability to stop "bad" regulations, it would not have been a very significant congressional power or a very troublesome intrusion on the executive. In the fifty years of the legislative veto's life, Congress approved only 125 resolutions vetoing presidential or agency actions. More than half of those (sixty-six) were rejections of presidential spending deferrals (impoundments). Twenty-four were disapprovals of presidential reorganization plans. Only thirty-five vetoes were of agency regulations, projects, or decisions.[16]

Even when Congress overtly used the veto, the process did not necessarily comport with the model Wallace and Burnley imagine. When the House voted on the resolution to veto the four Education Department regulations in 1980, it did so under suspension of the rules that require the presence of a quorum (at least 218 members) and a two-thirds vote for passage. After a brief explanation of the resolution of disapproval by Education and Labor Committee Chairman Perkins, another member of the committee spoke even more briefly in its support. When the speaker called the question, the yeas and nays were demanded. The vote tally in the *Congressional Record:* "Yeas, 8, nays, 0."[17] Expedited procedures will not ensure the participation of the full membership if Congress does not enforce its own rules, and no other actor in our political system has the power to force Congress to obey them. Anyone who has watched the House and Senate in action would not be surprised by this level of participation even when "lawmaking" is occurring.

Conclusion

It is important to reemphasize that this analysis of the legislative veto has been confined to its exercise over executive branch departments and agencies or independent agencies. The veto's effects, problems, and advantages differ considerably when the target is the president and especially when the area of concern is foreign policy. Presidents are in a far stronger position to resist and counter congressional veto power. Agency heads, as subordinates of the president, must get his attention and support (and that will need to be sustained attention and support—a near impossibility) to counter the weight added by a legislative veto provision to their perhaps not constitutional, but surely effective, bosses in Congress.

If an agency and its oversight committee were in agreement in opposition to administration policy, the legislative veto might prove a useful weapon. Occasionally, if an agency determined that the costs were worth the fight, it might be able to use the veto process to its advantage. In day-to-day administration, the legislative veto, as Congress was determined to use it and expand its use, could hardly be an attractive prospect for executive branch actors or, for that matter, for public policy in the national interest. Whatever the merits of the Court's legal reasoning in *Chadha* (and these, I believe, are open to debate), the executive branch should breathe a sigh of relief at the veto's demise.

Notes

1. *Washington Post*, February 21, 1981, Outlook, pp. D1, D5.
2. 103 S. Ct. 2764 (1983).
3. *Washington Post*, June 24, 1983, p. A1.
4. For a full discussion of the effects of different legislative veto forms, see Robert S. Gilmour and Barbara Hinkson Craig, "After the Congressional Veto: Assessing the Alternatives," *Journal of Policy Analysis and Management*, vol. 3, no. 3 (1984), pp. 373–92.
5. "Out of Control: Congress and the Legal Services Corporation," chap. 12.
6. Ibid.
7. See the discussion of the airbag veto effort in Barbara Hinkson Craig, *The Legislative Veto: Congressional Control of Regulation* (Boulder, Colo.: Westview Press, 1983), chap. 5.
8. For an account of this battle see ibid., chap. 4.
9. These requirements are the equivalent of a committee-level veto, although they now take the form of appropriations riders; that is, "appropriation caps set in the law may not be exceeded" without the permission of the appropriations committees.

10. Quoted in *Congressional Quarterly Almanac*, vol. 39 (1983), p. 562.

11. P.L. 93-492.

12. P.L. 94-25.

13. P.L. 95-335.

14. Harold Seidman, "Legislative Veto: Two Views—One 'Yea,' One 'Nay,' " *Congressional Staff Journal* (September/October 1980), p. 22.

15. U.S. Congress, House, *Report to Accompany the Elementary and Secondary Amendments of 1974*, Report 93–805, 93d Cong., 2d sess., 1974, pp. 72–73.

16. Gilmour and Craig, "After the Congressional Veto," p. 374.

17. *Congressional Record* (daily ed.), May 12, 1980, H 3487.

15

Special Interests, Regulation, and the Separation of Powers

C. Boyden Gray

Economic progress, innovation, competition, and the realization of opportunity are all goals essential to the maintenance of our quality of life and our role in the world, but they are not achievable without a certain amount of pain and suffering. For every winner in the marketplace of ideas and products, there is probably a loser; and even though winners will invariably outnumber losers in a growing economy, the losers are also motivated to complain the loudest to maintain the status quo.

Congress and Special Interests

It is my thesis that today's Congress is the champion of the entrenched special interest and the executive branch is the advocate for opportunity and innovation; that the ability of the United States to compete internationally in the future will depend in part on the executive's ability to reassert its constitutional role to represent all the people and to induce Congress to engage in internal reform of its own to reduce the fragmenting and paralyzing influence of special inter-ests.

The principal problem posed by special interests in the regulatory context is their exploitation of the regulatory process to solidify market share at the expense of new, often innovative, competition. Entrenched special interests not only oppose deregulation, which favors more open competition, but also are imaginative in suggesting new regulations to impose burdens on competitors that do not apply to them and that retard rather than advance progress in such areas as health, safety, and the environment. Ironically, health and safety goals are often invoked by those interested in preserving the status quo to block the very progress in health and safety that the relevant regulatory agencies were created to promote.

Before examining how this process works, we should first review why Congress has become so vulnerable to the paralyzing effect of special interests. Excellent front page articles in the *Wall Street Journal*, a number of pieces in the *Journal's* editorial page, and Hedrick Smith in his excellent book *The Power Game* are among the observers who have identified the issues with some clarity. At the heart of the problem is the loss of the influence and discipline of the party system, which has been the "glue" holding together our unique system of divided power, to borrow a phrase from Lloyd Cutler. But the decline of the role of the parties is more a consequence than a cause of the breakdown of the Congress. To understand the factors that explain the breakdown of the party system is also to explain Congress's current state of vulnerability to special interests.

One of the factors is simply the seduction and abuse of power held too long. Democrats and incumbents generally have controlled Congress for so long that most members of Congress have figured out how to achieve the rough equivalence of life tenure (if boredom does not strike long before death, as it is doing now more and more). Supporting this modern form of life tenure are a number of perquisites that members have made available to themselves but not to their challengers, such as the franking privilege, staff, travel, home office support, newsletter expenses, and the like that some have valued at one-half million dollars a year in campaign terms. These benefits have freed incumbents from dependency on the party (and congressional leadership) for financing, as have the post-Watergate campaign finance reforms that made political action committee (PAC) money directly available to the incumbent, thus almost directly converting dependency on party to reliance on special interests.

So-called internal reforms instituted in the early 1970s have provided a second source of difficulty. Elimination of the discipline of seniority has often meant no discipline at all: almost every congressman has a subcommittee and a separate staff to promote his own reelection and, of course, to be captured by some special interest eager to strengthen his life tenure. Hedrick Smith would add television to this mixture because it allows a highly staffed subcommittee chairman to create or augment his own publicity without the permission or help of congressional or party leadership. The campaign finance reforms have perversely reinforced this. W. Clement Stone may have given $1 million to Richard Nixon, but it is not clear he wanted anything more nefarious than invitations to White House state dinners. Modern managers want something more tangible for their money, and what they want is the same thing a congressman wants—namely, life tenure, which usually means life tenure for whatever it is they make or sell.

A third source of problems has been partly of the executive's own making. The embarrassment and vulnerability created by Watergate and Vietnam invited an enormous turf grab by Congress both in domestic policy (such as the 1974 repeal of the president's impoundment authority) and in foreign policy (such as the War Powers Act and the Boland amendments). The Ethics in Government Act, the independent counsel statutes, and related laws that were not vetoed also constituted a form of turf invasion, because they permit the Congress to try to manipulate the regulatory agencies directly and through revolving-door policies while prohibiting the executive branch from doing the same. The Freedom of Information Act and the assault on executive privilege are other examples of successful efforts to inhibit the executive branch without subjecting the Congress to the same constraints.

What are some of the broader consequences of these trends? Perhaps the most striking fact is the historically unprecedented control of the House of Representatives by one party for more than one-third of a century. With an incumbency reelection percentage that averaged over 90 percent for decades and rose to 98 percent in 1986, there is little likelihood of change. It is difficult to believe that the Founding Fathers had this kind of life tenure in mind when they created the two-year term for the House of Representatives. And apart from whether this state of affairs can be representative of anything other than entrenched power, it certainly guarantees fractured government for an indeterminate period, especially since there is no reason to believe the House leadership will be more beholden to, and therefore cooperative with, a Democratic president than a Republican one.

The implications of this, in turn, are the subject of this volume. Although the focus of my paper is regulatory policy, I wish to make a few budget and foreign policy observations. As to the budget, Lloyd Cutler has pointed out that the government as a whole has produced deficits of more than 3 percent of gross national product (GNP) in nonrecessionary peacetime nine times since the Second World War— and each time was when there was a divided government.

On the foreign policy side, confused congressional interference in foreign policy has reached the point that it is routine for someone to say what Senator David Pryor did after a particularly baffling vote on

Persian Gulf reflagging, "In the final analysis, I don't know what we are doing." The Boland amendments are another example of congressional confusion. Perhaps the best illustration of the meaning of the Boland amendments is Arthur Liman's anecdote about Robert McFarlane's offer to share all contra resupply information with House Intelligence Committee members on the condition that there be no staff present, knowing that his offer would be refused, as it was.

The trade bill vetoed by President Reagan in 1988 is a final example, where we were treated to the spectacle of 200 conferees meeting in seventeen separate subconferences; the next step is a 535-member conference. If the national interest can continue to survive this special interest free-for-all, it will be a near miracle. Luckily for the national interest, the primary results in both parties greatly strengthened the administration's free-trade hand, forcing Congress to drop the most extreme forms of protectionism, such as the Gephardt amendment. Indeed, the trade bill is an excellent example of how captured the House is by special interests and how out of touch it is with the general public. It may turn out that Vice President George Bush's primary victories against the protectionists in South Carolina and on Super Tuesday, which led directly to the demise of the Gephardt amendment, may constitute his most important contribution to the Reagan presidency.

Deregulation Efforts

Although trade restrictions are a form of regulation, most regulatory examples are not as easy to describe because of their inherent complexity. But regulatory problems remain important. Five examples of efforts at deregulation at different agencies are illustrative: acid rain, highway safety as reflected in the air bag and five-mile-per-hour bumper standards, labor restrictions as reflected in the so-called homework rules, new drug approval, and financial regulation.

There will be no extended discussion of congressional deregulation for the obvious reason that there has not been any sweeping congressional deregulation since the transportation initiative that began in the early 1970s—before the consequences of the factors discussed above had set in. Indeed, Congress's recent inaction on deregulation is as illustrative of the power of special interests as the administrative examples that follow.

Acid rain may well be a bigger diplomatic and public relations problem than a scientific one. Evidence is beginning to mount and a consensus beginning to form, not only here but in Europe as well, that the problem is more ozone than acid deposition. But since they share a common precursor, are otherwise scientifically related, and are both serious problems, it is worth examining Congress's treatment of acid rain for a moment.

The principal congressional provision of relevance is the so-called percentage reduction requirement enacted as part of an environmentalist–coal-industry–utility compromise in the 1977 amendments to the Clean Air Act. This aspect of the 1977 compromise has been dissected by Harvard Professor Bruce Ackerman in a classic diatribe called *Clean Coal, Dirty Air*. The provision in question requires all new coal-fired power plants to achieve 90 percent reduction in SO_2 emissions, not using the best method available to a utility (such as switching to low sulfur coal) but *only* by installing a scrubber (the option of using natural gas was cut off in 1978 by the Fuel Use Act). A scrubber, it should be noted, is a very inefficient and highly costly method of removing SO_2 from the flue gas that itself creates a waste disposal problem leading to severe long-term groundwater contamination.

It does not make much sense to impose a design requirement of this kind even on utilities located in high sulfur coal areas in the east, because it prohibits them from using the least costly clean-up approach. But it is absurd to apply this requirement in the west. Indeed, some western coal is so low in sulfur that engineers actually have to add sulfur to the scrubber to make it work.

This ridiculous provision is an example of the exploitation of an otherwise totally unopposable "health" regulation to enhance the competitive position of a product or process, in this case high sulfur coal in the East, to the severe disadvantage of low sulfur western coal or any other competing alternative for reducing SO_2 emissions. The result, of course, was predictable: a virtual freeze on technological development toward more efficient electricity generation and support for this state of affairs by the environmentalists who should be the most forceful advocates for technological advance. As a further consequence, the taxpayer is now footing a multibillion dollar bill for the United States to demonstrate new clean coal technology, much of which may never make it in the marketplace because it was not developed with the real world in mind.

The worst consequence of the provision, however, is that in setting a design rather than a performance standard—that is, in denying utilities any flexibility in deciding how to reduce emissions— Congress has been costing the public (and Canada) more than 5 million tons of pollution annually. In other words, if utilities were free to choose the means of pollution control including the use of ordinary emissions trading that is routinely allowed for other pollutants, the industry would be producing at least 5 million tons less acid rain annually than is now the case.

It is this kind of micromanagement that lies at the heart of the problem of congressional overreaching. In domestic or in foreign affairs, Congress has a role in setting overall policy guidelines, but when it begins to manage the operational details, which more properly belong to the executive, it becomes a prisoner of its fragmented committee system and the special interests that have captured it.

Needless to say, efforts to modify this statute failed in 1981. While it is also true that the special interests have produced a gridlock on acid rain issues in the Congress since then, there is every indication that even if Congress could act, it would only aggravate the problems of the 1977 law, not solve them. Congress unintentionally undid some of the damage of the 1977 amendments in 1987 when it repealed the Fuel Use Act, thus permitting utilities to avoid the scrubber requirement by burning natural gas. This was unintended because the Fuel Use Act "belongs" to a different committee in the Senate (Energy) than that which has jurisdiction over the Clean Air Act and the Environmental Protection Agency (Environment and Public Works), and the former generally has no interest in environmental issues. The repeal, as a result, has attracted little attention as an environmental measure, even though the Canadians benefit twice—once through expanded markets for their own ample natural gas supplies and again through reduced cross-boundary emissions. Accordingly, these benefits may go unnoticed, an unfortunate occurrence because the Congress may enact acid rain controls in a manner that could undermine the benefits of the Fuel Use Act repeal for both the environment and energy security.

As this example indicates, the special interest fragmentation on the Hill makes it difficult for the government to see or act upon relationships between related subjects—here, natural gas and clean air. Thus, because the congressional committee that dominates the EPA's acid rain agenda is dominated by coal, EPA's own acid rain approach tends to be dominated by coal; while the Department of Energy, which is dominated by the Energy Committee that is precluded from considering the environment, is similarly discouraged from touting the environmental benefits of natural gas. The White House has been able to link some of these issues together, but it is always having to combat the divisive influence of the special interests and congressional committee fragmentation.

A second example can be found in two highway safety issues. The first, air bags, is as much a question of insurance company profits as it is consumer safety. Air bags do increase safety, but they also cost a great deal more than safety belts, which, if worn, provide equal or greater safety. It was in the insurance industry's clear economic interest to see whether it could persuade the federal government to require air bags at no cost to the industry, because the resulting "free" benefits (in the form of reduced accident claims) would flow straight to the bottom line. As long as there was a chance of government action, the insurers saw no incentive to offer premium discounts to drivers who purchased bag-equipped cars or higher insurance awards to drivers who were wearing belts at the time of an accident. Indeed, the insurers refused to say to the Department of Transportation (DOT) whether or how much they would reduce their premiums if a federal air bag rule were adopted, even as they were telling DOT what the safety benefits would be. In this instance, they were relying on the fact that the states regulate the insurance industry, while the federal government is the primary regulator of autos.

The insurance industry won an almost unqualified victory by nudging Congress repeatedly to try to influence the DOT's deliberations. Behavior of this kind by the White House would have triggered cries of unethical "political" interference. The "cover" was highway safety, but the motivation was insurance industry lobbying, which was able to do more than hold its own against the auto industry, which has historically not been popular in the Congress. In the end, with some White House counterpressure, DOT reached a compromise version, which encouraged the states to pass seat belt laws and wage campaigns against drunken driving and encouraged the auto companies to continue experimenting with more effective passive restraint systems. If Congress had not had to contend with the White House, however, it might have frozen passive-restraint technology where it stood in 1981, dulled local initiative to address drunken driving and seat belt use, and virtually abandoned the huge public investment in seat belts already installed in every car on the road.

The five-mile-per-hour bumper standard was another example of a design specification that had its roots in congressional micromanagement. It resulted initially from congressional pressure, which in turn resulted from a combination of lobbying by the insurance industry (again) seeking to get a free ride on reduced repair costs without reduced premiums and interference from Senator Robert Byrd, whose state was host to the principal manufacturer of the five-mile-per-hour bumpers that were required by DOT's design team proponents. Underscoring the special interest nature of this regulation was its justification as a "safety" standard even though consumer safety was not remotely involved.

217

Understandably, the Reagan administration was able to eliminate the standard only with great difficulty. As it turns out, five-mile-per-hour bumpers do provide more cost-effective dent protection than two-and a half-mile-per-hour bumpers, and auto companies have been forced by the market generally to install bumpers that provide more protection than the two-and a half-mile-per-hour variety. But the current bumpers are cheaper than the old, being designed by the demands of the marketplace rather than by the bureaucrats at DOT, and they are not all manufactured in West Virginia.

The famous homeworker regulations prevent home manufacturing of various classifications of women's apparel. Ostensibly designed in the 1920s to eliminate the abuses of sweatshops, they operate now to prevent the spread of nonunionized work competition to the winter home apparel industry in Vermont, where knitting ski caps is a favorite snowbound pastime, or the sunny Midwestern farm, where wives are often isolated from urban manufacturing centers. Since these regulations do not apply to men's apparel, they also have the effect of granting tenure to a specific union, in this case the International Ladies Garment Workers Union (ILGWU). Despite President Reagan's direction early in his term to deregulate these rules if a supportive record could be developed, congressional pressure, or perhaps more precisely ILGWU pressure, has staved off deregulation of most of the restrictions. The only consolation is that without White House counterpressure, none of the homework regulations would ever have been reviewed at all.

Another target of the regulatory reformers has been the highly rigid, time-consuming, and health-threatening new drug approval process at the Food and Drug Administration (FDA). The first term produced only minor improvements, but the second term hit pay dirt with the promulgation of the Treatment IND regulations, which will make experimental drug therapies available much earlier (that is, in about half the time) to terminally and seriously ill patients. Predictably, this provoked critical hearings on the Hill and the passage of a bill in the Senate that was intended to convert the FDA from an executive branch agency to an independent one responsive only to Congress.

Although it is impossible to prove cause and effect, this change probably could not have been made without Congress's repeal in 1986 of the export restrictions on drugs not approved by the FDA, even if the drugs were approved in the foreign country. This change put international competitive pressure for reform on the FDA. Equally important, it reflected congressional openness to reform, at least in some quarters. But it is doubtful that Congress could have enacted the 1986 change without the pressure of the 1986 midterm elections. Challenger Ed Zschau was poised to use the old law as ammunition against Senator Alan Cranston and the Democrats in California, which is one of the two most important sites of the emerging biotechnology industry. The fact that Senator Edward Kennedy represents the other site was not lost on Congressman Henry Waxman, who acceded to Vice President Bush's request to let the legislation go through.

The point is that, as in the case of the demise of the Gephardt amendment after Super Tuesday, it took statewide or broader elections (California is big and diverse enough to be considered a region for this purpose) to force action on legislation that probably would have been stalled by special interests in the ordinary legislative process. Even so, one biotechnology firm tells the story of having to raise $10,000 to attend a particular senior lawmaker's fund-raising reception in order to get the export ban repeal scheduled for floor action.

Why would there be any special interest resistance to accelerating the drug approval process or to repealing export restrictions? The reason is that current law benefits the large, well-established companies to the disadvantage of the new high-tech startups. That is, only the large companies had the capital and staffing necessary to overcome the old bureaucratic hurdles at FDA for new drug approval and to build and operate plants abroad. The new biotechnology firms had neither and were poised to license their technology overseas when these two changes allowed them to continue and expand their operations here.

The last example is financial regulation, which has been very much in the news as a result of Black Monday and other developments. With all due respect to Wendy Gramm, who made enormous contributions to regulatory reform when she was in the Office of Management and Budget and who won a promotion to the chairmanship of the Commodities Futures Trading Commission (CFTC), it is difficult to believe that one would divide the regulation of trading in stocks and options on stocks from trading in stock index futures and similar futures between the CFTC and the Securities and Exchange Commission (SEC), subject to separate congressional oversight, if one were able to start over and erect the ideal regulatory structure. But the interests influencing the Agriculture and Commerce Committees are so entrenched that it is hard to see how the thrust of the Brady Commission recommendations to consolidate these agencies can be implemented politically. The compromise that may develop in the form of the new interagency group led by Treasury is certainly workable and is probably the best that can be devised in the circumstances. But it is not the way one would do it if one had an entirely free hand.

Banking regulation similarly reflects the stamp of special interests. The restrictions of the Glass-Steagall and bank holding-company statutes are classic examples of restrictions ostensibly enacted for one purpose—safety and soundness—but whose actual effect is to protect market advantage and agency power while undercutting safety and soundness. Those who would preserve the competitive insulation advantage provided by Glass-Steagall (namely to some investment banks) use the rhetoric of safety and soundness to argue that commercial banks are too fragile to handle new opportunities. In fact, the reverse is probably much more accurate, namely, that the banks would be in much better shape today if they were not prohibited from diversifying their risk in terms of both product and geographic markets.

Similarly, the commercial banks that seek the protection against competition or acquisitions provided by the Bank Holding Company Act (and the Federal Reserve) use rhetoric seeking to enshrine the "separation of banking and commerce" as a key to both safety and soundness and proper regulation of banking. Among the negative effects of the act is prohibiting acquisition of troubled U.S. banks by virtually all U.S. corporations (all those that are not pure banks), while freely permitting foreign firms with diversified operations in every nonfinancial field to acquire these banks. One result is the steadily growing foreign ownership of the U.S. banking system.

Do not the current proposals in Congress, however, now enacted by the Senate to deregulate Glass-Steagall, undercut the thesis that Congress is incapable of major deregulation? Probably not. In the first place, it has not happened yet. But more important, it is happening only where the special interests are willing to let it happen—that is, in the investment banking area but not in insurance and not in every market even in investment banking. The fact is that certain Wall Street firms want to go into commercial banking, which requires them to allow commercial banks onto their turf, and they are willing to let the banks in on some of the less lucrative underwriting markets. But the insurance industry does not yet have similar interests, so the legislation actually increases restrictions on bank holding companies competing in insurance markets.

Financial regulation is useful as a last example because it underscores the point made at the beginning about exploiting health and safety rhetoric to undermine those very values. Time and time again regulatory agencies are publicly implored not to authorize some new product innovation, whether it be a cleaner fuel at EPA, a breakthrough in heart treatment like TPA (Tissue Plasminogen Activator) at the FDA, or a new financial instrument that banks want to have permission to market, because these innovations are not proven to be risk free. Because it is always impossible to prove perfection, regulatory bureaucracies must concede that the new approvals pose some risk. This risk is frequently found to be unacceptably high; but agencies rarely compare the risks of new products to the often much higher risks of existing products enjoying current market approval.

Of course, part of the reluctance to approve new things is the risk-averse nature of bureaucracies. But an ever-present factor is the effort made by existing product makers to impose very high health or safety standards on their emerging competition that they themselves could never meet. This is called "letting the perfect be the enemy of the good," and it helps explain the regulatory drive to zero risk. It is the most often invoked strategy of the entrenched special interests, a strategy that regulatory agencies must always view with the healthiest of skepticism.

Executive Branch Successes

As these examples suggest, the executive branch has made some successful counterattacks against the tyranny of the special interests. The Justice Department successfully argued in the Supreme Court against the legislative veto in the *Chadha* case, thus eliminating one of the means by which Congress both enacted policy and retained partial control over how that policy was implemented. Judge Laurence Silberman, the Reagan appointee who wrote the appeals court decision invalidating independent counsel (since reversed by the Supreme Court) also had a hand in burying the Rupert Murdoch bill of attainder that endangered his media holdings in New York and Boston; that attempt was an especially egregious example of special interest congressional meddling in the regulatory agencies.

Finally, the executive branch has successfully implemented and judicially defended Executive Orders 12291 and 13498, which allowed the executive office of the president for the first time to communicate the president's philosophy to the agencies and to coordinate their interaction. Imagine that: a president actually talking to one of his appointees directly or through staff on regulatory matters! As bland as this may seem today, Executive Order 12291 was considered revolutionary at the time—indeed, many critics insisted that it was entirely illegal. It has survived, however, and has earned the reputation as one of the most far-reaching government changes made by the Reagan administration.

221

In part as a result of these initiatives and in part as a result of wise personnel choices, the Reagan administration has made important strides in improving the regulatory process and reducing regulation in the absence of, indeed in spite of, help from Congress. Under the leadership of the Presidential Task Force on Regulatory Relief, led by Vice President Bush, the administration dramatically slowed the growth of new regulation, cut existing regulations for savings of over $150 billion (including 600 million worker hours of paperwork) in a decade, and spearheaded at least some isolated but nevertheless important statutory changes.

The most important of the changes in existing regulation include Davis-Bacon deregulation, a package of auto industry deregulation in 1981 that helped that industry refocus on product quality to meet foreign competition, the so-called Treatment IND regulatory changes at the FDA discussed above, and the alternative fuels initiative that will greatly alleviate the regulatory burdens associated with meeting the ozone and carbon monoxide air quality standards while advancing the cities' compliance with these standards at lower cost. In a related development, the task force also oversaw development of several important deregulatory proposals at the Department of Energy, the Federal Energy Regulatory Commission, and the Environmental Protection Agency to remove the disincentives to the adoption of clean coal technologies and other pollution reduction measures (including use of natural gas) that will lower both acid rain and ozone emissions.

On the legislative front, Congress repealed the Fuel Use Act, enacted during the Carter years to prohibit utility use of natural gas. As indicated above, repeal of this curious statute will level the playing field for competing fuels and will lower emissions in connection with the task force's acid rain changes. As noted above, Congress also repealed restrictions in the Food, Drug and Cosmetic Act that prohibited exports of new drugs not approved by our FDA even if they are approved by the recipient country. This change, the FDA's Treatment IND regulation, and an interagency regulatory monitoring process established at the task force's initiative have gone a long way to maintaining the U.S. biotechnology industry's ability to keep its worldwide leadership role in recombinant DNA technology. Other legislative changes included the lifting of the ceiling on interest rates in 1983 and the deregulation of bus lines.

Although it is hard to measure the bottom line, the remarkable resurgence of manufacturing productivity over the past few years, which is running higher here than in either West Germany or Japan and which is playing an important role in our current export boom, surely reflects some of the effort that has been made.

There is, of course, much more to be done, much more than can comprehensively be described here. Further substantive changes in both the existing set of regulations and the underlying statutes will depend on further strengthening of the executive branch vis-à-vis the Congress. The EPA still responds more to the dozens of reviewing subcommittees on the Hill than it does to the White House, except when the latter can muster an interagency effort like the Alternative Fuels Working Group. Moreover, efforts like defense procurement deregulation at the Pentagon will inevitably run up against pork-barrel politics. To achieve improvement, therefore, internal discipline must be reestablished on the Hill, together with a streamlining of the proliferation of subcommittees, reform of campaign financing, reduction of staffs and perks, and revision of micromanagement statutes.

These, in turn, will probably depend upon a publicly supported reassertion of responsibility by the executive that is won in the political arena, such as by outright repeal of the War Powers Act or changes in the 1974 Impoundment Control Act following a national election campaign that has raised these issues. Only then will innovation and competitive opportunity truly have a fair chance in the marketplace to go head to head against the entrenched special interests and their ability to make the perfect the enemy of the good.

16

The Impetuous Vortex: Congressional Erosion of Presidential Authority

Theodore B. Olson

The single most important characteristic of the U.S. Constitution, responsible for the preservation of individual freedom and liberty for 200 years, is its carefully balanced structure of divided yet interdependent powers. One principle with which most Americans found themselves in agreement in 1787 was that "no political truth is . . . of greater intrinsic value, or is stamped with the authority of more enlightened patrons of liberty, than that . . . [t]he accumulation of all powers, legislative, executive, and judiciary, in the same hands, whether of one, a few, or many . . . may justly be pronounced the very definition of tyranny."[1]

To avoid the accumulation of power, the first three articles of the Constitution allocated legislative, executive, and judicial power to three separate, coordinate branches of government. The legislative department, created by Article I, vested with the authority to make all laws and appropriate all funds to be drawn from the Treasury, was the most feared of the three branches:

> [W]here the legislative power is exercised by an assembly, which is inspired, by a supposed influence over the people, with an intrepid confidence in its own strength; which is sufficiently numerous to feel all the passions which actuate a multitude, yet not so numerous as to be incapable of pursuing the objects of its passions, by means which reason prescribes; it is against the enterprising ambition of this department that the people ought to indulge all their jealousy and exhaust all their precautions.[2]

Because the legislature's powers are "at once more extensive, and less susceptible of precise limits [than the other branches], it can, with the greater facility, mask, under complicated and indirect measures, the encroachments which it makes on the coordinate departments."[3]

In short, while governmental power was carefully divided among three branches, the framers nonetheless forewarned that the "legislative department [would be] everywhere extending the sphere of its activity, and drawing all power into its impetuous vortex."[4] The framers also appreciated that "parchment barriers" would be insufficient protection from the legislature's "encroaching spirit of power." Therefore, along with the judicial and executive powers allocated to the president and the courts, respectively, each of those branches was given authority and protections presumed to be sufficient to resist encroachments by the legislature. The judiciary, for example, was given life tenure. The executive power was vested by Article II in a president who, among other things, was given the exclusive authority to "take care that the Laws be faithfully executed." Thus, the "entire legislature . . . can exercise no executive prerogative."[5]

The first section of this chapter explores the framers' decision to vest all executive power in a single individual, partly to ensure that executive decisions would be effective and efficient, partly to provide strength to counterbalance the power of the legislature, and partly to focus responsibility and accountability. Next the chapter catalogs some of the ways in which Congress has eroded presidential power, through a variety of "complicated and indirect measures," weakening the president, enhancing the strength of the legislature, and producing the kind of enfeebled, disorganized, and unaccountable executive establishment feared by the framers.

A Unitary Executive

The decision to vest executive power in a single individual was thoroughly and thoughtfully considered in a debate culminating on June 4, 1787. On that date, by a vote of seven states to three, the Constitutional Convention in Philadelphia approved a resolution offered by Pennsylvania delegate James Wilson that "the Executive consist of a single person."[6] During the discussion preceding that vote, the framers squarely confronted and explicitly decided the question whether executive power should be divided among several people or lodged exclusively in one person.

The debate leading to the decision of June 4 on this "point of great importance,"[7] as it was characterized by Benjamin Franklin, was prescient and enlightened, the decision between conflicting concepts of executive power, deliberate and informed. The substance of the debate on the form of government the framers intended to create in 1787 as contrasted with what the government has become in the two succeeding centuries is most revealing.

Casual historians tend to characterize the American Revolution as an insurrection against King George III and the abuses of a despotic monarch. Ample evidence supports this perspective; the litany of grievances against the king contained in the Bill of Rights is certainly exhibit A. This point of view, however, obscures the concerns that the framers harbored regarding the legislative power. As James Wilson argued during the Constitutional Convention, "The People of America did not oppose the British King but the Parliament—our opposition was not against a Unity but a corrupt Multitude."[8]

The Constitution was created against the backdrop not only of the Revolutionary War but also of the weak, ineffective government created by the Articles of Confederation. Many of the delegates, moreover, had direct experiences with colonial governments, which in many instances were characterized by powerful legislative bodies and weak, divided executives. The delegates had seen how such governments had become feeble. They wanted a national government that was effective yet accountable.

In his *Notes on Virginia*, written during 1782 and 1783 and published in 1784, Thomas Jefferson, who had served as governor of Virginia during the period 1779 to 1781, described the Constitution of Virginia as having been formed "when we were new and inexperienced in the science of government. It was the first . . . which was formed in the whole United States. No wonder then that time and trial have discovered very capital defects in it."[9] Among those defects was the fact that:

> All the powers of government, legislative, executive, and judiciary, result to the legislative body. The concentrating of these in the same hands is precisely the definition of despotic government. . . . An *elective despotism was not the government we fought for* . . . .[10]

During the Constitutional Convention James Madison argued that state governments tended to "throw all power into the legislative vortex. The Executives of the States are in general little more than Cyphers; the legislatures omnipotent."[11] At the same time that the framers worried about the legislature's potential for acquiring tyrannical powers, they were also concerned that if the legislature became involved in the execution of the laws, government would grind to a halt. Here again the sentiments of many of the delegates to the convention are best expressed in the writings of nondelegate Thomas Jefferson:

> I think it very material, to separate, . . . the executive and legislative powers. . . . The want of it has been the source of more evil than we have experienced from any other cause. Nothing is so embarrassing nor so mischievous, in a great assembly, as the details of execution. The smallest trifle of that kind occupies as long as the most important act of legislation, and takes place of everything else. Let any man recollect, or look over, the files of [the Continental] Congress; he will observe the most important propositions hanging over from week to week and month to month, till the occasions have past them, and the things never done. I have ever viewed the executive details as the greatest cause of evil to us, because they in fact place us as if we had no federal head, by diverting the attention of that head from great to small objects.[12]

Thus the delegates in Philadelphia were familiar with governments with powerful legislatures, which tended to strangle government through preoccupation with trivia, and with impotent, divided executives. When they turned to the task of describing the qualities they intended to establish in the executive component of the new national government, several criteria were repeatedly expressed: "energy [or vigor,] dispatch and responsibility."[13] In short, the framers expected the executive power of the new government to ensure strong, decisive, efficient, and accountable decision making.

While those who participated in the debate seemed to agree that energy and efficiency were best served by a single executive, some delegates expressed concern that accumulation of too much power in a single individual would, as Edmund Randolph of Virginia stated, become "the foetus of monarchy."[14] George Mason argued in favor of a three-person executive, which, in his view, would help prevent cabals and provide a check against the aspirations of "dangerous and ambitious men."[15] Several delegates called for a council to advise the executive and share in the executive responsibilities. James Madison apparently favored the motion for a unitary executive but leaned toward adding a council "who should have the right to advise and record their proceedings, but not to control [the executive's] authority."[16]

These concerns were overridden. The proponents of a unitary executive responded that "unity in the Executive instead of being the foetus of monarchy would be the best safeguard against tyranny" because responsibility for executive decision making could readily be fixed. It would be easier for the public to monitor the performance of a single executive and therefore control abuse.[17]

Pennsylvanian James Wilson added that if the executive were divided, he foresaw "nothing but uncontrolled, continued and violent animosities, which would not only interrupt the public administration, but diffuse their poison through the other branches of government." He added that the "only powers he conceived strictly executive were those of executing the laws, and appointing officers."[18] He argued that if "appointments of Officers are made by a single executive he is responsible for the propriety of [them;] not so where the Executive is numerous."[19]

A single individual was also perceived as better able to check the ambition and the natural tendency toward encroachments by the legislature. If the executive were divided, it would be weak; if weak, it would become dependent on the legislature. That, in turn, would render the legislature the executor as well as the maker of laws. As a result, according to James Madison, "Tyrannical laws may be made that they may be executed in a tyrannical manner."[20]

The final vote reflected a clear and conscious decision that effectiveness in government would be best ensured and liberty best preserved by a single executive. A unified chief executive authority would be more effective, forceful, energetic, efficient, and, because more accountable, less dangerous. As James Wilson later explained to the Pennsylvania Ratifying Convention:

> We may discover from history, from reason, and from experience . . . executive power is better to be trusted when it has no screen. . . . [W]e have [created] a responsibility in the person of our President; he cannot act improperly, and hide either his negligence or inattention; he cannot roll upon any other person the weight of his criminality; no appointment can take place without his nomination; and he is responsible for every nomination he makes.

Wilson added that with a unified executive "we secure *vigor*. We well know what numerous executives are. We know there is neither vigor, decision, nor responsibility, in them."[21]

The most comprehensive analysis and defense of the decision in favor of a single executive were set out in *Federalist* 70. Entitled "Advantages of a Single Executive," it contains Alexander Hamilton's perceptive and persuasive explanation of the convention's decision. It began with the proposition that "energy in the Executive is a leading character in the definition of good government. It is essential to . . . the steady administration of the laws . . . [and] to the security of liberty. . . . A feeble Executive . . . must be . . . a bad government."

Hamilton argued that "unity" is one of those indispensable ingredients of energy in the executive:

> Those politicians and statesmen who have been the most celebrated for the soundness of their principles . . . have declared in favor of a single Executive and a numerous legislature. They have . . . considered energy as the most necessary qualification of the [executive] and have regarded this as most applicable to power in a single hand.

Federalist 70 goes on to itemize the disadvantages of a plural executive. First, "the mere diversity of views and opinions would alone be sufficient to tincture the exercise of the executive authority with a spirit of habitual feebleness and dilatoriness." Second, a plurality in the executive

> tends to conceal faults and destroy responsibility. . . . [T]he multiplication of the Executive adds to the difficulty of detection. . . . It often becomes impossible, amidst mutual accusations, to determine on whom the blame or the punishment of a pernicious measure . . . ought really to fall. It is shifted from one to another with so much dexterity, and under such plausible appearances, that the public opinion is left in suspense about the real author.

Finally, a plural executive

> deprives the people of the two greatest securities they can have for the faithful exercise of any delegated power—first, the restraints of public opinion, which lose their efficacy . . . on account of the uncertainty on whom it ought to fall; and, secondly, the opportunity of discovering with facility and clearness the misconduct of the persons they trust, in order either to their removal from office, or to their actual punishment.

In 1797, John Adams wrote that "the worst evil that can happen in government is a divided executive. As a plural executive must forever be divided, . . .[that] is a great evil and incompatible with liberty."[22]

Commenting on the strength of the American Constitution in 1829, William Rawle observed that weak executives often led to monarchies: "In some republics, the fear of evil from a single head, has led to the creation of councils and other subdivisions of executive power, and the consequent imbecility and distractions of those governments have probably contributed to lead most of the nations of Europe to the preference given to monarchies."[23]

Congressional Erosions and Usurpations of Presidential Power

The thoughtful, considered decision of 1787 to vest executive authority in a single individual has been under siege almost from the moment it was made. Congress began almost immediately to involve itself in executive decisions and to erode presidential power. After two centuries of unrelenting encroachments by Congress, concerns that are occasionally expressed concerning an "imperial presidency" are simply misplaced. Today's executive has been diluted, divided, fragmented, and parceled out to literally scores of agencies, commissions, "independent" officials, boards, and corporations. Those powers that have not been taken from the president altogether have been so encrusted with congressional or congressional committee involvement or tangled with procedural impediments to vigorous decision making that the president can exercise little real authority. President Kennedy, speaking nearly thirty years ago, captured what the presidency had become then when he said, "Well, I agree with you, but I'm not sure the government will."[24]

Congress has so adeptly and persistently eroded and disassembled executive power that a comprehensive chronicle of legislative encroachments on executive power with corresponding examples would be a book in itself. The following, however, touches some highlights.

Undermining Presidential Law Enforcement Authority. Congress has created an array of techniques designed to diminish the president's ability to enforce the law. It has set up numerous "independent" regulatory agencies, for example, with the express purpose of removing from the president the power to enforce legislation in various fields. Generally, the president's control is stripped from him by the device of restricting his ability to remove those with law enforcement power: "Once an officer is appointed, it is only the authority that appointed him that he must fear and, in the performance of his functions, obey."[25] If the president must prove incompetence or some other specified cause to a court to justify removing an official who will not comply with his policies, the president has lost all effective control of that official. The clearly stated congressional purpose behind creating agencies whose heads cannot be removed at the president's will is to "require them to act in discharg[ing] their duties independent of executive control."[26]

Agencies that have been given substantial independence from the president include the Federal Trade Commission, the Securities and Exchange Commission, the Federal Election Commission, the

Federal Reserve System, the National Labor Relations Board, the Tennessee Valley Authority, the Federal Communications Commission, and the Federal Maritime Commission. Thus, the power given to the president by Article II to "take care" that the laws of the United States are faithfully executed no longer extends to vast areas of federally regulated conduct and behavior. While arguments continue to be made that withdrawing the president, and therefore "politics," from law enforcement is a beneficial system, it is most decidedly not the system created in Philadelphia in 1787.

These erosions of presidential power mean that it is virtually impossible for the president to have an impact upon vast areas of American life. Two agencies, for example, one controlled by the president (the Antitrust Division of the Justice Department), another not controlled by the president (the Federal Trade Commission), enforce the antitrust laws. The president cannot, therefore, implement a uniform antitrust policy. The same is true for communications, energy, and many other areas.

Another result of fractioning the presidency is that it has become exceedingly difficult to effect policies through elections. Indeed, it is often impossible for the public even to know who is responsible for many of our most vital national policies. The U.S. Court of Appeals for the District of Columbia Circuit recently expressed the constitutional ideal:

> Under the Constitution, the President, as the head of the Executive Branch, is the person ultimately responsible for a decision to initiate a criminal prosecution. . . . If that decision is contrary to the mores and customs of the community, the community has a visible target for its grievances. No anonymous directorates hold sway here, no impenetrable bureaucracies or commissions obscure the identity of the responsible official; the chain of command leads directly upward to the President.[27]

How contrary to this ideal today's reality has become.

William Greider, author of *Secrets of the Temple: How the Federal Reserve Runs the Country*, offers another pungent example. He observes that American economic policy is a "repetitious and pathological conflict" in which a "cycle of continuing disorder originates in the governing structure itself—the divided nature of government's management of the economy . . . one driver operating the accelerator while the other controls the brake."[28] As he concisely and accurately observes, this "is a bizarre way to govern."[29] His point was recently reinforced by congressional testimony from the chairman of the Federal Reserve Board bitterly complaining that a member of the executive branch had had the temerity to express in writing an opinion as to what steps the board should take respecting the economy. The executive was accused of political interference.

Another tool for interfering with presidential prerogatives is the Independent Counsel Act. The independent counsel provisions of the Ethics in Government Act contain numerous intrusions on the executive's fundamental and exclusive authority to enforce federal criminal laws. First, the act vests power in a court to appoint special prosecutors to investigate and prosecute a wide range of present and former federal officials for alleged violations of federal criminal laws and authorizes the court to define the prosecutorial jurisdiction of the prosecutor. Second, the act insulates the independent counsel from removal except by the personal action of the attorney general (not the president) and only for good cause—physical disability, mental incapacity, or other condition that substantially impairs the performance of the independent counsel's duties.

At its core, the act removes the president's power to enforce the law—the essence of his constitutional function. An independent counsel is free to spend unlimited resources to investigate and prosecute in circumstances in which the executive would not deem an alleged violation worthy of prosecutorial resources. The independent counsel law was held unconstitutional by the U.S. Court of Appeals for the District of Columbia Circuit on January 22, 1988.[30] That decision was reversed by the U.S. Supreme Court on June 29, 1988.[31]

In addition, legislation is often proposed, and occasionally passed, that would strip the president's discretion to decide not to prosecute a particular offense. The laws relative to contempt of Congress are examples. They make a prosecution mandatory if there is a congressional certification that there has been a contempt of Congress.[32]

Interference with the President's Appointment Power. Congress has devised a number of ways to hinder presidential appointments; among them are the appointments, incompatibility, and ineligibility clauses. The appointments clause of the Constitution, Article II, section 2, provides that "Officers of the United States" must be appointed by the president by and with the advice and consent of the Senate or, where authorized by Congress, by the president alone, the courts, or subordinates of the president. The methods of appointment set forth in the appointments clause are exclusive; officers of the United States therefore cannot be appointed by Congress or by congressional officers.[33] Persons who "exercise significant authority pursuant to the laws of the United States" or who perform "a significant governmental duty . . . pursuant to the laws of the United States" must be officers of the United States[34] and therefore must be appointed in accord with the appointments clause. In *Buckley v. Valeo*, the Supreme Court struck down as unconstitutional attempted appointments by Congress of its own members to the Federal Elections Commission.

Congress, nevertheless, frequently establishes commissions, agencies, advisory boards, or other entities, the functions of which include advisory as well as operational responsibilities, and provides for the appointment of officers of such entities in a manner inconsistent with the appointments clause. When signing such legislation, presidents have often responded by taking the position that bodies of this nature may perform only advisory, investigative, informative, or ceremonial functions and may not perform regulatory,[35] enforcement, or other executive responsibilities. Nonetheless, even advisory councils imposed upon the presidency are appendages that were rejected by the Constitutional Convention, and they are an awkward embarrassment to the president.

Similar problems have arisen with disturbing frequency in connection with commemorative commissions. In those situations, the House or the Senate has frequently appointed its own members to these commissions in violation of the incompatibility clause of the Constitution, Article I, section 6, stipulating that no person holding any executive office may be a member of either house of Congress. The appointment of members of the Senate or the House to newly created positions also violates the provision of the ineligibility clause barring members of Congress from holding an office created during the term for which the member was elected or from holding an office the compensation for which was increased during the member's term.

President Reagan, following precedents set by his predecessors, has insisted that members of Congress could participate on such commissions only in an advisory or ceremonial capacity.[36] Where the members of a commission appointed in violation of the appointments or incompatibility clauses of the Constitution have constituted a majority of the commission, the president has stated that the commission itself could perform only advisory or ceremonial functions.[37]

Another way that Congress blocks presidential powers of appointment is by restricting the list of nominees. Congress occasionally imposes significant limitations on the pool of candidates from which the president may make appointments. Congress has attempted to restrict the president to selecting an official from lists submitted by the Speaker of the House and the president pro tempore of the Senate or other officers of Congress, for example. The president has typically not construed such provisions as limits on his ultimate responsibility for the selection of the officer, and he can reject all individuals on the list if he finds them unsatisfactory. Because it is politically quite difficult to reject an entire list of tendered candidates except in compelling circumstances, however, these provisions have a serious corrosive effect on presidential appointment power.

In the case of the bankruptcy amendments and Federal Judgeship Act of 1984, Congress not only attempted retroactively to reinstate bankruptcy judges whose terms and offices had expired with the expiration of the old Bankruptcy Act but also created new Article III judgeships with limitations on the president's power to appoint persons to fill these positions.

Moreover, agencies such as the Securities and Exchange Commission may consist of no more than three members of the same political party. A major universe of potential appointees, including those most likely to be in resonance with the president's policies, is foreclosed to him by such restrictions.

Other Methods of Eroding Presidential Power. With ever-increasing frequency, Congress provides for commissions composed of members or appointees of the legislative and executive branches. These commissions are not clearly a part of either branch. The president's statement, upon the signing of the U.S. commission on the Civil Rights Act of 1983, objected to the creation of "agencies which are inconsistent with the tripartite system of government established by the Framers of our Constitution" and stated that the "Civil Rights Commission is . . . unique in form and function [and] should therefore not become a precedent for the creation of similar agencies in the future." Unfortunately, the reconstituted Civil Rights Commission has become such a precedent. Similar provisions were included in an amendment to a House bill to change the tariff treatment with respect to certain articles, which would have established an International Trade and Export Policy Commission; the Patent Law Amendment Act of 1984; the Health Promotion and Disease Prevention Amendments of 1984; the Older Americans Act Amendments of 1984; and the Public Works Improvement Act of 1984.

In many instances, the problems created by a hybrid commission are aggravated because the representatives of the legislative branch on the commission typically far outnumber those of the executive branch. An example is the recently created federal commission to find ways to reduce the federal deficit. The panel was created to have fourteen members, only two of whom are selected by the president. Four are selected by congressional Republicans, six by congresssional

Democrats, and two by the person elected president in November. The new president will have to deal with this strange hybrid body's report in March 1989. As William Safire expressed it, "Thus, the next Presidency [will] be emasculated at birth." He adds, "If we are about to fix responsibility for the budgetary mess the Congress has placed us in, let's do it at the polls—and not rig the next economic policy with some stultifying consensus beforehand."[38]

• In addition to frequent attempts to place restrictions on the power of the president to appoint officers of the United States under the appointments clause, Congress has attempted to constrain his power under Article II, section 2, to "fill up all Vacancies that may happen during the Recess of the Senate, by granting Commissions which shall expire at the End of their next Session." Thus, for example, a provision in an appropriations bill mandated continued funding for grantees of the Legal Services Corporation unless action was taken by directors *confirmed by the Senate*. This provision interfered with the president's recess appointment power to the extent that it disabled recess appointees from performing functions that could be performed by directors confirmed by the Senate. This device weakens presidential powers because the recess appointment power is an important counterbalance to the power of the Senate. By refusing to confirm executive appointees, the Senate can cripple the president's ability to enforce the law. The recess appointment power is often his only recourse. If this constitutional power is vitiated, the presidency itself will be weakened materially.

• As noted earlier, Congress restrains the president's power to control an official by restricting the circumstances when the official may be removed. There are literally hundreds of manifestations of this form of restriction on presidential power. Significantly, it is precisely this issue that led to major confrontations between President Washington and the First Congress, President Jackson and Congress, President Andrew Johnson and Congress (leading to impeachment), President Roosevelt and Congress, and other serious controversies throughout our history.

• The proposed Senate Reconfirmation Act of 1984 would have prevented cabinet members and several other high officers in the executive branch from serving during the succeeding presidential term unless reappointed by the president by and with the advice and consent of the Senate. This provision would have required the president to start over with his administration, giving major leverage to Congress in the process.

• Congress consistently attempts to obtain access to the most sensitive executive branch information and opposes with every resource at its disposal arguments that the executive branch, like Congress and the judiciary, must enjoy some measure of protection for confidential exchanges of information if it is to function effectively.

Among the many examples of congressional overreaching in this area are the relatively continuous demands by one committee or another to require the Department of Justice to produce documents from its files relative to current criminal investigations. These demands extend to cases under active investigation before sitting grand juries. Premature release of the material from investigative files may severely damage the confidence and cooperativeness of witnesses, the integrity of the case development, the independence of prosecutorial decisions, and the strategy of future prosecution.

• With increasing frequency Congress is using concurrent reporting requirements to insert itself into the executive branch decision-making process. A concurrent reporting rule requires an agency to transmit simultaneously to Congress a budget recommendation or legislative proposal that it transmits to the Office of Management and Budget or the White House. Thus, for example, a recent bill required the National Institute of Education, an executive branch entity, to submit certain reports directly to Congress without prior review within the executive branch. One section of the bill provided:

> Notwithstanding any other provision of law or regulation, such reports shall not be subject to any review outside the National Institute of Education before their transmittal to the Congress, but the President and the Secretary may make such additional recommendations to the Congress with respect to the assessment as they deem appropriate.[39]

Similar provisions in recently enacted laws have required the Federal Aviation Administration administrator to submit budget information and legislative recommendations directly to Congress at the same time as they are submitted to the secretary of transportation[40] and have applied similar requirements to the Railroad Retirement Board and Securities and Exchange Commission. This is now a common requirement.[41]

• In the aftermath of the Supreme Court's decision in *INS* v. *Chadha*, Congress has attempted on several occasions to recoup what it apparently perceives to be power lost because of the Court's decision. Over objections raised by the executive branch, Congress has continued to include, although with decreasing frequency, some forms of legislative veto devices in legislation. In signing the 1985 appropriations bill for the Department of Housing and Urban Development and other agencies, the president objected vigorously to the inclusion in the bill of *seven* legislative veto devices and urged Congress to cease including such devices in legislation.

Another example was reported in the *Wall Street Journal*:

> In the omnibus spending bill passed in the dead of night late last December, Congress included a provision requiring the Reagan administration to notify the congressional appropriations committees before sending aid to Jamaica; the committees could then block the aid at the request of any member.
>
> When a request came to send $100,000 for a Jamaican housing project earlier this year, Mr. Wilson, a member of the subcommittee that controls foreign aid, simply said no, and the committee suspended the aid.[42]

• Congress has passed or considered legislation granting executive branch agencies or components thereof (for example, the Special Counsel to the Merit Systems Protection Board, the Chief Counsel of the Small Business Administration, the Environmental Protection Agency, and the Comptroller of the Currency) authority to sue other executive branch agencies in federal courts. Such legislation undermines the president's ability to supervise effectively the affairs of the executive branch by making it possible for the president's subordinates to submit intrabranch disputes for resolution by the judiciary. While it is not clear what the courts would do with such an unusual proceeding, the concept of pitting the president's subordinates against one another in court in connection with the "faithful execution" of the law sets the notion of a unitary executive on its head.

Congress has also diminished the president's power to represent the United States in the courts by dispersing authority to control government litigation to literally dozens of separate agencies. Without centralized control, it is impossible to articulate consistent and uniform policies in the courts.

• In recent years, a number of provisions have been considered or enacted that had the intent of limiting the Department of Justice's presentation of legal positions in court. The 1984 Appropriations Act, for example, prohibited the expenditure of funds for "any activity, the purpose of which is to overturn or alter the *per se* prohibition on resale price maintenance in effect under Federal antitrust laws."

A similar provision was included in the Department of Justice Appropriations Authorization Act for fiscal year 1982, which passed the Senate in 1982 but was never enacted by the House. One section of that bill provided that no funds appropriated to the Department of Justice could be used to bring or maintain any action to require, directly or indirectly, the transportation of any student to a school other than the school nearest to the student's home, except for students requiring special education because of mental or physical handicap.

A third example was the Department of Justice Appropriations Authorization Act for fiscal year 1984, which sought to prohibit the attorney general from proceeding in any action in which he determines that the Department of Justice would contest or not defend the constitutionality of any law.

• Under Article II of the Constitution, the president is directed to recommend for legislative consideration "such measures as he shall judge necessary and expedient." Just as courts have occasionally infringed upon this power by ordering executive branch agencies to readjust their budget priorities or seek additional funds from Congress to implement a program in a manner satisfactory to the court, Congress has occasionally attempted by statute to control the executive's legislative priorities. A statute requiring the secretary of health and human services to assign the highest budget priority and funding to a particular project, for example, interfered with the president's constitutional power to submit only those budget proposals he deems necessary and expedient.

Another example was a 1983 bill to amend the Rural Electrification Act of 1936. That proposed law would have required the secretary of agriculture to include in each annual budget estimate a request for funds to continue a project known as the Rural Electrification and Telephone Revolving Fund.

• Since the 1970s, Congress has increasingly attempted to assert itself in the president's foreign affairs powers at the expense of the authority traditionally exercised by the president. The history of recent congressional action in this area has been succinctly summarized in the following excerpt from an article by Senator John G. Tower, former chairman of the Senate Armed Services Committee:

> The 1970's were marked by a rash of Congressionally initiated foreign policy legislation that limited the President's range of options on a number of foreign policy issues. The thrust of the legislation was to restrict the President's ability to dispatch troops abroad in a crisis, and to proscribe his authority in arms sales, trade, human rights, foreign assistance and intelligence operations. During this period, over 150 separate prohibitions and restrictions were enacted in Executive Branch authority to formulate and implement foreign policy. Not only was much of this legislation ill conceived, if not actually unconstitutional, it has served in a number of instances to be detrimental to the national security and foreign policy interests of the United States.[43]

One ongoing problem is the War Powers Resolution, enacted in 1973, which provides for congressional oversight "in any case in which United States Armed Forces are introduced into hostilities or into situations where imminent involvement in hostilities is clearly indicated by the circumstances." The president is required to submit a written report to Congress detailing the circumstances of U.S. involvement, and Congress is authorized to order U.S. troops removed by concurrent resolution. After sixty days, the War Powers Resolution provides that the president must automatically terminate the use of U.S. armed forces except in very narrow circumstances.

Similarly, a section of the International Security and Development Act of 1984 would have required the president during fiscal years 1984 and 1985 to advise certain committees of Congress thirty days in advance of assigning or detailing troops for the purposes of "commencing joint military exercises with the armed forces of any Central American country." While this section was not enacted into law, it is noteworthy that it went beyond the consultation and reporting requirements of the War Powers Resolution. The War Powers Resolution imposes procedural requirements of consultation and reporting on certain presidential actions involving the deployment of U.S. armed forces in certain situations but does not attempt to limit the president's power to act unilaterally in the first instance. In contrast, the section of the International Security and Development Act would have created a thirty-day waiting period during which the president would have been disabled from deploying troops for joint military exercises in Central America.

Other examples of congressional interference in the president's foreign affairs power have involved attempts to restrict his power to negotiate with or recognize foreign governments or governmental entities. A recently passed continuing resolution, for example, contains a provision arguably preventing the president from negotiating with or recognizing the Palestine Liberation Organization (PLO) until the PLO recognizes Israel and complies with other requirements set forth in the provision. Another recent law much in the news lately required the president to close the PLO's mission to the United Nations. The prospect of the enforcement of this law drew near unanimous disapproval in the United Nations because it was said to have violated the treaty obligations of the United States. A 1983 bill would have precluded the president from establishing diplomatic relations with the Vatican. Yet another proposed law would have forced the president to move the American Embassy in Israel from Tel Aviv to Jerusalem.

• Congress may interfere with existing investigations, foreign policy, domestic policy, or all three by conducting parallel, intrusive, or clumsy investigations. An example was reported in the *Washington Post*:

> While pursuing their own probe into Wall Street insider trading, four of Rep. John Dingell's investigators cut short a trip to Switzerland last week after being reprimanded by Swiss officials over their attempts to obtain information from a Geneva bank.
>
> The incident briefly threatened the cooperation the Swiss are providing to U.S. agencies investigating insider trading, according to a Washington lawyer who represents Swiss banks.[44]

Moreover, whatever the merits of the Iran-contra congressional investigation, it exposed and therefore affected a wide range of government policies. The defenders of this investigation undoubtedly believe that it was a proper use of congressional investigative powers, and the merits of that proposition can be debated. It is certainly true, however, that the process illustrated by this investigation is an unusual, embarrassing, and awkward way to conduct or alter foreign policies.

The congressional oversight mechanism provides Congress with an opportunity to interdict executive policy making in the formative process, precludes confidential and candid predeliberative discussions in many cases, occupies inordinate time of policy makers, and otherwise involves Congress and its sizable staff in the minutiae of executive decision making. The result is a tendency toward paralysis of both branches.

• Congress has the power to force congressional—and now, through the Independent Counsel law, criminal—investigations of those whose conduct displeases its members. Congress can intimidate, punish, and wreak retribution against those who assist the president in resisting legislative encroachments. Especially when there is political capital to be gained, this phenomenon is becoming an increasingly fashionable way to drive executive policies through threat and intimidation.

• Congress has also placed restrictions on the president's ability to gain advice. In 1972, for example, the Federal Advisory Committee Act (FACA) provided, among other requirements, that any committee, conference, panel, or group established by statute, the president, or any agency to give advice to the president must comply with a long list of burdensome, onerous formalities. Among these are the requirements that the advisory groups must have a "balanced membership" "in terms of the points of view represented and the functions to be performed," must conduct meetings in public unless formally exempted from doing so, must permit public participation in meetings, and must make materials generated available to the public under the Freedom of Information Act. It also requires that a designated government official attend every meeting. A court has invalidated a report of a presidential advisory commission for failure to satisfy the balanced membership requirement.[45]

• Congress frequently attempts to lodge executive power in officials, such as the comptroller general, who are actually agents of Congress. Its effort to do so in connection with the Gramm-Rudman-Hollings Act was rejected by the Supreme Court in *Bowsher* v. *Synar*. A similar effort to empower the comptroller general to exercise executive and quasi-judicial powers in connection with the awarding of government contracts is now before the Supreme Court.

Conclusion

This review shows how Congress has given life to the fears of the framers by attempting to absorb and weaken presidential power through innumerable complicated and indirect measures. It has vested executive authority in individuals not subject to the president's supervision and more subject to the will of Congress. It has eroded the president's relationships with those who do serve the president by making it impossible for them to report in confidence to the president and making them report instead or simultaneously to Congress. Congress restricts or impinges on the president's power to appoint his subordinates and penalizes those subordinates who serve the president too faithfully.

Those who examine the presidency today will see an institution that is becoming increasingly ineffective and inefficient and less responsible for the management of government, the antithesis of the model created in Philadelphia in 1787.

Notes

1. *Federalist* No. 47.
2. *Federalist* No. 48.
3. Ibid.
4. Ibid.
5. *Federalist* No. 47.

6. Max Farrand, *The Records of the Federal Convention of 1787*, vol. 1 (New Haven, Conn.: Yale University Press, 1911).

7. Ibid.

8. Notes of Rufus King, June 1, 1787, quoted in Wilbourne E. Benton, ed., *Drafting of the U.S. Constitution* (Texas A & M University Press, 1986), p. 1108.

9. *The Life and Selected Writings of Thomas Jefferson, Notes on Virginia*, "Query XIII, The Constitution of the State and its Several Charters?" (Modern Library, 1944), p. 237.

10. Ibid.

11. Notes of James Madison, July 17, 1787, quoted in Philip B. Kurland and Ralph L. Lerner, eds., *Founders' Constitution*, vol. 3 (University of Chicago Press, 1987), p. 496.

12. *Life and Writings of Jefferson* (Letter to E. Carrington, August 4, 1787), pp. 427–28.

13. Farrand, *Records of the Convention*, p. 65.

14. Notes of James Madison, quoted in Benton, *Drafting of the U.S. Constitution*, p. 1099.

15. Kurland and Lerner, eds., *Founders' Constitution*, vol. 3, p. 492.

16. Notes of Pierce, June 2, 1787, in Kurland and Lerner, *Founders' Constitution*, vol. 3, p. 492.

17. Notes of James Madison, June 1, 1787, in Kurland and Lerner, *Founders' Constitution*, vol. 3, p. 491.

18. Ibid.

19. Notes of Rufus King, June 1, 1787, in Kurland and Lerner, *Founders' Constitution*, vol. 3, p. 492.

20. Notes of James Madison, July 17, 1787, in Kurland and Lerner, *Founders' Constitution*, vol. 3, p. 495.

21. Jonathan Elliot, *Debates in the Several State Conventions on the Adoption of the Federal Constitution*, Burt Franklin Reprints (New York: Lennox Hill Publishing and Distributing Corp., 1974), p. 480.

22. John Adams to Thomas Pickering, October 31, 1797, *Works of John Adams*, vol. 8 (New York: AMS Press, 1972), p. 560.

23. William Rawle, quoted in *Founders' Constitution*, vol. 4, p. 129.

24. Roger Hilsman, *The Politics of Policy Making in Defense and Foreign Affairs* (New York: Harper and Row, 1971), p. 1.

25. Synar v. United States, 626 F. Supp. 1374, 1401 (D.D.C. 1986) (three judge court), *aff'd sub. nom.* Bowsher v. Synar, __ U.S. __ , 106 S. Ct. 3181 (1986).

26. Humphrey's Executor v. United States, 295 U.S. 602, 629 (1935).

27. *In Re Sealed Case* (January 22, 1988), reversed, *sub. nom.* Morrison v. Olson, 108 S. Ct. 2597 (1988).

28. *New York Times*, February 28, 1988.

29. Ibid.

30. *In Re: Sealed Case*.

31. Morrison v. Olson, 108 S. Ct. 2597 (1988).

32. For a discussion of the extent to which the Supreme Court has determined that Congress may restrict by legislation the executive's decision whether or not to enforce a law, *see* Heckler v. Chaney, 53 LW 4385.

33. Buckley v. Valeo, 424 U.S. 1, 124-41 (1976).

34. Buckley v. Valeo, 424 U.S. at 126, 141.

35. An example is the president's statement when signing the law re-creating the U.S. Commission on Civil Rights Act, 19 Weekly Comp. Press. Doc. 1926, 1627 (1983).

36. See, for example, signing statement dated September 23, 1983, relating to the establishment of the Commission on the Bicentennial of the Constitution, 19 Weekly Comp. Press. Doc. 1362 (1983).

37. See, for example, signing statement dated August 27, 1984, relating to the establishment of a Commission on the Commemoration of the First Legal Holiday Celebration of the Birth of Martin Luther King, Jr., 20 Weekly Comp. Pres. Doc. 1192 (1984).

38. *New York Times*, March 3, 1983.

39. Section 403(c).

40. Pub. L. 97-248.

41. See 7 U.S.C. § 4a(h)(1) (Commodity Future Trading Commission); 15 U.S.C. § 2076(k)(1) (Consumer Product Safety Commission); 21 U.S.C. § 11(j) (Interstate Commerce Commission).

42. *Wall Street Journal*, March 2, 1988.

43. John C. Tower, "Congress versus the President: The Foundation and Implementation of American Foreign Policy," *Foreign Affairs* (Winter, 1981/82), pp. 229 and 234.

44. *Washington Post*, February 27, 1988.

45. See Nat. Anti-Hunger Coalition v. Exec. Comm. of the President's Private Sector Survey on Cost Control, 711 F.2d 1071 (D.C. Cir. 1983).

17
Commentary and Exchanges on Regulatory Policy

Commentary by Jim Burnley

I am in the uncomfortable position of coming as the client ex post facto to say that the *Chadha* decision in which the legislative veto was declared unconstitutional as an intrusion by Congress into the executive branch prerogatives did not work out exactly the way we might have hoped. I will describe what has happened at the Department of Transportation since the *Chadha* decision and then return to the underlying question of how the relationship between the executive and the congressional branches should be structured.

The legislative veto is a mechanism Congress created because it did not trust the executive branch to exercise its discretion in implementing the legislation once that legislation was enacted. In effect, the legislative veto was a string on a yo-yo, so that Congress could pull the executive branch back. When that string was cut, we found that the same distrust was still there. The Congress then felt the need to create new devices, or at least to amplify considerably its reliance on existing but seldom used devices, such as in the appropriations process.

Since *Chadha*, Congress has constrained the Department of Transportation in many ways, virtually all via the annual appropriations bills. These bills are themselves often buried in huge continuing resolutions making it difficult if not impossible for the president to get after them.

In fiscal year 1985, for example, congressmen prohibited us from spending any money on a pending rule that would have considered lowering the annual passenger cap at National Airport in Washington, D.C. They also required the Coast Guard to obtain written warranties for anything it procured of any size and expense, which ruled out the possibility that the Coast Guard might get a better price for a given procurement by not demanding a written warranty.

In fiscal year 1986, Congress told us that even though Miami had not met certain published criteria that we were applying to every new metropolitan mass transit rail system in the country, we were simply to sign a letter of intent to commit the funds to Miami for its metro system.

In fiscal year 1987, Congress used the appropriations bill to terminate the responsibility of the Linden, New Jersey, airport to use the federal grant money (with which it had purchased land over the years) for continuing airport purposes. When an authority spends federal grant money from the Federal Aviation Administration (FAA), whatever is bought is supposed to be used to serve aviation. Even though the FAA had ruled that Linden, New Jersey, had violated that understanding, Congress saw fit in the appropriations bill to overrule that finding. Congress terminated an FAA enforcement action against Florida's Pompano Beach Airport for a violation similar to the Linden, New Jersey, problem. In addition, Congress prohibited Secretary of Transportation Elizabeth Dole from spending any funds whatsoever to set up an advisory commission to study ways that we might privatize part or all of Amtrak, a prohibition that continues in our appropriations language to this day.

In fiscal year 1988, Congress continued the annual prohibition on the sale or transfer of Union Station in Washington, D.C., without our getting committee approval in advance. Congress mandated that we reopen eight flight service stations in New England and upstate New York that we had closed as part of a modernization program. Congress prohibited us from spending any funds on planning or implementation of any changes in our transportation research center in Cambridge, Massachusetts. We were also prohibited from spending any money to plan or implement any change in the status of the Federal Highway Administration's research facility in northern Virginia. We were prohibited from having the FAA do any further contracting out of maintenance work on the air traffic control system. We had our funding automatically cut by 5 percent in the Office of the Secretary if we failed to meet deadlines in our appropriations language for putting out rule makings on transponders and the use of cockpit voice and data recorders on smaller, commuter-sized aircraft.

Perhaps one could argue the merits of each of these as a matter of public policy. But I think the explosion of restrictions that we have seen just at the Department of Transportation since the *Chadha* decision is indicative of Congress's unwillingness to be denied in this area. Where Congress does not trust the executive branch, congressmen will often find ways and means to control policy more perverse than the legislative veto. In retrospect, then, the Reagan administration's victory in *Chadha* has had the practical outcome of less discretion in the executive branch rather than more.

Two other examples perhaps loom over those already described. These legislative veto statutes, which were on the books at the time of the *Chadha* decision, are somewhat different from the cases just enumerated. One was the question of selling Conrail. In 1981, in the Northeast Rail Service Act Congress instructed the secretary of transportation to devise a plan for the sale of the stock in Conrail. The legislative veto provision was a two-house provision requiring sixty legislative days of review. With the *Chadha* decision, there is clearly a question unanswered to this day of "severability"—as to whether that statute as a whole would fall. But as a practical matter severability was not a question we had any interest in litigating because we wanted to sell Conrail.

We could have tried to assert severability by simply letting the Congress review this matter for sixty days and then going forward. The Office of Legal Counsel at the Justice Department recommended this approach assuming a reasonable basis for arguing severability in each of the statutes that include legislative vetoes. But had we done that, no one would have wanted to discuss buying Conrail because lawyers for any prospective buyers would have doubted our legal authority to sell the stock under that scenario. As a practical matter the only way to find out whether we did have such authority would have been for a willing buyer to sign a contract to perform and then have the buyer refuse to perform because the lawyers would not give him an opinion. Then we could have sued the buyer, and some years hence a court ruling would decide whether the legislative veto provision and the Conrail legislation were severable and whether we had the authority to go forward with the sale.

The practical effect was that the administration had to seek prior approval from the Congress, despite Congress's 1981 judgment that the administration should devise a plan to sell Conrail and than present it to Congress for sixty legislative review days. Compare that approach to the approach we had to take. A persuasive argument can be made that we ended with much less discretion than we had before.

Another case in which *Chadha* did not work out quite the way we might have hoped concerns fuel economy standards. Since 1974, a statute has required the Department of Transportation to tell the automobile manufacturers once a year what the gasoline mileage per gallon must be, on average, for all the cars they sell in this country.

The statute decreed that by 1985 new cars sold in the United States had to average 27.5 miles per gallon. That is, General Motors was to ensure that all the cars it sold would average out to that standard, and Ford, Toyota, and all the others would do likewise. We found, however, that 27.5 miles per gallon was not reachable by 1985 but that, fortunately, Congress had left a safety valve.

When it passed this law, Congress said that the average had to be 27.5 miles per gallon unless the secretary of transportation found that practical, economic, or technical reasons prevented a particular manufacturer from reaching this level. The secretary had discretion in making such a finding. But the secretary's discretion was unfettered only between 26 miles per gallon and 27.5 miles per gallon. The discretion to go below 26 miles per gallon was fettered by a legislative veto mechanism. Again, the practical effect of *Chadha* is that we have been constrained, regardless of what the marketplace might dictate, to require manufacturers to achieve mileage somewhere between 26 and 27.5 miles per gallon.

Interestingly, even though this requirement forced the automobile makers to make bizarre decisions contrary to what the marketplace dictated about how cars were designed, how big the engines were, and how much they weighed (raising the question of metal versus plastic), the manufacturers did not want the department to test our legal authority post-*Chadha* to go below 26 miles per gallon. They reasoned that once a car is sold in a given year, it is sold and that whatever its average is, it cannot be changed. If another secretary of transportation or I were to assert that the standard should not be 26 but 25 miles per gallon instead, some years later a court would tell us whether, post-*Chadha*, we had that authority—whether the legislative veto provisions, again, were severable from that statute.

If the court ruled that we had guessed wrong, then the only question would be which day of the week a manufacturer had to show up with a check to pay a massive penalty to the U.S. government. The fuel economy statute provides a penalty derived from this formula: for every one-tenth of a mile per gallon for which the manufacturer's average falls short of the standard, he must pay $5 times the number of cars he sold. For instance, if General Motors, which sold 3.5 million cars last year, were to miss the standard by 2.5 miles per gallon, General Motors would owe the federal government more than $400 million in penalties for that one year. It is easy to understand why the manufacturers were not anxious for us to test this theory under the circumstances. Again the practical effect has been that the executive branch's discretion—its ability to react to the realities of the marketplace—was restrained as a result of the loss of the legislative veto mechanism.

We must recognize that one way or another Congress will assert certain prerogatives. Congress will assert the right to second-guess the executive branch in areas where it does not trust us to get it right. Therefore, when we consider which device we want to challenge in court as the most perverse, it is important to work through the practicalities of the various alternatives.

I apologize to former Attorney General William French Smith and to Theodore Olson, who were instrumental in litigating *Chadha*, for exhibiting the worst kind of Monday-morning quarterbacking. But at least in the case of the Department of Transportation, a compelling argument can be made that we would have more discretion today if the Reagan administration had lost the decision and the legislative veto mechanism had survived. Certainly in the cases of Conrail and the enforcement of the fuel-mileage standards, we would have had more discretion. Moreover, many of the examples I listed of these particular provisions in our appropriations bills in recent years might not have shown up had the legislative veto mechanism been available as an alternative. The somewhat less intrusive device of the legislative veto might have been used.

WILLIAM FRENCH SMITH: Listening to Secretary Burnley's reference to the host of examples concerning congressional micromanagement of his department, I think I can top his parade of horribles. During the time I was in office, the Justice Department had a case before the U.S. Supreme Court, for which one of the arguments involved resale price maintenance. Our position supported resale price maintenance. A group of senators, however, apparently had a bundle of discount stores as constituents—that is the only reason I can understand for their intensity. They strongly objected to our position, so they sneaked into the continuing resolution funding the Justice Department a prohibition against the spending of any funds that would be used to argue that point in the brief in that case before the Supreme Court. This was a blatantly unconstitutional prohibition, which we could have ignored, but as so often happens in Washington, D.C., we did not because the consequences of not paying attention would have been worse. This strikes me as the ultimate for Congress in designating where the executive branch can and cannot use funds—saying we cannot use them to argue a particular point in a brief in court.

NORMAN ORNSTEIN: Pre-*Chadha*, Congress could give great discretion to the executive branch. Congress could say, in effect, "We have a lot of things here we cannot foresee; there are many problems here, and we can't get into great detail. Use your best judgment within the framework of the set of intentions that we are clearly prescribing to you, and go ahead and act. We trust you to carry out your responsibilities in good faith and in consideration of legislative intentions." The legislative veto was a way of saying, however, that Congress wanted a little insurance that if the executive branch strayed dramatically from congressional intentions, Congress could suggest to the executive branch that it had gone too far and had not done the right thing.

Pre-*Chadha*, the legislative veto was functionally equivalent to a parent who gives a teen-age child the keys to the family car on a Friday night and tells him to have a good time, not to get drunk, to come back by midnight, and not to drive too fast or break any laws. And if that parent finds later the child has disobeyed, he takes away his driving privileges and grounds him for the next six weekends.

I am not suggesting, of course, that Congress is the parent and that the executive is the child but that the legislative veto added to an atmosphere of trust and gave both the Congress and the executive branch something they valued and wanted very much. Post-*Chadha*, Congress is quite obviously not going to delegate great authority to an executive branch it does not trust without maintaining some control over what happens. Clearly, the Court's sweeping decision in *Chadha* ushered in many of the situations that Secretary Burnley has suggested have happened. At the time many suggested that the executive might come to regret the sweeping nature of that decision by the Supreme Court and that it would leave Congress in a position to search for alternatives to keep the government functioning. Those alternatives involve greater detail written into law and more so-called micromanagement in many instances; these and other mechanisms do not have the same legal effect as a legislative veto but have the same underlying effect. They will probably be less forthright and more damaging, perhaps, than the legislative veto itself.

What can we do to restore a balance of trust between the branches? One of the great culprits here is an excessive legalism, which has come largely from the courts. Many of the devices that developed naturally between the legislative and the executive branches when they hit an impasse, informal approaches that left both branches comfortable, have begun to be rejected willy-nilly by the courts, which are using a much too narrow view of what the law-making process is supposed to be.

THEODORE OLSON: Although Congress has used appropriations riders and other devices and techniques to control executive decisions since the *Chadha* decision, the same thing was happening before *Chadha*. As Barbara Craig points out, the legislative veto was a device that started as a trickle and had become a torrent, in which executive micromanagement had been taken over by Congress; legislative vetoes were used in an increasingly broad variety of circumstances to control the most minute executive decision making. I am not sure why Secretary Burnley would believe that there would not have been the same degree of tinkering, or even more, by the legislative branch had the legislative veto decision not come out the way it did.

While some of these things that Congress has done make it difficult, inconvenient, even burdensome, to make certain decisions, our system of government is not necessarily intended to be the most efficient and unburdensome way to get things done, because there are some higher values, including the preservation of liberty, that are embodied in the Constitution. The effort is made over and over again to say, "Let's be practical. Let's not be so formalistic. Let's be less technical." I do not think Secretary Burnley would have more discretion today if the *Chadha* decision had come out differently. I think Chairman X and Chairman Y would make a great deal more of his decisions for him and that, furthermore, the chairmen of those committees would be making those decisions without recorded votes. Let's remember what legislative vetoes were: one house acting through a resolution, both houses acting through a resolution, or committees acting through a resolution. In many cases, congressional vetoes were articulated by one house of Congress or inaction by a committee chairman. These unrecorded, unaccountable, irresponsible, or nonresponsible actions by Congress controlled actions by the executive branch.

In response to Mr. Ornstein's comments, if the framers of our Constitution understood anything, they understood human nature. They did not expect that our decision-making processes would be perfect. They expected, however, that if they built systems, then the bad decisions would not be worse decisions; the bad decisions would be checked, the people making those bad decisions would be discovered, and something would be done about them.

Congress can be more effective in the policy decisions it should be engaged in making if it is not also involved in the fine tuning that the executive branch was created precisely by our constitutional system to do. Congress should not have engaged in the excessively broad delegations of power that it did when it had the legislative veto. As Justice Antonin Scalia pointed out well in advance of the *Chadha* decision in *Regulation* magazine, Congress was engaged in passing

251

laws that said no product shall be unsafe and then delegated to the Consumer Product Safety Commission the task of effectuating product safety through regulations, which Congress then tinkered with through legislative vetoes. That, in my judgment, and as Justice Scalia put it at the time, is not the kind of legislation that is effective. Although members of Congress can easily vote for a law that says no product shall be unsafe anymore, that does not require them to make hard, accountable choices—to stand up and decide, How much will it cost to make all products safe? What does "safe" mean? Does it mean there will never be any accidents? And what will the effect of that be on our economy? It is supposed to be the function of Congress to deal with those important policy judgments, and it is not demeaning Congress to suggest that they ought to be engaged in that process.

With regard to the analogy of the parent and the child and the car on the weekend, the Supreme Court in *Chadha* did not prevent the parent in this metaphor from taking away the keys to the car. *Chadha* simply said that if Congress is going to take away the keys, both houses of Congress must stand up and vote on taking away the keys to the car and the president must have an opportunity to veto that legislation, which the Congress can then override. Mr. Ornstein used the term "extralegal devices," which I think is about all that needs to be said about them, that they are extralegal devices. They are also extraconstitutional devices because they shield accountability and responsibility and are not the correct and constitutional way for decisions to be made.

18

Independent Counsel Provisions of the Ethics in Government Act

William French Smith

The Ethics in Government Act was enacted in 1978 as part of the congressional overreaction to Watergate. Part of the act established a mechanism whereby a defined group of the highest officials in the executive branch of the federal government, including the president and vice president, would be treated differently from all other citizens if allegations were made that they had engaged in wrongdoing. If a very low evidentiary threshold, not necessarily related to culpability, is reached—namely, a finding that there are "reasonable grounds to believe that further investigation is warranted"—this further investigation and possible prosecution are removed from the normal law-enforcement process of the executive branch and transferred to the judicial branch. A three-judge panel of circuit-court judges then appoints an independent counsel, universally referred to as a "special prosecutor," who investigates and prosecutes as he or she sees fit. This independent counsel, as a practical matter, is beholden to no one for how the immense powers of investigation—empaneling grand juries, issuing subpoenas, conferring immunity, and so on—are employed. Nor is the independent counsel restrained with respect to the resources used, the money spent, or the time within which action must be taken.

Much of the debate about the act establishing independent counsel centered on whether it violated the constitutional scheme of separation of powers. The Supreme Court has ruled that it is constitutional, but insufficient attention has been given to whether the legislation is *good* legislation or good public policy. In my opinion it is neither, and I say that as one who, longer than any other attorney general, has had the responsibility for administering the act. The scheme established by the act is an unsatisfactory and unwise response to a perceived problem and a serious threat to the fair, evenhanded administration of justice.

We all agree that the law must be enforced in an impartial manner, without bias, and without politicization of the process. But this legislation has not served the ends of justice; it is cruel and devastating in its application to individuals, falsely destroying reputations and requiring the incurring of great personal costs; it has applied artificial standards often unrelated to culpability and to that extent has prevented the use of normal standards of prosecutorial discretion; it has been used more for political purposes and media appetite than to achieve justice; it has been a nightmare to administer; and it has caused a needless and substantial waste of taxpayers' money.

Because of the high profile of the targeted officials and their cases, the independent counsels have believed it necessary to undertake massive investigations. These have required the establishment of legal and investigative bureaucracies and have resulted in lengthy processes of from six months to over two and a half years—at tremendous personal anguish to individuals ultimately vindicated and at great cost to the taxpayers. In some instances independent counsels have roamed beyond the scope of the matter originally assigned to them, converting investigations into endless microscopic examinations.

Certainly some cases, because of their magnitude or the high position of those involved, require the appointment of an independent counsel. This appointment should be made by the president, as it has been in the past. There is no historical justification for the legislative morass created by the act. When in the past it has been necessary to have an independent counsel one has been appointed—from Teapot Dome to Watergate.

The triggering event for the passage of this legislation was the firing by President Nixon of Archibald Cox, the first special prosecutor during the Watergate fiasco. But that aberration was quickly corrected by the designation of a successor special prosecutor. Those special prosecutors fully accomplished what was intended and what the public expected: the indictment and conviction of those who had violated the law. And this had happened before. Whenever an investigation or prosecution had to be handled differently from the normal process, a special investigator or prosecutor was designated. The results fully satisfied the public.

The Ethics in Government Act establishes artificial standards requiring the attorney general to set in motion a cumbersome and expensive process that so far has damaged reputations but produced little else that could not have been handled by the usual process. Its principal vice is that the required process prevents those charged with enforcing the law from doing what they normally do—namely, exercising prosecutorial discretion to determine professionally whether proceedings should be undertaken. A case that after an appropriate inquiry would formerly have been dismissed out of hand must, once the act has been triggered, run its entire many-months-long process irrespective of ultimate vindication. Furthermore, virtually every inquiry under the act results in high-intensity and seriously damaging publicity to the individual under investigation, against which there is little defense.

Cumbersome Requirements and Unnecessary Expense

Most of the cases handled so far by special prosecutors could have been conducted by the criminal division of the Department of Justice, which would normally handle such matters. I have found no effort whatever among the prosecutorial and investigative career personnel in the Department of Justice, under any circumstances, to do anything other than act professionally regardless of the rank of the official being investigated. Indeed if there is any tendency it is to lean over backward to be fair the higher the official's position. This applies to politically appointed officials as well.

Consider the first two cases in which independent counsels were appointed—not during the Reagan administration but during the Carter administration. In neither case would the allegation—the use of a drug on a specific occasion—have received such intensive, resource-draining investigation under normal department standards. It is extremely rare for the federal government to conduct a full-scale grand jury investigation to determine whether an individual used marijuana or cocaine on a specific occasion, particularly when the allegations are received well after the fact, are of dubious credibility, and will not lead to seizure of any drugs or money related to the purchase and sale of drugs. In both cases, however, the statute mandated full preliminary investigations and the appointment of a special prosecutor, who virtually duplicated the preliminary investigation. In both cases, the targets were subjected to great expense and damage to their reputations, only to be cleared at the end. Individuals should not be subjected to this sort of treatment merely because they hold public office. On the contrary, our system of justice is premised upon equal treatment of all individuals, a principle that was in great measure turned on its head in these two cases.

In each instance, because of the strict time limitations in the statute, the preliminary investigation took priority over other department matters. The statute, of course, requires that all covered investigations be treated as highest priority whether or not the allegation would otherwise warrant such treatment. Obviously, this requirement has diverted scarce investigative, prosecutive, and financial resources away from other pressing matters.

With no budgetary restraints Lawrence Walsh, independent counsel in the Iran-contra matter, organized a staff of twenty-nine lawyers, seventy-three administrative staff members, thirty-five FBI agents, eleven Internal Revenue Service agents, and six agents from the Customs Department and in less than a year spent some $4.7 million not counting the cost of the FBI, IRS, and customs agents. That figure compares with an annual budget of $2.35 million for the Public Integrity section of the Department of Justice, which is responsible for investigating and prosecuting public officials in the entire United States.

There is simply no need for the extremely cumbersome mechanism created by the act. For the investigation and prosecution of every other federal offense, ranging from treason and murder to petty misdemeanors, the system depends, quite properly, on the integrity of Department of Justice personnel. The department employs career law-enforcement officials who serve without interruption under many presidents and politically appointed officials. They do not allow the discharge of their duties to be influenced by politics. The assumption on which the independent counsel law is premised—that the Department of Justice should not be trusted to investigate or prosecute certain federal offenses—is simply unfounded.

Even if there is no actual conflict of interest in most situations, many people believe that the appearance of conflict alone is enough to justify the statutory independent counsel procedures. In almost all situations where appearance questions are raised, however, the dangers of conflict are more apparent than real. There is no basis for assuming that Department of Justice personnel cannot fairly and thoroughly investigate crimes by public officials. Given the tremendous costs of routine, automatic independent counsel appointments in terms of reputation, fairness, time, and money, the problems of appearance are not sufficiently compelling to justify the present statutory problems. Where a reasonable danger of conflict might exist, it can always be handled by individual disqualification or, in the most egregious cases, by resort to nonmandatory temporary independent counsels such as were used in Watergate and the Carter warehouse investigations.

The Stigma of a Criminal Investigation

The removal of normal prosecutorial standards subjects public officials with extremely vulnerable reputations to the stigma and expense of criminal investigations in circumstances where, absent the statute, criminal investigations probably would not be warranted. An innocent person can never emerge whole from a criminal investigation, even when it results in a decision not to prosecute. This may be the price society pays for a free press and an open criminal justice system that provides due process at all stages. But where normal standards of prosecutorial discretion are eliminated for a certain class of cases and the added stigma and publicity of a special prosecutor is present, the cost to innocent people becomes greater than is necessary, and serious questions of fairness and justice are raised.

Proponents of the statute often argue that those who have been subjected to this process and vindicated should be grateful because the mechanism was there to clear them. That argument of course is specious. It assumes that they would not have been cleared under the usual, far-more-efficient, normal processes. It also ignores the fact that they could well not have been embroiled in the process at all except for the artificial standard established by the act. But most important is the tarnish that attaches to the vindicated victim of a special prosecutor designation, a tarnish that is impossible to remove.

It is also often stated that the target of such an investigation has frequently asked that a special prosecutor be designated to clear him and that the designation is merely a response to his wishes. In the first place, the wishes of the target are entirely irrelevant to the operation of the act. Furthermore, in my opinion, when the target of an investigation has made such a request it was because he knew the act was about to be triggered, and this was a way of putting the best face on the situation. Otherwise I cannot imagine anyone volunteering to submit himself to this gruesome process.

The act sets up a system of independent counsels who possess the same powers as presidentially appointed and legislatively confirmed U.S. attorneys and attorneys general with none of the myriad checks and balances that today control prosecutorial discretion and action. That is a dramatic departure from normal accountability standards.

The scheme as established by the act creates a procedural nightmare that anyone familiar with the problems of criminal law enforcement considers unworkable. The act requires the attorney general to jump through a series of procedural hoops almost every time anyone alleges wrongdoing by a government official; it makes no effort to distinguish the important from the trivial; and it assumes that virtually every allegation of wrongdoing by a federal official carries with it the potential of becoming another Watergate. I believe that, as presently constituted, the Department of Justice can effectively investigate and prosecute wrongdoing by government officials. Should a conflict arise, as occasionally it will, there are adequate procedures in place to accommodate the eventuality. These procedures will not satisfy those who believe that the department has a vested interest in hiding official corruption from public view, but I doubt that any procedure would serve that purpose.

Moreover, I believe that to the extent any officer or attorney of the department is disqualified, including the attorney general, the department would still be able to carry out its responsibilities. The Department of Justice has an established record of prosecuting prominent political figures irrespective of party. Should a grievously exigent set of circumstances comparable to Watergate arise in the future, there is now an established precedent whereby the president can name a prosecutor of independence within the executive branch.

Attorney General Edward H. Levi testified in 1976 when this legislation was proposed: "It would create opportunities for actual or apparent partisan influence in law enforcement; publicize and dignify unfounded, scurrilous allegations against public officials; result in the continuing existence of a changing band of multiplicity of special prosecutors; and promote the possibility of unequal justice." He was right then, and he is right now. In enabling the criminal investigative process to be transformed into a media event each time high officials are involved, the act casts aside one of the most decent traditions of our criminal law system. This procedure for spreading improper charges contributes to a public attitude of cynicism and distrust of government officials—again a problem the act is intended to help solve.

The Power and the Politics of the Independent Counsel

Some supporters of the act expected that it would rarely require the appointment of special prosecutors. But what has happened so far and is likely to happen in the future shows the contrary to be true. The existence of a multitude of special prosecutors each with only one case to pursue creates the inevitability of unequal justice under the law. Individual rights are clearly undermined when the special prosecutor is charged with focusing on one person and almost by definition has an incentive to prosecute. Each prosecutor is beholden to no one and, having no central authority, applies his own brand of justice. The concept of equal justice for all becomes a fiction.

It is true that under the 1982 amendment to the Ethics in Government Act the prosecutor is supposed to follow Department of Justice prosecutorial policies. But that is such a general standard that its de facto effect in many cases could be minimal. In the Iran-contra case Independent Counsel Walsh has indicated that he would seek indictments if he believed he had evidence to establish probable cause that a crime has been committed. But the prosecution manual of the Department of Justice states that fundamental fairness requires that an indictment issue only if the prosecutor believes that an unbiased jury would convict. Even then a federal prosecutor should not seek an indictment if no substantial federal interest would be served by a prosecution. Those are not the same standards announced by Mr. Walsh.

Although not responsible to anyone, the independent counsel has enormous investigative powers. We have already seen the independent counsel tangle with our foreign policy interests and procedures in the Iran-contra and Michael Deaver cases. In the event of a contest between the prosecutorial goal of an independent counsel and, for example, the State Department, who resolves the issue? Normally, it would be the president. Could it be the three-judge court that appointed the independent counsel? If so, does that mean that the judicial branch would have become enmeshed not only in the prosecutor's function but in our foreign policy as well?

As evidence that this is more than speculation, consider the statement of the chief deputy to Independent Counsel Walsh in response to a question by the U.S. Court of Appeals of the D.C. Circuit considering the constitutionality of the act:

> Court: So if the President and the Independent Counsel have a disagreement over foreign policy and its implications for a prosecution, then the Independent Counsel has the last word?
>
> Mr. Struve: That's right, that's right. If I understand the hypothetical, I think in principle the answer has to be yes.

An effort was made by the independent counsel in the Michael Deaver case to subpoena the Canadian ambassador. The State Department strongly objected to this effort. In the Iran-contra matter an effort was made to obtain information from four Israelis amid objections from the Israeli government.

Some have attempted to respond to the charge that the independent counsel is responsible to no one by referring to the fact that he is removable by the attorney general for good cause. It is well known, however, that it would be politically impossible for the attorney general to exercise this power absent conduct that was so egregious that the independent counsel would have to resign anyway. Reference is also made to provisions requiring reports to Congress and to the special court that appointed the independent counsel, to grand jury, judicial, and other relationships, and in given cases to efforts to comply with Department of Justice policies and to seek guidance from appropriate officials. None of these provisions affect the independent counsel's power, however, only his *modus operandi*.

Equally disquieting is the continuing tendency of members of Congress and others to use this act for essentially political purposes—in some cases blatantly. In one area where politics should play no role—the administration of justice—the Ethics in Government Act provides a convenient mechanism for politicians to practice their trade. And there is no indication that this practice will change. Some members of Congress seem to be poised whenever they sense any vulnerability on the part of an official in the executive branch to cry for an independent counsel, and it is usually worth a headline. The act has become a political weapon. Every subcommittee chairman who thinks he can exploit that vulnerability and who sees some political advantage—or even a possible spot on the nightly news—can claim enough evidence to warrant invoking the act. And it is the kind of juicy news that the media delight in covering. The damage to the individual is secondary.

Other attempts to use the act to achieve political ends have been more serious. Perhaps the outstanding example was the outrageous "investigation" conducted over a two-and-one-half-year period by the Democratic majority of the House Judiciary Committee. It was prompted by a running dispute in 1983 with the Department of Justice over the production of documents and the invoking of executive privilege in a continuing investigation of the Environmental Protection Agency. At least two staff members of that committee working full time, and using "star chamber" methods (for example, allowing only an interviewee's personal lawyer to be present during an investigative interview and requesting that the interviewee not discuss the subject matter with other Department of Justice staff), produced a 3,129 page report at tremendous expense to the taxpayers, to say nothing of disruption to Department of Justice operations. With that report the committee majority sought the appointment of an independent counsel to investigate four individuals. Those 3,129 pages actually produced nothing of substance—not even enough to meet the extremely low threshold of information necessary to trigger the act in three cases, and in my view not enough in the fourth case, although the attorney general did trigger it in that one case.

The motive was pure vengeance on the part of the committee majority because they had not received the obeisance from the Department of Justice to which they thought they were entitled in connection with the production of records. The investigation was political from beginning to end. The committee minority had no knowledge of the majority's activities until an executive summary of the report was leaked to the press. The vote was according to party lines with the minority voting against it. It was a blatant misuse of public resources and a blatant misuse of the act. (If the act had covered members of Congress it should have been invoked to investigate this conduct. But as it has with every major piece of legislation since the National Labor Relations Act of 1935, Congress has exempted itself from its coverage.)

Interests of the Public Not Served

These and other applications of the independent counsel law have turned its presumed purpose on its head. An act that was supposed to take political considerations out of law-enforcement matters has itself become a political instrument. It is of course true that in times of great doubt about the ability of the administration of the Department of Justice to function, an independent counsel may be necessary. In the past, one has been appointed on those occasions. The law must rest upon public confidence. People may well judge differently when events demand this unusual remedy or when the aftermath of such events makes the creation of such a remedy necessary. But such exigencies do not require the legislative scheme established by the act.

What I have said here I believe parallels the views of almost all of the attorneys general who have had experience with the act. The predominant experience has been that this legislation is not in the public interest and does not serve the ends of justice. Nor do I believe that most who have been involved in the day-to-day administration of this act and of the criminal law in the Department of Justice would have views very different from those that I have expressed here. And since only those involved in the administration of the act can really know how it works, I submit this weight of opinion is entitled to substantial respect.

Unfortunately, the problems created by the legislation were not eliminated by the Supreme Court decision holding that the act does not violate the Constitution. That decision only increases the obligation to weigh carefully the burden, injustices, and expense of this legislation against its potential for doing justice.

PART THREE
Political Debate

19
Legalistic Constitutionalism and Our Ineffective Government

Paul M. Bator

The subject of this volume is the fettered executive branch. My own theme is a bit broader: what might be called "our fettered government." My thesis is that the executive branch itself too frequently participates in and is thus complicit in the subordination of the powers of government to an ever more severe and rigid regime of moralistic legalisms that make effective government virtually impossible.

I begin with what is an entirely conventional and well-known account of some of the ills that beset our processes of government and then sketch what might be called the special and creative contributions that the legal system is making to the existence and persistence of those ills.

The conventional account—and I believe it is entirely accurate—goes something like this. The federal government is becoming ever more powerful. The tools available to government to intervene in our private, domestic, social, and economic lives are more powerful today than they have ever been, and as we know, in the past twenty-five years, these interventions have become more and more comprehensive. Even since 1970, there has been a phenomenal growth in federal government programs and in the bureaucracy staffing them. The various federal, state, and so-called cooperative programs and the direct federal command-and-control programs such as Title VII and the Occupational Safety and Health Administration (OSHA), put the federal government into a direct supervisory position in the American household and work place.

This expansion of power has been accompanied by huge growth in the federal law governing private rights and liabilities, and thus private litigation—so much so that the federal judiciary, too, should be perceived as a part of the federal bureaucracy that participates in the life plans and the economic plans of most Americans.

Federal interventions now occur at a level of frequency and detail that would have been unthinkable even as recently as the mid-1960s. Nevertheless, the stunning irony is that government conceived of as a purposive enterprise seems to be becoming less and less effective. We used to think of government as capable of getting things done, of problem-solving, but our endemic habit today seems to be to create processes that make it more difficult for the government to accomplish anything or to solve problems.

The reasons for this are, again, conventional and well known. The system of dispersed powers and checks and balances is of course primarily designed to prevent tyranny, and in this it has been brilliantly successful. This accomplishment is not to be sniffed at. The price we pay, however, is that we make it stupendously difficult for government to create and carry out any coherent program of government policy, or to plan and execute any purposive enterprise whatsoever.

Our luxurious proliferation of different centers of power, a riot of countervailing checks and balances, transforms the task of formulating and carrying out a purposive policy into a complex exercise of multilayered, multicentered, interest-group politics. What is lost in this process is not only effectiveness, but also accountability. The lines of responsibility are so dispersed and obscure that they are singularly unresponsive to democratic controls. Indeed, we have allowed the notion of the dispersal of powers to become a principal engine of our governmental system rather than a limitation on that system. It seems as if the very purpose of government today is to develop new and ingenious ways to stop, break down, or delay the processes of government.

The modern flowering of checks and balances has been immeasurably aided by the proliferation of new centers of power. Looking at the cast of characters that now formulates and executes our national policy, it is not difficult to understand why notions such as coherence, purpose, and energy are so foreign to the scene.

A quick catalog of the executive branch shows that the Executive Office of the President itself is now a rather complex and many-layered bureaucracy, with different constituencies and lines of responsibility and interest. The White House and the Office of Management and Budget are no longer a picture-postcard example of the energetic executive. Within the departments and agencies, the slow acculturation of the political officers of the department to the culture of the bureaucracy is a phenomenon well known in political theory and history. The resulting additional diffusion of power and responsibility is enormous, even within the executive operation.

The past thirty years have produced another well-known phenomenon, a breakdown within legislative government. The breakdown of purposive legislative government is remarkable, a consequence of the breakdown of the party system and discipline of the leadership along with the replacement of the seniority system by the enormous diffusion and dispersion of authority among the members of Congress, the committees, and the subcommittees. This breakdown in purposive legislative government has been immeasurably aided by the growth of the congressional staffs, which are yet another layer of substantive bureaucracy executing the laws within the various substantive fields. There are also committees and subcommitees attached to particular interest groups in substantive fields.

Outside government, the organized interest group is another well-known participant in the processes of lawmaking and policy formulation and execution by both the executive and the legislative branches. The other nongovernmental agent that should also be listed as part of the phenomenon of the dispersion, complication, and layering of power is the powerful media, especially television.

Lawyers and Judges as Policy Makers

My special interest is in the role that lawyers, judges, and litigation play in this dispersion and proliferation of power centers. After all, many societies have rendered themselves ineffective by their inability to organize centers of power that can act, but we are first in one respect: We are the first society in which the courts and the litigation system have played an active role both as one of the important independent centers of policy formulation and execution and as the generator and the enforcer of canons whose primary function is to negate the possibility of energetic government.

It is well known today that the federal courts are important, sometimes front-rank, and often the decisive players in determining the content of public policy and how it will be executed. The legislative process is simply act one of a drama of policy formulation and the executive's role in executing the law is act two. These are really just preamble to the next three acts of the drama in which the litigation process takes over and eventually the federal judges decide what the law means, whether it is valid, and if so how it will be executed.

The federal courts, it should be remarked, are themselves only a metaphor for a complicated subbranch system of interest-group politics in which lawyers, organized interest groups, public interest law firms, and other participants in the litigating system eventually, together with the judges and their law clerks, play a decisive role. In other words, in this country we have created the remarkable phenomenon of an independent policy-making power generated out of the American litigation system and the federal judiciary. Central planning is central in the sense that, in the federal-state dynamic, it is an element of *federal* command-and-control. Many societies have adopted similar systems, but never has a society adopted central planning through litigation.

The legal system not only plays a central substantive role in the formulaton and execution of policy, but in itself has become centrally committed to developing more comprehensive and effective weapons for fighting government. We seem to have committed ourselves to the notion that it is a major function of law to bring government to a halt or at least to delay its processes. The widening system of judicial review has included the enormous widening of our system of access to the courts through changes in the law of standing. These changes now allow almost any disgruntled citizen or member of Congress independently to litigate a large number of complicated and abstract constitutional questions.

Remarkable changes in the procedural law governing litigation that make litigating attractive—most importantly the elaborate provision of attorneys' fees—have generated a cottage industry of persons who in one sense are lawyers, but who in another sense are the clients, too. That is, there are lawyers who are simply in the business of litigating their public policy views, as so-called public interest representatives. We have whistle-blowing statutes, sunshine laws, and myriad other rules whose purpose is to provide weapons against government. The net result is that there is no governmental endeavor that cannot be delayed, transformed, or even stopped by resort to the legal system.

Government by Cooperation

This array of rules and formal and legalistic norms are usable in constitutional litigation to undo or at least to qualify many important public enterprises. My complaint about the executive branch is that it feels free to use these weapons and rules when they serve its parochial interests; it has recently participated extensively in undoing, delaying, or complicating the solution of problems through government.

A rigid and fundamentalist approach to the doctrine of separation

268

of powers, rather than being an effective instrument for eventually making government more effective, has been transformed into a severe and abstract set of rules that perpetuate the notion that an adversary culture, particularly between the president and the Congress, is an important element of American constitutionalism. My own intuition is that history shows that for government to be effective in solving problems the mode must be cooperation rather than legalistic adversary confrontation.

Take the example of Gramm-Rudman-Hollings, the budget-balancing law. This law can be criticized as a false step. Nevertheless, it was an attempt—a rather creative attempt in a situation of complete political gridlock—to solve a vastly significant and difficult public policy problem. The Congress did this through a technique that of course immediately made the legalistic and moralistic American lawyer sniff. It said essentially, "Well, we're not going to take the poison pill today, but we will create a situation in which it is almost certain that we will have to take it the day after tomorrow." It was a temporizing solution. When we do not have the courage to do something courageous today, we try to create conditions in which it will be almost impossible not to be courageous tomorrow. And that was the political horse sense of Gramm-Rudman.

Without getting further into the question of whether the bill was ingenious or creative, it was a step in the direction of dealing with a significant public policy problem. It was, however, immediately unhorsed on a ground that is bizarre and would immediately appear bizarre to every foreign observer of the American scene. The fatal flaw in Gramm-Rudman was that the comptroller general, who had an important part in the execution of the law, operates under ancient congressional statutes allowing Congress to remove him from office for cause. The comptroller general had never actually been removed by Congress, but within that rather abstract flaw, the various lawyers, including the Justice Department's lawyers who were on the lookout for separation-of-powers heresy, saw a fatal obstacle, which they persuaded the Supreme Court to see as well.

It is not necessary to discuss whether the Court's opinion was legally correct, but it is a remarkable cautionary tale to anyone who can manage to step out of the American legalist culture and see the Gramm-Rudman solution as an attempt by the political system actually to *solve* a problem. The attempt was wrecked upon the shoals of this extremely formal proposition that did not in the real world affect the fundamentals of the solution in any way.

Another example involves something not as well known as Gramm-Rudman, the United States Sentencing Commission, which I represent in court. Gramm-Rudman was an emergency solution, a patched-up solution to a problem believed to be a crisis, and it was undone by the courts. The story of the Sentencing Commission is very different. The commission and its work are the product of an extremely elaborate, sophisticated ten-year bipartisan effort by both the executive and the legislative branches to creatively address what had become an open scandal in the administration of justice in the United States: the completely unequal, arbitrary, irrational, and unpredictable system of sentences, which were meted out by a combination of federal judges and executive branch officials called parole officers. To deal with the problem, Congress created a commission to which the president appointed people, including judges. The commission was designated to be in the judicial branch, and under standards created by Congress it has promulgated some guidelines that are meant to rationalize, by making more equal and predictable, the system of sentencing in the federal criminal law.

The work of the commission is controversial, but oddly, the debate is not over whether it did a good job and whether the changes it proposed are for the better or for the worse. The fate of the commission and its guidelines is now subject to an extremely arcane constitutional litigation the judges are going to have to decide. The fate of this enterprise will not be determined by substantive policy. Instead, the commission, the Justice Department, and the public interest law firms (which are extremely hostile to the commission) will debate the constitutionality of Congress's creating an institution that formally is in the judicial branch, the members of which are appointed by the president (some of whom are judges and some of whom come from the executive branch), and all of whom are removable by the president, but only for cause.

The commission is an untidy but highly functional attempt to solve a problem in an area that has always been untidy. Sentencing has always been a field in which the legislature, the executive, and the judiciary have played a rather complicated mix of roles. This has never been a field in which rigid or abstract separation-of-powers doctrines have operated. The commission is trying in this litigation to ward off the other two parties, who—simplifying the argument—are trying to reorganize everything according to their notion of a constitutionally tidy table of organization, in which there is a rigid separation between branches. If the commission is in the judicial branch the president can not remove its members; if it is in the executive branch there can be no judges on it. It has to be absolutely in accord with certain fundamentalist tenets. .

In fact, if we are really going to try to tidy up our separation-of-powers act, we should understand that we have a formidable task ahead of us. For many years no one has bothered to ask whether the Smithsonian Institution is in the legislative or the executive branch, for example. The point is that the various formal constitutional pseudo-doctrines that are being pressed more and more aggressively do not permit creative problem solving through cooperative government.

The habit of subjecting our policy-making modes to the rigid, formal, and legalistic norms of the legal system is spreading from domestic policy to military and foreign affairs. In the wake of Vietnam, Watergate, and the Iran-contra affair, the inevitable tendency is to curb presidential powers, and—in reaction—to curb congressional powers too, because of this complicated minuet of litigation and constitutional theorizing between Congress and the president. But what will be the consequence of trying to subject powers of the branches in international political, economic, and military matters both substantively and procedurally to our system of highly legalistic, carefully cabined, and publicly monitored system of checks and balances and separation of powers? The result will be that it will become more and more difficult to formulate and carry out coherent and bold world diplomatic strategy, and for the president and Congress to work out cooperative arrangements for the solution of some of these problems.

In the minds of many this is a cause for rejoicing, because it means—and this is something that is to be taken seriously—that the "rule of law" is spreading its hegemony. But this carries its own risks. A powerful government is of course dangerous, but a powerless government can also lead to ruin. And I believe it is true, historically, that more societies have foundered because of ineffective government than because of tyrannical government.

In a tense and volatile world, it is not necessarily a happy prospect that a thousand cooks, including not only legislators but also judges, the media, and interest-group lawyers, will attend the cooking of every foreign policy and military broth. We are witnessing an expansion of the hegemony of our highly legalistic system of formal constitutionalism over an ever-widening domain of government policy making. While the happy result is to widen the rule of law, an ironic result seems to be the widening of the hegemony of our complex, unstable, and antidemocratic system of dispersed interest-group politics and interest-group litigation.

Our efforts to make the president more accountable—to the courts, to Congress, to the media—leads to a dispersion of responsibility. It is at least doubtful whether the result is to increase account-

271

ability in the political system as a whole. Checks and balances guard against conventional tyrannies, but they do not guard against Madison's fear of the rule of unruly faction. It may be that we can make our way in the twenty-first century without a government that can formulate and carry out policy as a coherent purposive enterprise, but we ought be at least a little worried about it. Our legalistic and moralistic constitutionalism gives our legal system a thousand legal and ideological tools for striking blows at our own government and the attempts it makes to solve problems. This is a blessing, but like all blessings, it is a mixed one.

20

Legalism versus Political Checks and Balances: Legislative-Executive Relations in the Wake of Iran-Contra

Michael J. Malbin

Legislative-executive relations clearly broke down during the Iran-contra affair. What is most interesting, however, is not the mere fact of a breakdown, but its character. The Reagan administration made a series of imprudent, impolitic, short-sighted decisions. In the course of pursuing those decisions, some steps taken by the National Security Council (NSC) staff may also have skirted the edge of the law. The resulting conflict raised tough questions about the behavior and operating style of both branches. When Congress chose to investigate, however, it did so almost solely to portray the administration's behavior as illegal. The legal judgments underlying the investigation almost all involved assertions, made with unswerving confidence, that serious lawyers can and will honestly debate. These legal disputes are fairly reflected in the majority and minority reports of the Iran-contra investigating committees.[1] The majority's recommendations and Congress's subsequent actions to change the laws about congressional oversight of covert action flowed directly, in turn, from the legalistic character of the committees' work.

Missing so far has been an analysis of how and why the two branches let the situation reach such an impasse. Without such an analysis, Congress seems doomed to pass—and the president to veto—"corrective" legislation that will only invite future conflict. It would be far better if Congress and the executive branch thought more systematically about the underlying political and institutional issues raised by their respective courses of action. Although no manner of good will can wish substantive disagreements away, I shall argue that there already are more than enough levers available for each branch to deter the other from letting disagreement degenerate into mutually harmful procedural warfare.

Iran-Contra: Nicaraguan Issues

The argument of this chapter does not require a detailed rehash of the Iran-contra affair. A few key features will be needed, however, to set the stage for what follows.

Congressional Division. At the heart of the Nicaraguan side of the Iran-contra affair was an intense dispute over the wisdom of President Reagan's policy of providing U.S. support to the Nicaraguan resistance, or contras. That policy has divided Congress almost evenly for most of the Reagan administration.[2] The Senate has consistently supported the president, sometimes by narrow margins. In the House, the votes typically have been close. About 190–200 members have consistently lined up on one side or the other. The proadministration side has included almost all the House Republicans and two to three dozen Democrats, mostly from the South. The consistently antiadministration side includes about three quarters of the Democrats and a handful of Republicans. The remainder of the House—about 20–30 Democrats and 10 Republicans—have changed their votes with the context and therefore have held the balance of political power.

The close division has given each side an incentive to look for procedural devices that will give it an advantage in gaining the votes of the swing members. In addition, because neither side can feel certain of winning a vote with enough margin to settle the issue definitively, each has an incentive to avoid final decisions. The aim, particularly for the president's opponents, has been to avoid giving the impression that any one vote will be the last. By portraying their decisions as being subject to further review, swing members who vote against the president could protect themselves from blame if developments in Central America went badly.

The intensity of the members' opinions has been at least as important as the narrowness of the vote division. President Reagan and his supporters believe that the Sandinista regime in Nicaragua is controlled by Communists who are dedicated to their self-proclaimed goal of a "revolution without borders" and who were giving material

274

assistance to leftist guerrillas in El Salvador. A pluralistic, democratic Nicaragua would be less likely to pursue such policies, the administration has argued. The most likely way to achieve pluralism, in turn, is if the Nicaraguan resistance can put significant military pressure behind its desire for negotiations about internal political reform. Unless the United States helps the resistance maintain military pressure, the administration has maintained, U.S. national security interests will eventually compel some future president to take more forceful steps, including the use of American troops.

On the other side, most congressional Democrats have been convinced that the Sandinistas can be persuaded, through negotiations, to drop their support for revolution in neighboring countries—but only if the United States stops intervening in Nicaraguan affairs. Some also believe that an end to the civil war would be more likely than its continuation to lead to political reform. Whatever their views about the chances for democratization, the president's opponents generally believe that giving aid to the contras means supporting what will inevitably be the losing side in a protracted war. If the contras are bound to lose eventually, the realistic choices for the United States are to accept Sandinista control inside Nicaragua and negotiate regional issues, to continue to back the contras until the Sandinistas win without negotiating regional issues, or to intervene eventually to overthrow the regime by force.

Thus, each side has seen the other's approach as a prescription for eventual war. Under the circumstances, neither has been willing to go very far to accommodate the other. The result has been a vacillating policy toward Nicaragua that has changed almost every year for the past decade. The shift that was most important for the Iran-contra affair, of course, was the one that resulted in the now famous Boland amendment of 1984.

The Boland Amendment. The Boland amendment is a good example of how each side has used the procedural levers at its disposal to achieve what it wants. The House had passed an amendment to the Intelligence Authorization Act of 1983 prohibiting the U.S. intelligence community from spending funds directly or indirectly to help the resistance's military efforts. The Senate rejected the prohibition, and the result was a $24 million compromise that no one expected to be enough for the full fiscal year.

In 1984, the House again passed an intelligence authorization act with the same prohibition. Interestingly, there was no separate vote in the House on aid to Nicaragua—a ploy that let swing members from conservative districts avoid the election year political risk of voting against contra aid. When the Senate refused to compromise on the authorization bill, the House position was made part of the Defense Department Appropriations bill, which in turn was made part of a 1200-plus-page, year-end continuing resolution that packaged nine of the normal thirteen appropriations bills together with an omnibus crime control measure. Once again, there was no separate House vote on contra aid.

The Senate continued to support contra aid, but by this time it was October during an election year. Some of the key senators on the conference committee were concerned about public works projects in the continuing resolution. Others just wanted to get home to campaign. When the House refused to give in, the Senate accepted a compromise that embraced the substance of the House position but also set up expedited procedures for a vote the following February on a $14 million aid package. Many people thought the president should veto the bill to force public debate on the issue, but the president decided to sign the continuing resolution. It is not at all clear that a veto would have been sustained so close to the election, given the anxiety of members wanting to go home, and the provision expediting a vote the following February.

The language adopted in October 1984 read as follows:

> During fiscal year 1985, no funds available to the Central Intelligence Agency, Department of Defense, or any other agency or entity of the United States involved in intelligence activities may be obligated or expended for the purpose or which would have the effect of supporting, directly or indirectly, military or paramilitary operations in Nicaragua by any nation, group, organization, movement or individual.[3]

This wording was both convoluted and strange. One can appreciate just how strange by comparing Boland with the 1976 Clark amendment:

> *Notwithstanding any other provision of law, no assistance of any kind* may be provided for the purpose, or which would have the effect, of promoting or augmenting, directly or indirectly, the capacity of any nation, group, organization, movement or individual to conduct military or paramilitary operations in Angola [emphasis added].[4]

The clarity of the Clark amendment stands in vivid contrast to the difficulties of Boland. The amendments differed in at least three ways. First, the Boland amendment was a rider to an appropriations bill that prohibited only the expenditure of funds, while the Clark amendment prohibited assistance of any kind. Second, the Clark amendment clearly and unequivocally applied to the entire U.S. government, while the Boland amendment reached only the Central Intelligence Agency (CIA), Department of Defense, and other agencies or entities involved in intelligence activities. Third, the Clark amendment prohibited any assistance, anywhere, that would have augmented the capacities of the Angolan resistance, but the Boland amendment prohibited only assistance that would have had the direct or indirect effect of supporting military or paramilitary operations inside Nicaragua. It is therefore easy to see why the debate over the Boland amendment's meaning during the Iran-contra investigation centered on two issues: which federal agencies were covered and precisely what activities were prohibited.

Administration's Reaction. The administration reacted to the Boland amendment by all but eliminating CIA support of the contras. The National Security Council staff, however, took a number of steps intended to help keep the contras alive until the next congressional vote:

• National Security Adviser Robert McFarlane and Lt. Col. Oliver L. North, an NSC staff aide, met with third country representatives to encourage contributions to the resistance.

• North also met with potential contributors to private fund-raising networks to describe how private funds could help the contra cause.

• North encouraged retired General Richard Secord to set up a private air resupply operation for the contras, helped obtain secure communications equipment for the operation, sought the construction of an emergency air strip in a neighboring country, and engaged in detailed discussions with Secord about the contras' specific supply needs. The communications devices were supplied after Congress specifically changed the law in December 1985 to permit the U.S. government to give communications assistance to the contras. By this time, Admiral John Poindexter had succeeded McFarlane as national security adviser.

• North also supplied the contras with intelligence information for the resupply effort, some of which was also militarily useful for defensive purposes.

• Finally, North gave strategic military advice to the resistance.

Many of North's actions might well have been legal. No one would maintain, however, that Congress knew about, much less approved of, the level of North's daily involvement. Every effort was made to ensure that Congress did not know. The record of the NSC staff's efforts to keep Congress in the dark is well documented in the

Iran-contra committees' majority report.[5] There was little dispute between the majority and the minority of the Iran-contra committees on these points. The minority did believe, however, and I share the belief, that the motive for deceiving Congress was not to cover up activities the NSC staff believed to be illegal, as much as to prevent Congress from knowing about, and closing, legal loopholes the NSC staff was exploiting. The aim was to keep the contras alive, while efforts were being made to persuade Congress to renew direct federal aid.

In the short term, the strategy worked. Opponents of contra aid in Congress tried to investigate North at the time of the next major vote, in 1985. Through various deceptions, the NSC staff kept Congress in the dark and contra aid was gradually renewed. In 1986, Congress passed a $100 million package that included a significant amount of military support. Then, the contra resupply effort and all the NSC staff deceptions became known, along with the unraveling of the administration's arms sales to Iran and the use of some proceeds from those sales to help the contras. The unraveling and subsequent congressional investigation changed the political dynamic. In late 1987 and early 1988, the administration failed, after several close votes, to renew military aid for the resistance.

Iran

The political background to the Iran arms sales was almost the opposite of the background to the NSC staff's efforts to help the contras. Instead of an intense political division, the Reagan administration had managed to fashion a broad, bipartisan consensus on a tough, publicly articulated antiterrorism policy.

The Carter administration had imposed an embargo on arms sales to Iran on November 14, 1979, in response to the seizure of the U.S. embassy and its personnel in Tehran. On December 14, 1983, after three years of war between Iran and Iraq, the State Department began a vigorous program called Operation Staunch to persuade other countries to join in the arms embargo. In addition, on January 20, 1984, the secretary of state declared Iran to be a sponsor of international terrorism. Four days later, the department announced in the *Federal Register* that this declaration would subject Iran to a limit on the export of U.S. military equipment to "countries that have repeatedly provided support for acts of international terrorism."[6] The restrictions were tightened in September. Beginning in October, 1984,

278

the administration began articulating an increasingly tough public line toward terrorism and terrorists. On June 30, 1985, two weeks after Shiite terrorists hijacked a TWA airliner, the president said: "The United States gives terrorists no rewards and makes no guarantees. We make no concessions. We make no deals."[7]

About a month later, the United States agreed to a small Israeli shipment to Iran of arms originally supplied to Israel by the United States. By November, the United States became involved directly by helping to arrange details for an Israeli shipment that had run up against shipping problems in a European country. In January, the president signed a covert action finding, as required by law, to authorize the United States to sell arms to Iran directly. The shipments were opposed by Secretary of State George Shultz and Secretary of Defense Caspar Weinberger. They were supported by CIA Director William Casey, Attorney General Edwin Meese, and National Security Adviser Poindexter. Between January and the end of October, there were three different arms sales—the first two using Manucher Ghorbanifar as an intermediary and the third using a so-called "second channel." The sales stopped when information about them was leaked by a disgruntled faction inside Iran to a Lebanese news weekly.

The motivation for supporting the arms sales varied with different participants. For Oliver North, the idea of generating profits to divert to the contras appears to have been one important motivation. This motivation was not shared by others, however. Poindexter did not know about and did not authorize the diversion until after the president signed the finding of January 17. Nor did anyone else involved in the finding know about the diversion at the time. The president was strongly motivated by a desire to see Iran secure the release of Americans being held hostage by the Iranian-supported Hezbollah forces in Lebanon. One of those hostages, the CIA Beirut station chief William Buckley, was of particular concern to the president and to CIA Director Casey. Buckley eventually died under torture.

Most of the participants were also motivated, however, by a genuine desire to pursue relations with factions inside the Iranian government that were open to cooperation with the West. The United States had developed no reliable intelligence and no good connections inside Iran since the fall of the shah in 1979. Inaccurate rumors were rampant about the Ayatollah Khomeini's health, combined with more accurate ones about factional divisions inside Iran and potential Soviet inroads among some of the factions. There was a legitimate policy reason, therefore, to pursue some initiative with Iran at this time.

That reason might not have been enough to justify the specific tactic of selling arms, but combining the policy interests with hostages produced the covert operation.

Through the full ten months of the program, the U.S. government publicly continued to reaffirm its strong posture against terrorism, and the State Department continued to pressure other governments not to sell arms to Iran. During the same period, the president invoked his authority not to inform congressional leaders of the finding he had signed in January. After the information became public, the administration said that its decision not to notify Congress was based on a concern that leaks would lead to the death of the hostages. There was legitimate reason to be concerned about leaks. Even under the most narrow statutory interpretation, notification would have to include the chairmen and ranking minority members of the House and Senate Select Committees on Intelligence, and both figures then on the Senate committees have been suspected of leaking.[8]

Apart from this concern about leaks, however, there is considerable reason to think that the administration simply did not want to tell congressional leaders about the operation because the whole program ran counter to the administration's expressed public policy. Once all the hostages were freed, perhaps all would be forgiven. But unless and until that happened, there was every reason to expect that the congressional intelligence committees would strongly object.

It is impossible to separate a concern about leaks from concerns about political controversy. The simple fact is that the more controversial a program is, the more likely it is to leak. In this case, the arms sales obviously raised questions about their consistency with the administration's public positions about dealing with terrorists and selling arms to Iran. These questions fueled the public's reaction after the operation was disclosed. It is true that the administration distinguished between dealing with the Hezbollah in Lebanon, who held the hostages, and dealing with a government that gave support to and influenced the Hezbollah. But that distinction was a hard one to make publicly, after the fact, and in any case it was a distinction that did not address the decision to sell arms.

Of course, part of the problem may have been with the rhetoric as well as with the arms sales. One can easily imagine a less categorical, subtler public face that would have explained the importance of, and the hard choices involved in, protecting the lives of individual Americans abroad. Alternatively, the administration might have taken an approach, similar to Israel's, of being open to negotiations, but also showing an ability and willingness to engage in effective punitive retaliation. Either approach might have produced a more forgiving public reaction. That, however, would have implied a form of presidential rhetoric quite different from the one that was the basis of Reagan's power and popularity.

"In Ronald Reagan, America found the rhetorical president," wrote Jeffrey Tulis in a recent book on the presidency.[9] The use of public rhetoric is an essentially modern (post-Woodrow Wilson) tool, according to Tulis, that carries with it the inevitable dilemma of maintaining a consistency between what is said in public and the subtler arguments appropriate for deliberation among knowledgeable policy experts. Too sharp a disjunction, let alone inconsistency, is bound to come back to haunt the president. In this case, President Reagan's ability to control the future political debate was dealt a crippling blow from the public revelation of the Iran arms sales. As with the contra resupply program, the short-term benefits did not come close to matching the long-term political and policy costs.

Congressional Reaction

The congressional reaction to the Iran-contra affair was devoid of the just described, or any other, political and institutional analysis. In contrast with the Tower Board's decision to contract for a series of studies of past National Security Council operations,[10] the Iran-contra committees made no effort to examine other examples of tense or harmonious contemporary relationships between the legislative and the executive branches. Such studies could have provided benchmarks for dissecting precisely what was different about these events and for making useful, broadly informed recommendations for the future.

Instead of taking a comparative approach, the congressional committees decided early to hire criminal lawyers to run their investigations. Although I am in no position to know what motivated the committee leaders, the staffing made sense from a short-term political point of view. Whenever the committees moved beyond "the facts" and "the law" in public hearings, it became clear that the members' points of view were too diverse to have permitted a clear majority opinion to emerge on broader issues. In contrast, as long as the committees could concentrate on the law—defined not only to include statutes but also those vague emanations known as the "intent" or the "will" of Congress—the committees could rely on the members' concern for their own branch's power to provide the glue for an institutionally jealous majority.

Whatever the motivation, the majority report made obedience to the law its central theme, to the exclusion of almost all others. This is evident from the report's overall structure. The first "finding and conclusion" in the executive summary at the beginning of the report was: "The common ingredients of the Iran and Contra policies were secrecy, deception and disdain for the law."[11] The executive branch was described as having been engaged in "a lawless process"[12] and the president as having failed "to take care that the laws be faithfully executed."[13] The next 400 pages were in large part a legal-style factual brief to support these assertions. Chapter 27, the rhetorically overstated conclusion of the majority's analysis, was entitled "Rule of Law" and was an appropriate capstone for all that had preceded.

The alleged violations described in the report, and the indictments by Independent Counsel Lawrence E. Walsh, fall broadly into two different categories. The first category includes a series of alleged actions, none of which were authorized by the president, that constitute traditional crimes if the facts and the necessary criminal intent can be proved in court. These include such alleged crimes as destroying government documents, deceiving Congress, misappropriating government funds for personal use, and so forth. None of the actions leading up to these indictments were necessary to the government's policies toward Iran and the contras, and Congress probably would have objected to the underlying policies every bit as much without them.

The second category of alleged crimes involved conspiracies to violate laws that in themselves were civil rather than criminal. For every one of these, a reasonable case—we in the minority often thought that the better legal argument—could be made to show that the law was not violated, even though in some cases the edges of the law were admittedly skirted closely. Without reviewing all the disputes here, I believe the three following examples give a flavor of the committees' debate:

• The majority argued that all actions taken by the staff of the National Security Council were covered by the Boland amendment. The minority said that the clear language of the 1976 Clark amendment did cover the NSC staff's actions toward Angola but that the Boland amendment used language ("agency or entity of the United States involved in intelligence activities") originally crafted for the 1980 Intelligence Oversight Act *specifically to exclude the NSC and its staff.*

• The majority described all NSC staff efforts to encourage third country and private party contributions to the resistance as efforts to evade Congress's constitutional control over the purse. The minority said that the Constitution prohibits Congress from regulating the president's diplomatic communications or communications by any of the president's designated agents. This would include communications that lead to third country contributions for causes the president supports, as long as the contributions do not pass through, or under the control of, the United States. Similarly, the minority said that the president and his employees could not be prevented from encouraging private contributions, as long as the contributions were entirely private and not otherwise prohibited by U.S. law.

• The majority found that the transfer of Israeli-owned arms of U.S. origin to Iran violated the Arms Export Control Act, which requires that the president must approve and Congress must be notified of all such transfers from the original purchaser to a third country. The minority said that the Arms Export Control Act was never intended to apply to covert transactions governed by the National Security Act, that the attorney general had notified Congress of this legal interpretation in 1981, and that Congress had subsequently affirmed this interpretation.

As these three examples should make clear, the general tenor of the majority's argument, following the style of a legal brief, was a series of legal conclusions asserted as if there were no room for doubt. The minority than replied to every important legal point in kind. The intense legal dispute, however, let the committees slip away from the harder questions. That becomes obvious when one turns to the subject of remedies.

Flawed Remedies

Two different kinds of remedies have flowed out of the Iran-contra committees' work. The nostalgic remedy is a call for bipartisan consensus; the other approach is statutory and punitive.

Although consensus may be generally desirable, a call for it does not go very far. Bipartisanship comes easily when a clear-cut majority accepts common principles for action and then negotiates on the fine points. But there is no such consensus on Nicaragua. If there were, people would be willing to look for a common ground and stick to it. Instead, the policies have vacillated because neither side sees vacillation as being worse than the other side's policy. Under these conditions, the underlying interbranch issues have to be redefined, not as a search for consensus but as an attempt to manage interbranch conflict and to foster a spirit of procedural comity.

Proposed Forty-Eight-Hour Bill. Congress has responded to the challenge by trying to write legislation that would prohibit the specific

283

form President Reagan's uncooperative behavior took in the Iran arms sales. Most members believe the president abused the reporting discretion he was given under the 1980 Intelligence Oversight Act. The proposed solution is to tighten the law to deprive all future presidents of exercising any reporting discretion at all.

Under the present law, the heads of the CIA, Department of Defense, and all other agencies and entities involved in intelligence activities are supposed to report all significant activities, other than pure information gathering, in advance to the House and Senate Intelligence Committees. Under unusual conditions, the president may choose to limit notification to the chairmen and ranking minority members of the two committees and the four leaders of the full House and Senate. The 1980 act also specifically notes, however, some conditions under which prior notice would not be given to anyone. In those situations, the law requires the president "to fully inform the intelligence committees *in a timely fashion* [emphasis added]."

The 1980 law does not claim to give Congress the right to approve covert operations in advance. Nevertheless, the two intelligence committees do conduct a project-by-project budget review of all ongoing operations. On occasion, they will use the budget review to terminate operations with which they disagree. But both oversight and budget review rest on the important assumption that the executive branch will tell Congress what it is doing.

For eleven months after the Iran arms sale finding, President Reagan did not notify Congress. Even if some initial delay may have been justified, it stretches credulity to describe this as "timely" under the terms of the statute. Once one acknowledges this much, however, it is not at all obvious what response should follow. The congressional response so far has been to "get back" at the president or presidency by rewriting the Oversight Act. As of this writing (in mid-1988), the Senate had passed, and the House was soon to consider, bills that would require the president under all conditions, with no exceptions, to notify Congress of all covert operations within forty-eight hours of their start. To make sure the last disaster will never again repeat itself, Congress is willing to deprive future presidents of all possible discretion under conditions Congress cannot possibly foresee.

Unfortunately, the bill raises constitutional difficulties that would all but ensure future confrontations between the legislative and the executive branches. Presidents are sure to argue that the Constitution gives presidents the authority to initiate covert or overt actions, with the resources placed at their disposal, to protect American lives abroad and to serve other important foreign policy objectives short of war. If the president has the inherent power to initiate such actions, however, then the same interpretive rule about implied powers that gives Congress the right to demand information as an adjunct of its legislative role, also gives the president the implied powers he may need to put his acknowledged powers into effect.

In almost all cases, there is no conflict between the notification of Congress and the president's power to initiate action. In some rare circumstances, however, there can be a direct conflict. A good example is the Carter administration's decision to withhold notification of particular hostage rescue operations in Iran. In one case, notification was withheld for about three months until six Americans could be smuggled out of the Canadian embassy in Tehran.[14] Interestingly, the Canadian government made withholding notification a condition of its participation.[15] President Carter was faced with a stark either-or choice: accept the Canadian terms or risk the six Americans who were being given safe haven in their embassy.

The example shows that whether withholding notification is proper may depend not on how much time has elapsed but on the character of the operation itself. There can be no question that when other governments place specific security requirements on cooperating with the United States, the no-exceptions aspect of the proposed forty-eight-hour rule would be equivalent to denying the president his inherent power to act. Unfortunately, that kind of a stark either-or choice is common in intelligence. Cooperation may depend on meeting someone else's terms. Other countries or foreign nationals have to risk their own lives and interests to cooperate with us. If they feel nervous about participating, our laws cannot change their assessment of the risks they have to take.

Who should have the power to decide when notification must be withheld? Congress can retain the power to judge after the fact whether a particular decision to withhold was appropriate. The initial decision, however, must by its nature rest with the president. Only the president can decide, for example, whether meeting another party's terms is essential to an operation or whether meeting the terms would impose too high a cost. The president obviously cannot consult with Congress about whether to consult. That would itself be a form of consultation.

The logic creates an inevitable conflict between statutory law and presidential responsibilities. Presidents will feel bound to disobey statutory law when they believe their higher obligation to the law of the Constitution requires it. Because courts prefer to avoid deciding these kinds of conflicts between the legislative and the executive branches, Congress will need some extrastatutory enforcement mechanism to make the proposed statute stick. But if Congress has extrastatutory means available, does that not make the proposed statute redundant at best and a potential new source of conflict at worst? It is futile to use statute law to close all loopholes. The attempt, in this case, merely draws attention away from political mechanisms that would be more likely to produce results.

Defending the Presidency

In the resolution of conflict, it can be useful to get back to the source. On one level, the source of the interbranch conflict over Nicaragua and Iran was the constitutional separation of powers. That could be changed by adopting the recommendations of some constitutional reformers to move the country toward a parliamentary system of government. As I have argued elsewhere,[16] however, such a "solution" would bring costs of its own. Countries with disciplined two-party systems may not normally show as many annual vacillations over specific policies as the United States, but they are more subject to polarized politics and to complete shifts in policy direction with the alternation of governments. Multiparty systems, on the other hand, too often replace vacillation with paralysis and stagnation. A parliamentary model, in other words, would not necessarily improve foreign policy. In any case, there is little reason to believe the required constitutional amendments would ever pass Congress. Why should the members voluntarily amend the Constitution to make themselves less powerful?

Realistic analysis, therefore, should be about making the separation of powers work better, not about replacing it. Two obvious points have to be stressed at the outset. First, representatives, senators, and the president each have their own independent bases of political power. Second, courts are reluctant to adjudicate disputes over the allocation of legislative and executive powers over foreign policy. In Locke's terms, the two observations mean that the two branches are in the position of being the judges of their own cases, with no common judge or authority above them. That means Congress and the president must be treated as independent actors who generally will have to work out their differences on their own.

In general, the branches of government have an interest in containing conflict and working cooperatively because legislative and executive power are not zero sum. For example, Congress began delegating more rule-making discretion to the executive branch during the late nineteenth century because increasing the president's delegated power went together with Congress's increasing its own and the whole federal government's power under the commerce clause.

Normally, there is also a policy as well as a power basis for cooperation. That situation exists when both sides in a policy conflict believe that compromise, or even the other side's policy, would be better than no policy or an impasse. But with Nicaragua, as with many other post-Vietnam foreign policy issues, each side sincerely believes the other's policy would be a disaster. As a result, each side is willing to pull out the procedural stops to achieve its objective. House Democrats have used their control over the agenda to pass major limitations on presidential power without separate floor votes. They have also used their control over the informal oversight levers available to committee and subcommittee chairmen to pressure for maximalist interpretations of ambiguous statutory language. In response, the president and his staff implemented a minimalist interpretation of the same language without telling Congress what it was doing.

Unfortunately for the president, relying on procedural levers does not work equally well for both sides. There are two basic reasons for the asymmetry. First, the president's power ultimately does have to rest on political support and public persuasion. Second, in the absence of either elite consensus or public support, our system gives the advantage to incremental or short-term decisions rather than overt decisions requiring long-term commitment and sacrifice.

Thus, members of Congress who opposed the president's Nicaraguan policies could engage in procedural warfare without threatening their underlying policy objectives. Assertions of congressional power that resulted in policy vacillation were perfectly consistent with preventing a sustained program of U.S. military support for the contras. In contrast, the president's objectives were to sustain and support action, not prevent it. That left him with a more complicated position: the short-term steps needed to sustain specific program objectives one fiscal year at a time were not the best ones for maintaining the long-term political powers of his office.

Consider the choices with which the 1984 Boland amendment left the president. First, the president could have vetoed the continuing resolution three weeks before election day. That would have stimulated a public debate that probably would have helped the president, given the size of his lead over his opponent, but a veto did carry the risk of an override. Second, the president could have signed the bill under protest, announced his view that the NSC staff was not covered, and then proceeded openly with the policy he did adopt covertly. Again, the public confrontation could have helped the president's long-term goals, but it did risk a tighter, loophole-free statute. Third was the approach he and the NSC staff took. Fourth would have been to capitulate to those in Congress who were pushing the broadest interpretations of the Boland amendment.

The fourth choice had nothing to recommend it from the president's point of view. The first two would let the president challenge Congress's use of appropriations riders directly. They probably would have been best, therefore, for preserving the institutional powers of the presidency. The danger is that either choice would have risked short-term help for the contras and thus might have led quickly to their defeat. The third option was the best for the contras but hurt the presidential office.

What makes this kind of choice particularly difficult is the importance of presidential power for the president's own foreign policy objectives. The president gave priority to Nicaragua because he was concerned about the long-range danger of Communist expansion in the Western hemisphere. But a strong presidency—one that builds public support for the exercise of discretionary power—may well be a prerequisite for defending against foreign policy threats over the long term. Thus, the immediate policy that the president thought would leave the country in the best strategic position involved risking political support for the institutional powers he and his successors would also need to achieve the *same* long-term objective.

What should the president have done? Congressional opponents of any activist president can easily maintain a consistency between their policy goals and their desire for institutional power. They have no reason not to assert themselves, so they can be expected to do so. Therefore, I believe the president should let it be known in advance, before the specifics of particular policy conflicts come into focus, that he intends to defend his own institutional power whenever that power is challenged by Congress. He needs to engage in what game theorists would think of as a strategy of tit for tat.[17] That is, he needs to make it clear, through his actions, that he will respond predictably and effectively to any congressional action that he considers a usurpation of presidential power. For example, massive continuing resolutions that do *anything* more than continue past funding levels should be vetoed, no matter what, because these "must pass" money bills are used as legislative vehicles precisely to weaken the veto power. Or, when the House leadership uses the Rules Committee to prevent an open vote on an important presidential issue, the president should use his own powers within the bureaucracy to retaliate.

The president can avoid being forced to weigh policies and institutional power against each other only if he staunchly and predictably defends his office without reference to the specific policies at issue. Such a defense would almost certainly help both branches, producing a better relationship between them. Predictable response is a mechanism for enforcing a spirit of comity. By way of contrast, ambiguity in interbranch (as in international) relations leads to probing and anger. Indeed, a predictable and open defense of the office may result in some policy outcomes the president will find hard to swallow. In Nicaragua, for example, it might well have led to an early defeat for the contras. But defending the office is too important for shortcuts—not just for procedural reasons but for the substantive policies only a strong president can pursue.

Notes

1. U.S. House of Representatives, Select Committee to Investigate Covert Arms Transactions with Iran, and U.S. Senate, Select Committee on Secret Military Assistance to Iran and the Nicaraguan Opposition, 100th Cong., 1st sess., *Report of the Congressional Committees Investigating the Iran-Contra Affair, with Supplemental, Minority, and Additional Views*, H.Rept. 100–433, S.Rept. 100–216 (Washington, D.C.: 1987). Hereafter cited as *Report, Majority Report*, or *Minority Report*.

2. Note that this essay was written shortly after a consensus vote the end of March 1988 to provide only humanitarian aid for the duration of a sixty-day cease fire that was intended to facilitate negotiations during April and May between the Nicaraguan government and the resistance. The result of those negotiations remained in doubt at the time of this writing. In any case, these events and congressional votes occurred after the ones analyzed in this essay.

3. Pub.L. No. 98-473; 98 Stat. 1837, 1937(Oct. 12, 1984),Continuing Resolution, Department of Defense Appropriations Act, Sec. 8066 (a).

4. 22 U.S.C. 2293, emphasis added.

5. *Majority Report*, pp. 117–53.

6. *Majority Report*, p. 160, citing 15 C.F.R. 385.4 (d).

7. Ibid., p. 161. The information in this paragraph all come from the *Majority Report*, chap. 8.

8. *Minority Report*, p. 577. All of chap. 13 in the *Minority Report* is about leaks from Congress.

9. Jeffrey K. Tulis, *The Rhetorical Presidency* (Princeton, N.J.: Princeton University Press, 1987), p. 189.

10. The still classified studies are referred to in the *Report of the President's Special Review Board*, John Tower, Chairman (Washington, D.C.: Feb. 26, 1987), Appendix E.

11. *Majority Report*, p. 11.

12. Ibid.

13. Ibid., p. 21.

14. U.S. House of Representatives, Permanent Select Committee on Intelligence, Subcommittee on Legislation, 100th Cong., 1st sess., Hearings on H.R. 1013, H.R. 1371, and Other Proposals Which Address the Issue of Affording Prior Notice of Covert Actions to the Congress, April 1 and 8, June 10, 1987, p. 45. See also pp. 46, 49, 58, 61.

15. Ibid., p. 158.

16. Michael J. Malbin, "Factions and Incentives in Congress," *The Public Interest*, vol. 86 (1987), pp. 91, 107.

17. See Robert Axelrod, *The Evolution of Cooperation* (New York: Basic Books, 1987), passim.

21
Talking about the President: The Legacy of Watergate

Suzanne Garment

If the institution of the American presidency has grown enfeebled over the past two decades, it is not only because of battles with its opponents over policies or institutional prerogatives. Its adversaries have also waged a crucial and more or less continuous attack on the underlying moral legitimacy of the office, its occupants, and the president's allies in the executive branch. The moral attack has not come from antipresidential partisans who deliberately set out to make war on the idea of federal executive power per se. Rather, it began as an incidental though large part of the ideological and policy struggles of the 1960s, especially the attack on the foreign policy pursued by U.S. presidents from World War II to Vietnam.

In a fight as bitter as this one has been, it is no surprise to find that the antipresidential troops have been using poisoned arrows or that our current national politics has become to a significant extent a politics of scandal and radical moral delegitimation. The changes that produced this state of affairs have been general. They affect more than the institution of the presidency, and their consequences cannot be reversed by narrow institutional changes. But institutional factors have placed a disproportionate burden on the executive branch and have helped perpetuate the current climate. Some of these can be altered if there is the political will to do so.

The Rising Temperature

Scandals are perennial in public life. But moralistic fervor in American politics waxes and wanes, and the temperature rose fairly steadily

291

throughout the 1960s. There were big national political scandals, of course, even in the early years of the decade. The two major landmarks were the cases of Billie Sol Estes and Bobby Baker. Each of these scandals was, in its way, an American classic. And each was from a present-day perspective almost genteel.

Certain elements in the story of Billie Sol Estes sound familiar in the 1980s. Estes was a creative Texas entrepreneur who figured out how to make money off the U.S. government through such devices as nonexistent fertilizer tanks and the illegal purchase of cotton-growing rights. He was exposed in 1962 by a local newspaper engaged in a circulation war with a competing paper owned by Estes himself. Republican congressmen clamored for an investigation of Estes' connections with the Kennedy administration's Agriculture Department. Not long after a congressional subcommittee began such an investigation, the committee's Democratic majority, in a gesture known to us all, fired its Republican minority counsel for leaking an incriminating document to the *New York Herald Tribune.*

Bobby Baker had been a longtime secretary to the Senate and a particularly close associate of Vice President Lyndon Johnson. The scandal came to light in 1963 when Baker was sued by a vending machine firm, which alleged that he had taken money from a competing firm to influence the allocation of defense plant vending machine contracts. The *Washington Post* took up the story, and the ensuing congressional investigation went on for two years. Republicans on the investigating committee accused the Democratic majority of a cover-up. Republican Representative John W. Byrnes of Wisconsin, drawn into the investigation's net when he was found to have bought some Baker-connected stock at a very low price, behaved like many current figures in similar circumstances when he excoriated the press for having "prosecuted, judged, and hung" him.

Much of this sounds familiar. But in some ways these big scandals of the early 1960s look strange when observed from twenty years later. When it seemed that President John F. Kennedy's secretary of agriculture, Orville Freeman, was about to be implicated in the Billie Sol Estes scandal, Kennedy came to Freeman's defense unequivocally and unwaveringly. "I could have found no one of stronger conviction or greater dedication to the national interest," he said as the crisis heated up, "than Secretary Freeman." At his next press conference, Kennedy pointedly repeated, "Secretary Freeman I think has a matchless reputation . . . and I have the greatest confidence in the integrity of Secretary Freeman." These signals from Kennedy played a significant role in limiting the scandal's spread. A counselor to a more modern president would have made certain that his boss substituted some ambivalent and self-protective formula for Kennedy's enthusiastic and high-risk endorsement.

In the Baker scandal Republicans complained that the majority Democrats would not properly broaden the investigation to include subjects like the "party girl" ring that Baker was said to have operated out of his Senate office. The *New York Herald* publicized testimony that implicated President Johnson and Representative Sam Rayburn of Texas in Baker's activities. Such inviting leads did not bring about what would have occurred today in such a situation—a veritable stampede to nail the president to the wall.

In the years after 1963 national politics began to feel the profound effects of Kennedy's assassination, of the increasingly divisive issues facing the civil rights movement, and of a fledgling consumer politics based on the idea that the chief threats to the American consumer derived from the nefarious motives of the American corporation. By the middle of the decade, even before the antiwar movement had stirred up a frenzy against President Johnson, the scandals that most occupied the Congress had become more bitter and inflammatory.

The dominant scandals of the mid-1960s involved Representative Adam Clayton Powell, Jr., Democrat of New York, and Senator Thomas Dodd, Democrat of Connecticut. It is hard to imagine two more different American political figures. Dodd had been assistant to five U.S. attorneys general, had served as chief trial counsel for the United States at Nuremberg, and was a thundering anticommunist. Powell, a minister politely described as a "flamboyant" figure and a man of the left, was the second black committee chairman in the history of the House of Representatives. He had gained this unusual degree of seniority because his Harlem constituents had elected and reelected him by large majorities since 1944.

Senate action against Dodd grew out of events in 1966, when the columnists Drew Pearson and Jack Anderson got hold of some 4,000 documents taken from Dodd's files by former employees. The columnists used the documents to charge that Dodd had diverted contributions from testimonial dinners to his personal use, accepted gifts from a contracting firm for helping it get government business, and double-billed for trips he took. A Senate committee began an investigation and solemnly appointed a former Supreme Court justice, Charles Evans Whittaker, as a consultant. President Johnson, a guest at the two testimonial dinners involved, pointedly distanced himself from Dodd.

When the issue finally came to the floor of the Senate, Dodd's chief defender, Senator Russell Long, argued that Dodd was in some respects being convicted ex post facto on the basis of acts that had violated no clear rule. But the Senate voted to censure Dodd. It was an event of great drama, for in the history of the Senate, a body that has known its share of scoundrels and horse thieves, this was only the seventh time that a member had been punished so severely. The last censure had been that of Senator Joseph McCarthy in 1954.

Like Dodd, Powell aroused strong sentiments among his colleagues. He used committee funds to go to Bimini with a female staffer who was not his wife. He had a long series of tax disputes with the federal government. During the course of a defamation suit against him, the New York state courts found him in criminal contempt in 1966. As a result he could not set foot in his home state.

Even so, his treatment by the House was striking. A House committee investigating him recommended that he be not only censured but fined, which was unprecedented. The House as a whole went further than the committee, voting to exclude him from the chamber altogether. This made him only the sixth member excluded in House history. Two had been shut out for aiding the Confederacy, one for selling an appointment to West Point, one for polygamy, and one for treason during World War I. This last man was a Socialist from Wisconsin, who later had his treason conviction overturned and his House seat restored. Powell, too, was reseated in 1969 after the Supreme Court overturned the House action against him as unconstitutional.

Each of these men aroused strong feelings, partly for personal reasons but also because each was associated with a body of ideas or forces that were causing increasingly bitter political divisions. In each case the ideological rancor, laid on top of the usual partisan and personal feelings and the traditional pursuit of scandal, made for a particularly dramatic reaction to offensive behavior. This was not the spirit of politics as usual.

Politics as usual finally collapsed almost entirely during the protests against the Vietnam War. Ideological resentment quickly turned into a pattern of violent personal accusation. Critics of the war did not limit themselves to objections on grounds of *Realpolitik* or humanitarian moral concerns. Many took the next step and assaulted the war as illegal—indeed, criminal. They hammered away at quasi-criminal issues like the deception behind the Gulf of Tonkin resolution, the lying to the press, the bombing of Cambodia, the wiretapping, the illegal counterintelligence activity of the Federal Bureau of Investigation, and the attempted suppression of the Pentagon Papers.

They treated the Vietnam War as a massive scandal, the U.S. government's pursuit of the war as a huge illegal conspiracy, and the president as the chief conspirator. As in the early 1950s, an underlying ideological battle was joined to the traditional and perennial American search for illegal or improper political behavior and produced a politics of scandal that was unusually intense.

Watergate was the climax of this developing view that obnoxious American policies could continue in practice only because they were being foisted illegally on the nation by presidents who were criminals. By the end of the Watergate proceedings, the ideological and policy-related motives of Richard Nixon's adversaries had almost completely disappeared from public view, lost under the mass of talk about the threat posed by the executive branch to legality and institutional balance. Only amid this sort of confusion could an old-fashioned Southern politician like Senator Sam Ervin, who had voted against all the civil rights measures of the 1960s, become a liberal hero.

Post-Watergate: The New Sex Scandal

The insistence that the crisis was institutional, a threat to the law on the part of the executive branch, produced a set of institutional remedies for what were really ideological and policy divisions. These remedies have increased public awareness of criminality and illegitimate acts by government officials. Because most of the remedies were devised for the executive branch alone, the executive has borne the brunt of this process of delegitimation.

Still, it is important to draw some distinctions and note that the seemingly endless official and journalistic preoccupation with wrongdoing in the government, particularly in the executive branch, does not come just from the institutional detritus of Watergate. Other changes have been at work.

First of all, broad cultural changes have helped create the current climate. Take one relatively entertaining example: Beginning around the time of Watergate, we have seen a series of sex scandals of a distinctive sort. The stories have faded from memory, but some of the names remain familiar: Fanne Foxe, Elizabeth Ray, Paula Parkinson, Rita Jenrette, Donna Rice. These were women of apparently dubious virtue whose names were linked with those of prominent politicians from Wilbur Mills to Gary Hart.

This sort of sexual connection is not exactly new in the political history of the world and was not absent from the period just before Watergate. Indeed, Judith Campbell Exner recently said in *People* magazine that she not only was President Kennedy's mistress but actually carried documents between him and mobster Sam Giancana. True or false, this is bigger sex scandal news than anything that the supposedly amoral Reagan years have managed to produce.

295

Note an interesting difference, however: Judith Exner did not kiss and tell during Kennedy's lifetime. During the early 1960s we still did not find many women prepared to accept the notoriety that comes from public revelation of this kind of sexual connection. The calculus changed after the 1974 incident involving Wilbur Mills and Fanne Foxe, in which Ms. Foxe dived into the Tidal Basin. She does not seem to have begun her involvement with Mills just to publicize herself. But after the affair became widely known, it gave a considerable boost to her career as an exotic dancer. The women who followed Ms. Foxe into similar situations and who had examples to emulate seem to have been more calculating in their search for the spotlight. In 1987 the nation saw what must surely be the logical end of this progression when Donna Rice showed up in a television commercial as a spokesperson for No Excuses blue jeans.

What happened in the quarter-century between Exner and Rice was the sexual revolution. Short-lived as it may have been in its active stage, the movement for sexual liberation left a considerable legacy. Today many more women than before are willing to bear whatever social cost still attaches to being mentioned in the same public breath with Paula Parkinson and Donna Rice. On the other side of the cost-benefit calculation, the benefits of notoriety have increased in the past twenty-five years as the appetite for gossip as mass entertainment has grown. Therefore, for perhaps the first time in our political life, it is the women in these episodes who are the more likely to kiss and tell. Our ever-adaptive society has developed a whole new channel through which political sex scandals can become public.

The increased publicity from this kind of scandal has so far not hit disproportionately at the executive branch. On the contrary, it has been in the main a congressional phenomenon. Just as it has been said that Democrats produce the sex scandals in American public life while Republicans give us the money scandals, it may soon be conventional wisdom that the executive branch has taken a big lead in money scandals while Congress has become the champion at scandalous sex.

The new-style sex scandals do not give any direct advantage to Congress in its current struggles with the executive branch. They do, however, affect the question of moral legitimacy in a general way. A majority of the American people were, for better or for worse, never fully liberated by the sexual revolution. Even some of those who were have become less tolerant of sexual indiscretions in recent years. Their decreasing tolerance has played an independent role in creating yet other kinds of sex scandals over the past decade. Incidents such as the Gary Hart affair, the publicly circulated stories about presidential hopeful Pat Robertson, and the decision by journalists to publicize the story of spousal abuse by John Fedders of the Securities and Exchange Commission testify to an increased willingness to pass judgment on matters of private morality. When this decreased tolerance among some of our citizens comes face to face with the still-liberated frankness of others, numerous opportunities arise for the less liberated to reaffirm their opinion that the moral tone of political life is very low indeed. This opinion makes it easier for people to believe accusations of all sorts about public officials.

More "Normal" Scandals: Prosecutorial Discretion

If some of the atmosphere of moral illegitimacy surrounding the executive branch comes from broad cultural changes affecting more than just the executive, another part of it comes from incidents that are fairly normal for many periods in recent American politics. That is, they involve actions that would have given offense before Watergate as well as afterward. For instance, when the conservative Republican Representative Robert Bauman was charged in 1980 with soliciting sex from a teen-age boy, observers were startled in the usual way and for the usual reasons.

Even when the offenses are perennial, though, much of the publicity surrounding them cannot be called a perennial phenomenon because it demonstrates some of the special features of the post-Watergate climate. Some executive branch scandals have come about because of the increasingly tough manner in which the post-Watergate executive branch, sometimes under congressional pressure, has used its prosecutorial discretion. In 1983, for instance, Paul Thayer, deputy secretary of defense and former head of LTV Corporation, came under investigation for possible obstruction of justice connected with insider trading that had occurred before he went into government. He resigned, was ultimately convicted, and got a stiff prison sentence of four years.

This was a serious case. It was also, when it started, a somewhat ambiguous one: Thayer had given the inside information to friends, including his mistress, and in the beginning it was not clear that he had profited personally from the transactions. Thayer was vigorously pursued by the SEC and the Justice Department at a time when the SEC was conducting a well-publicized campaign against insider trading. The vigor was unfortunate for Thayer, who soon became a staple item on the long lists that began to appear in the press of morally dubious actions by officials of the Reagan administration.

Another such instance of prosecutorial discretion was the case of James Beggs. In 1985 Beggs, former executive vice president of General Dynamics, was the aggressive, hands-on chief of the National Aeronautics and Space Administration (NASA). At the time the Department of Justice had embarked on a campaign to show that it was tough on the issue of waste, fraud, and abuse in the defense budget. As part of an effort by a special Justice Department military procurement unit established in 1982, General Dynamics and several of its officials, including Beggs, were indicted on charges of overcharging the government in the development of the DIVAD antiaircraft gun. The prosecutors discounted the insistence by General Dynamics that the Justice Department was using the wrong method of calculating how much the government owed to the company.

Beggs was forced to resign from NASA, shortly before the disastrous launch of the Challenger shuttle. Over a year later a Freedom of Information Act request by the company produced documents showing that General Dynamics had clearly been right all along about the cost calculations. The evidence was strong enough to make the government take the unusual step of dropping the case before trial. But the air of scandal remained, despite Beggs' exoneration. He joined Thayer on the lists of Reagan administration figures who had come under a legal or moral cloud.

More "Normal" Scandals: The Discovery Explosion

The reputation of government has also suffered because of ordinary offenses that would probably not have become known before the post-Watergate "discovery explosion." Part of the increased ease of discovery comes from more willingness on the part of public organizations to report impropriety by public officials or even to take special public note of their misconduct, instead of trying to treat these high-level sins discreetly (or, in more modern parlance, through cover-up). Moreover, although it is hard to amass aggregate numbers, journalistic organizations clearly seem to be devoting more resources to the job of digging up independent evidence of misconduct. Finally, for better or for worse, more of the information gathered by the press is actually reported to the public.

These changes, beginning or accelerating around the time of Watergate, have had effects beyond the executive branch. It is generally agreed that the publicity surrounding Wilbur Mills and the Tidal Basin incident of 1974 would have been highly unlikely a decade or even five years earlier. The same change was evident when in 1976 Representative Joe Waggoner in Washington and Representative Allen Howe in Salt Lake City were apprehended for soliciting undercover policewomen for purposes of prostitution. Even in 1976 Representative Waggoner was released without being charged because it was then standard police practice in the District of Columbia not to arrest members of Congress for misdemeanors while Congress was in session.

As for changes in press behavior, at the end of 1983 someone leaked to the *New York Times* transcripts showing that Charles Wick, head of the United States Information Agency and a close friend of President Reagan, had been tape recording some of his phone conversations with others. It quickly became evident that there was nothing criminal in Wick's motives. He was in the not-too-prudent habit of taping these conversations as a means of keeping records, especially of his own ideas. But the scandal very nearly drove Wick out of government. Journalists, intensely alive to the post-Watergate theme of wiretapping as an abuse of government power, treated the story as a major scandal by definition. They kept probing for additional detail, which meant that they kept covering the story. The extended coverage made the scandal seem more important and increased the opportunities for blunders on Wick's part. The examples of this pattern of press behavior and public figures' reactions form a long list indeed.

Another aspect of the discovery explosion is that public officials must by law, beginning with the Federal Election Campaign Act of 1974 for Congress and the Ethics in Government Act of 1978 for executive branch officials, make considerably more financial data publicly available than ever before and file continuing supplementary reports. This information is, of course, a rich new lode for researchers to mine for clues to a public official's financial connections and thus to possible sources of corruption. Just as important, the new reporting obligations create new possibilities for inconsistency and noncompliance. While these flaws may not prove actual corruption, reporting them even without comment affects public attitudes by creating the powerful impression that the public official involved has been acting in bad faith or has something to hide.

The executive branch has, however, of course felt this change keenly. To mention just one example, when presidential adviser Edwin Meese went through lengthy and painful confirmation proceedings for the job of attorney general in 1984, inconsistencies and omissions in his financial disclosure forms constituted a large part of the case against him.

This change has, however, affected Congress as well as the executive branch. "Rep. Donald Sundquist," says a typical *Wall Street Journal* story on the subject in 1984, is "a Tennessee Republican who doesn't yet see any opposition to his re-election. Yet Rep. Sundquist has raised. . . .from PACs, $174,593. . . . Rep. Martin Frost of Texas not only lacks opposition, he is a critic of the PAC system. . . . Yet even Rep. Frost has raised $122,750 from PACs, nearly one-third of his total campaign receipts." This information comes from a story by an excellent investigative reporter who spends a major part of his time in front of his computer screen, combing the public data for anomalies like these.

New Crimes, New Institutions

Sometimes the increases in scandal have stemmed not just from changes in procedure but from real changes in standards of legality. That is, new laws have created new crimes. Again, although the impulse behind such changes has not been directed exclusively against the executive branch, their main impact has often been on the executive. The reason lies in organizational and institutional factors. One very large difference is the body of lobbying provisions in the Ethics in Government Act, whose strict yet murky rules Congress has applied not to itself but exclusively to the executive branch. Two of the most serious scandals of the Reagan administration—the recent criminal convictions of Michael Deaver and Lyn Nofziger—came about directly or indirectly because of behavior that was not criminal before the passage of the Ethics in Government Act. Such behavior might still have been offensive without the act, but it would not have brought the official condemnation that is, as we shall see, especially important for the making of a major scandal in the post-Watergate era.

Other institutional changes disproportionately penalize the executive branch as well. Many times what drives a modern scandal is not only press interest but also the particular post-Watergate organizations that have been created to deal with scandalous activity, from the new inspectors general in federal agencies and the new public integrity section in the Justice Department to the office of the independent counsel.

In the summer of 1979 Steve Rubell and Ian Schrager, owners of the trendy nightclub Studio 54, were under indictment for income tax evasion. Their lawyers were negotiating a plea with the U.S. attorney's office. One of the defense attorneys made the charge that Jimmy Carter's White House chief of staff, Hamilton Jordan, had visited the club once and used cocaine there. The charges looked flimsy. But because Jordan was one of the high executive branch officials covered by the Ethics in Government Act, the attorney general had to send the FBI to investigate.

The beginning of the investigation was well publicized. It was not surprising, therefore, that new rumors and more alleged evidence soon began to emerge. Shortly after Thanksgiving Attorney General Benjamin Civiletti asked for the appointment of an independent counsel (then called a special prosecutor). The independent counsel he got—Arthur Christy—was a thorough professional. He had the subpoena powers that were missing in the preliminary investigation. He covered each of the myriad accusations in the case and concluded that none of them provided a basis for prosecution.

This process took six months—until the end of May 1980. It went on while Jordan was trying to negotiate with the Iranians for the release of American hostages. It went on as President Carter began planning his 1980 reelection campaign. It caused Jordan to leave the White House with a debt of $67,000—which, though it sounds picayune when compared with the investigation fees of today, was more than his entire annual salary.

The office of the independent counsel is now receiving a fair amount of critical examination. Even though the Supreme Court reversed the recent decision by the D.C. Circuit Court of Appeals declaring the office unconstitutional, that examination is likely to continue. The civil liberties problems with the office are serious ones, it is now clear, rather than just the inventions of disgruntled defense lawyers. But the institution is also coming under newer sorts of criticism. Some prosecutors and former prosecutors with Justice Department backgrounds now say that an independent counsel may prosecute crimes less rather than more effectively than the department does, because an independent counsel does not have full access to relevant expertise among Justice Department lawyers and because government investigative agencies like the FBI will not place as much confidence in an independent counsel and his staff as in a government prosecutor with whom they work regularly. Another argument is that independent counsels are dangerous to the development of the criminal law because they cannot choose among different cases with different facts when deciding whether and where to argue a legal question before the courts.

It has also became clear that the office of independent counsel has a distinct effect on public discussion of corruption in the executive branch. In the days following Watergate the case for establishing a special prosecutor's office was based on the argument that politics had to be kept out of criminal cases involving high executive branch officials so that they would be investigated and prosecuted in the ordinary way, as the rule of law requires. But the establishment of the independent counsel's office has had the opposite effect. The investigation and prosecution of cases involving high executive branch officials have become anything but regular and ordinary. Public discussion of these cases has followed suit.

A journalist who has found facts that lead him to suspect an official of corruption often finds himself with a surprisingly difficult story to write. Often the facts do not speak completely for themselves and do not make an open-and-shut case that the official's behavior is illegal or unambiguously offensive. In cases like these and at a time when American journalism is very much under scrutiny, a journalistic organization runs serious risks if it gives the story front-page treatment and thereby implies that major wrongdoing has been discovered. Such stories are much less vulnerable if they rely on information from government officials or reports of official government actions such as indictments or the opening of investigations. This need fits nicely with the sense among modern-day political progressives that if a moral wrong exists, there is or should be a law to invoke against it. The result is an increasingly close tie between modern scandal reporting and official legal action.

In the first decade after the office of independent counsel was established in 1978, the dependence of much scandal reporting on government action sometimes served as a protection for the executive branch. In a series of early cases, when an independent counsel took over an investigation, the atmosphere would calm down. The independent counsels themselves kept quiet, as befits a proper prosecutor. Other people who wanted to investigate the matter in a noisier way, like congressmen and their staffs, found it hard to do so. If they started their own highly publicized investigations, they could be criticized for impeding justice by prejudicing the investigation going on in the much-respected independent counsel's office.

The independent counsel would then issue a report. Typically— in the Raymond Donovan or the Edwin Meese case, for instance—the report would find that there was not enough credible evidence to warrant criminal prosecution. Such verdicts stopped well short of being moral exonerations. But for those who were certain that the moral failings of their opponents were so serious as to constitute crime, a verdict like this was a disappointment that broke a scandal's forward momentum.

This early pattern has probably been in part an artifact of the special solemnity with which the first independent counsels have been chosen and with which their investigations have been conducted. Over the course of the Reagan administration, though, the pattern has begun to change. Some counsels have started behaving more as early proponents of the office have hoped and early critics feared they would—as prosecutors with a single case and without real constraint by a higher authority.

It is probably not true that the more recent independent counsels and their staffs, because of some special desire for publicity, have leaked more information to the press than regular prosecutors do. Anyone who follows the activities of some of the Justice Department's U.S. attorneys knows how unlikely it is that such a proposition could be true. But when the independent counsel process is publicly invoked, several of events begin that are unambiguously newsworthy, that no journalist could be criticized for covering, and that the press has a positive obligation to report.

The chain of events starts when someone asks the attorney general to investigate a matter that falls under the independent counsel statute. The attorney general is by law given ninety days to do the job, during which time he does not have subpoena power. After the ninety days he must either ask the court to appoint an independent counsel or write a report to Congress explaining why not. He is very unlikely, because of his limited time and tools, to be able to report with certainty—even in a dubious case—that there are no relevant questions left unanswered. He knows that if he tries there will be people in Congress and the press ready to question his competence and character.

If the attorney general does ask the court to appoint an independent counsel, he is in effect stating publicly and officially that he is dealing with a suspicious matter requiring further investigation. That is worth reporting. It is especially worth reporting because the independent counsel's office deals with high public officials. Moreover, calling the independent counsel into the case necessarily suggests that some high political authority would otherwise be interfering, or perhaps has already tried to interfere, in the matter. This last, unspoken story makes the start of independent counsel proceedings seem especially important.

Each case handled by an independent counsel has about it the air of a significant struggle over the control of federal prosecution and the preservation of the rule of law. When a leak occurs from an independent counsel's office, the story seems especially significant. In addition, the office is likely to carry on its investigation for a relatively long time, since one of its jobs is to ensure thoroughness and to see that nothing gets swept under the rug. The opportunity for speculation and leaks is correspondingly long, as is the chance that the investigation will expand to include yet other public officials and instances of possible wrongdoing, which will generate yet more news. In theory, the independent counsel and his staff are unmoved by the pressures that such publicity may generate. In practice, this possibility is remote.

The process creates impressions that affect the perceived legitimacy of the presidency as a whole, and it is through organizational differences like this one that Congress has its greatest advantage over the executive branch. There has been increasing comment in the past few years over the fact that Congress has legislated harsh ethics rules for the executive branch but more or less left itself out of the movement for reform and moral purity. This is not to say that Congress has been scandal free during the post-Watergate years; on the contrary, because of all the changes that have taken place, post-Watergate scandals have involved Congress almost as much as the executive branch. What is missing in the Congress, though, is an institutional mechanism to drive a scandal forward, broaden its reach, and maximize its public impact and meaning. The House and Senate Ethics committees to which the task is given are not separate enough from the body as a whole and therefore do not have the proper incentives to do the job.

The executive branch is distinctly limited in what it can do to combat this relative advantage that Congress holds. Where Congress clearly crosses a constitutional line, usurping or abridging some well-established presidential prerogative, the executive branch can certainly protest far more vigorously than it has done so far. There is every indication that at this time the courts will take executive branch arguments on such issues seriously. At the least a new administration might persistently question why Congress does not extend ethics legislation to its own members.

People concerned about the larger problem posed by the politics of scandal cannot attack it, however, simply by contending that Congress is behaving in an unconstitutional manner. First, a good deal of what is continually putting the presidency on the moral defensive comes not from Congress but from cultural factors that affect all national political figures. Where congressional action is indeed the problem, the mechanisms Congress has established to eat away at executive branch authority are often perfectly constitutional, whether they are benign ideas or terrible ones. When Congress establishes new inspectors general in federal agencies, as it has done, or provides through legislation for special rewards to whistle blowers in the executive branch, or establishes a special public integrity section in the Justice Department, it is creating circumstances that cannot be simply changed in the courts.

This part of the executive branch's dilemma is nothing other than the old problem that the Constitution was designed to mitigate: Congress is indeed the most powerful, and therefore the most dangerous, branch. Government structures can be skillfully organized to mitigate the threat of legislative tyranny, and a clever president has many tools and stratagems at his disposal. But no other source of authority is as powerful as the law, because of the respect that its supposed neutrality engenders among all citizens. When a Congress starts using this respect in a tyrannical way—that is, when it starts using the laws to a significant degree in its own behalf, as weapons in its partisan struggles against opponents in the federal government or outside it—there is no way to avoid substantial damage.

Improvement will come only when critical numbers of people in Congress begin to shift the focus of their legislative and investigative energy. It will come when talk about enforcing a higher ethical tone in the executive branch becomes less politically profitable than other issues—that is, when other themes stir constituents and opinion makers more deeply.

Changes of this sort are not impossible. The Iran-contra investigation, our most recent attempt to reenact the passion play of Watergate, was ambiguous in its outcome. In public opinion no congressional investigator fared better than the quarry, Colonel Oliver North. Any future trial of North is unlikely to be a resounding victory for the morality-in-government forces. Watergate-style hearings, we can safely assume, have become less attractive.

Discussion in the legal community of the office of independent counsel is by now notably skeptical in tone. Issues from drugs to America's international competitiveness are beginning to stir the sort of widespread political anxiety that pulls canny politicians off one bandwagon and onto another. The moral attack on the executive in public discussion will end, when it ends, as it began—with a shift of attention by the political elite, perhaps this time to issues and attitudes that place the president at a greater advantage in the unending executive-legislative tug of war.

22
Commentary and Exchanges on Politics and Public Debate

QUESTION: I believe the present ideological polarization in foreign policy is unprecedented in American history. I would pose this question. Robert McFarlane pleaded guilty to four misdemeanor counts. One was that he lied to a congressional committee. Suppose McFarlane had done precisely the same sort of things to make funds available or assistance available to the French underground during World War II. Do you believe he would have been prosecuted for that? I think that Representative James Wright himself would have awarded McFarlane the Medal of Honor.

SUZANNE GARMENT: Two things: first, McFarlane pleaded guilty to four misdemeanor charges, but none of them was a charge of lying to Congress. He pleaded guilty to withholding information. There is a huge distinction here, which was argued over at great length before the pleas were made and accepted. Second, we should remember that before Pearl Harbor—even after the fall of France—President Franklin D. Roosevelt did not by any means find universal approval for the help that he was trying to give the democracies through Lend-Lease and other such measures. In retrospect it is very easy to see who should have been on which side, but that did not insulate Roosevelt from harsh political attacks at the time.

JEREMY RABKIN: Isn't there an underlying asymmetry between the branches, quite apart from politics and ideology? People in the executive branch feel responsible for running particular programs while people in Congress do not feel the same responsibility for how programs are run, because the programs are not literally their programs.

307

MICHAEL MALBIN: I think it trivializes the disputes going on, even in domestic policy, to say that congressional committees do not really care how programs operate or to suggest, as some critics do, that Congress simply cares about generating casework to help the members get reelected. The chairmen of committees are often themselves the authors of programs, and they care very much about how the programs work. Their conception of the program may not match that of all their colleagues who voted for it. Nor does it necessarily match that of the people who have to administer it. And it surely does not match the perspective of the politically appointed assistant secretaries, most of whom have significantly less experience with the programs than the career people in the agencies. But a real policy dispute should not be misdescribed as a dispute over efficiency. What we have are policy disputes in which the chairmen use their power to achieve their ends by making things work as they think they should work. It is not that they are cavalier about policy results or do not care whether things work. They do care. Executive officials must accept that there often are very real disputes, and they ought to wage their political battles with that in mind.

QUESTION: We have been talking about the struggles between executive and legislative officers and between Democrats and Republicans. What about the split between short-term political appointees, who often have little interest in institutions or in long-term cooperative relations, and the career bureaucrats? Have we gone too much in the direction of having short-term political appointees layers down into the agencies, without a long-term stake in their operations?

MICHAEL HOROWITZ: Too many administrations appoint people who have no intellectual capital, who do not know what the game is. They become the captives of others; they become irrelevant; they flail about, have no policy rudders, and have no long-term interest in issues. They may be interested in being "fair" in the exercise of power or in loyally serving the president, but they have no idea what is really at stake. In my judgment, however, the worse mistake would be to keep moving the career bureaucracy up and up the ladder to more senior administration positions. Deputy assistant secretaries ought to be political appointees, and elevating senior career people would be a great mistake. But political appointees who dismiss the "bureaucracy" and lock themselves up with a little band of trusted personal advisers properly feel the lash of the bureaucracy, if only because they lose the invaluable institutional memories of the career staff. One can, indeed often must, disagree with career staff advice, but making decisions without their input generates unnecessary enmity and loses for the decision maker often critical information. My own experience is that the career civil service is more eager to please good leadership than is commonly supposed by Republican administrations. And while they should not be placed in political positions if presidential elections are to be meaningful vehicles for change, it is also true that presidents need to appoint people capable of exercising good leadership—people with the intellectual capital to know what the programs they administer are about.

MR. MALBIN: I agree that the last thing we want is to say that the people who have to be the repository of executive branch wisdom are the career people, because their interest lies in serving the political masters who are going to be around to control their programs and their careers—and these masters will be at least as likely to be in the legislative as in the executive branch. In addition, Republicans tend to have a hard time finding capable junior-level political appointees. Assistant secretaries of both parties tend to stay on the job a short time, and Democrats have more people ready to take over these jobs than Republicans do. There are more of them in Congress, serving on congressional staffs, and they are more attracted to government as a career because in domestic politics they tend to believe in government activism. If the question is how a Republican administration can stand up to a Democratic Congress, a lot of the answer has to do with making sure Republicans get the skills and credentials to fill these posts. If an administration wants a chairman of the housing subcommittee to be dealing with somebody with equivalent political skills on the administration side and conflict-of-interest statutes prevent taking such people from industry, the administration has a real problem as things are now. The issue networks that keep people informed about such specialized issues are now overwhelmingly Democratic. But they need not be—no law of nature says they have to be.

QUESTION: You suggested that Congress was very interested in carrying out its policies. If that is so, why do we have such arcane procurement and personnel policies?

MR. MALBIN: I said that on the whole chairmen are interested in carrying out their own notions of what good policy is. I know nothing about procurement policy, and I am not prepared to say that my generalization applies to every area. But I will stand by the claim that the congressional committee chairmen, who are often the authors of new programs and policies, care about how those programs and policies operate. Often the programs do not work, or the policies are silly. But this does not show that the congressional sponsors of these programs do not care.

MR. HOROWITZ: I believe that the executive branch is generally the more responsible branch and Congress the more "irresponsible." But executive officials develop a kind of contempt for Congress, which, even if at times deserved, is nonetheless inappropriate and excessive. I have sat in too many meetings where executive officials talked about policy without sufficient recognition of the reality and the power of Congress as an institution. Any executive official who thinks Congress is irresponsible and proceeds to run his agency without regard to Congress is going to run his agency into the ground. Congress sometimes even plays a good role in executive branch decision making, it may surprise many to learn, but it will play a role one way or the other. It becomes extraordinarily irresponsible when it proceeds without understanding what is involved in running programs and making things happen on a day-to-day basis. But being "right" in controversies with Congress requires neither regular surrender nor, more to the point, arrogance and lack of bargaining skills.

I agree that there is gridlock between the branches, that it poses critical problems, and that in the battle between Congress and the presidency, the presidency has in the main been the loser. If we look at the Johnson, Nixon, and Carter administrations, we see essentially the collapse of an institution central to the success of the American political process. Reagan's second term is in serious trouble as we speak. I agree, too, that many of the wounds of the executive branch are self-inflicted. But I also believe that much of the problem is not a matter of personality or of particular avoidable mistakes. It is structural. It is the sort of thing that leads sensible and well-informed people like Lloyd Cutler to talk about replacing our constitutional system with a parliamentary government. We need to find our way out of this box.

I am very dubious about process solutions, and I am utterly dubious about court decisions. The *Chadha* decision overturning the legislative veto, for example, has largely shifted power from the legislative authorization committees to the Appropriations committees—the worst place for it to go. The Appropriations committees now have more power than they ever dreamed of before *Chadha*. In essence, the problem is that Congress is a decentralized institution dealing with a centralized executive branch under a single presumptive head. The congressional committees have learned to adapt to this situation. They come at the executive in many ways, and they shoot real bullets. No set of court decisions on process can or will stop Congress from working its will.

We cannot even expect the president to resist encroachments by vetoing the questionable measures now so often inserted in spending bills. When a president is confronted with a fat continuing resolution with lots of unconstitutional provisions and the House leadership tells him there is $25 million in there for El Salvador and it ain't gonna be there in any other vehicle, a veto requires him to be a lot tougher than any of us were—or requires that he not much care about the future of democracy in El Salvador. Moreover, if a president succeeds in resisting one form of congressional encroachment, he cannot often repeat his success. No single approach works more than once or twice, because Congress learns how to adapt. It is a continuing struggle.

What, then, is the way out? The key, in my view, is the application of democracy, lots of it, more of it. The principal problem is that the presidency is essentially owned by the Republican party and the Congress by the Democratic party. Elections have become predictable and not threatening to the people who win. Before the election begins, we know who is going to win. The winner does not have to tack and accommodate and be leavened by the moderating views of the electorate. The need to make voter choice real in the American democratic process, which over the past twenty years has increasingly become ritual and not meaningful, is at the heart of this problem of each branch dealing with the other as some hostile adversary toward which no accommodation is necessary.

On top of the predictable and expected and proper tensions between the branches built into the Constitution has increasingly been added an overlay of partisanship. When I used to sit in on White House meetings, people sometimes talked contemptuously about the House of Representatives as a body with 300 secretaries of state or HHS. But whatever their words, they were often also talking about their political opponents in the Democratic party, because the House has been under Democratic control for over forty years and looks as if it will remain under Democratic control for the next forty years, if current conditions continue. Similarly, when members of Congress talk about the executive branch, they do not think about an institution. They think about "that rat Nixon" or "that right-winger Reagan." More and more, each branch sees the other as being captive not so much to wrong-headed politics as to the other party.

The George McGovern reforms have essentially given the presidency to the Republican party. This means that congressional Democrats have no real sense of what it takes to run the executive branch. How else to explain the absurdity of the independent counsel bills,

311

particularly in their latest formulations? Sensible Democrats vote for those bills because they think of getting those right-wing guys in the Reagan administration—or the people to come in the Bush administration. If Democrats in the leadership of the House had had experience in the executive branch, or thought they had a fair shot at winning the presidency by means other than destabilizing a sitting Republican administration, we might again have bipartisanship in foreign policy. We might even have fewer public-hearing media events, more honest policy debate, less thundering rhetoric about one side or the other saving or destroying the Constitution. We would not have Kafkaesque independent counsel laws, because Democrats would understand the potential of those laws to do *them* in. As the independent counsel system now operates, three good lawyers with a bunch of gossip sheets can almost destabilize a democratic administration. But Democratic congresses pass these laws because they have no sense of what it is like for honorable men to try to run the executive branch. They do not see the people there now as honorable men. They see them as the other guys, the opposition party.

My first prescription, then, is for the Democratic party to take the steps needed to elect more Democratic presidents. The Democrats should not need advice on this. One would think, after all, that continuing losses in presidential elections would have taught their own lessons. They do not because Congress, particularly the House, is unaffected by what happens in presidential elections. Incumbent congressmen almost always get reelected—the 98 percent reelection rate in 1986 was the predictable outcome of the alarming trends of the past twenty years or so. A study done at Stanford University found that House incumbents have since 1964 become only half as vulnerable to party tides as were their predecessors during the 1946–1962 period. Indeed, the study found that if the conditions that applied over most of American history applied to House incumbents since 1964, the Republican party would have controlled the House of Representatives in the 1966, 1968, 1980, and 1984 elections. This then is what we need—more Republican Houses, more congressional incumbents going down to defeat, more Democrats winning the presidency. At that point the parties would not just be talking abstractly about trust. They would have lived in each other's shoes, would have had the responsibilities of being in each of the branches and controlling them. At that point accommodation would become real. It would be based on real experiences, real prospects, and the knowledge that the Constitution you hobble or demean today may be the one you earn your living with tomorrow.

Why has the power of incumbency increased so much? The causes are obvious. On the congressional side the staff explosion, the use of congressional franks, and the gerrymandering of electoral districts. If we care about the gridlock between the branches, we should worry less about *Chadha* decisions and more about the issue of gerrymandering. For those of us who lived with budgets and who see Congress working its will, the *Chadha* decision is of marginal significance. Many of the decisions that lawyers see as great constitutional landmarks do not turn out that way in the real world. But *Baker* v. *Carr*—the original one-man one-vote decision—was a major influence on the politics of this country, and so would be a comparable decision on gerrymandering.

Yet the Reagan administration, for terribly misguided reasons, did not even file a brief in the recent Indiana gerrymandering case. The next president must treat that as a central issue, and people must be prepared to litigate gerrymandering as effectively as Thurgood Marshall litigated racial segregation, taking the long haul, spending the millions of dollars involved in legal research, picking the right test cases, setting the climate of opinion, and so forth. Similarly the decision in *Buckley* v. *Valeo*, authorizing limitations on campaign contributions, made a big difference. Those are the decisions that count, not the separation-of-power cases. If we talk about judicial intervention, it ought to be in areas that directly affect the electoral system.

In the meantime other things can be done to restore political accountability and meaningful elections. Republicans in the House might just think about announcing that they will not ritually vote for the Republican senior candidate for committee chairman but will be prepared to vote for particular Democrats—and then try to pick up some moderate Democrats to vote with them in order to put the whole House and not merely the Democratic caucus in control of such selections. Many conservative Democrats know that, with the solid support of the Republicans, they could be elected committee chairmen by the whole House. There might just be a strategy to do that.

Another tactic would be to focus on a special aspect of the appropriations process. There are now thirteen appropriations bills, or there should be. One of them is the legislative branch appropriations act, by which Congress appropriates money for itself. There are 250 budget examiners at the Office of Management and Budget, including one who spends part of his time on the Battlefield Monuments Commission budget. None, however, study the multibillion dollar legislative branch appropriations bill. In the name of what is called comity the president simply signs whatever legislative appropriation he is sent. But the comity here, of course, is entirely one-sided. Here is a bargaining lever for the president, then, if he has the will to use it. Let the president use the budget process to focus on the expanded size of Congress and the ways that this bloated expense account is employed by Congress to reelect incumbents and finance the subcommittees that intrude on executive branch prerogatives.

In sum, we should be focusing not on so-called institutional adjustments but on making democracy real. The roots of the problems we face are not in the separation of powers but in our failing election processes. That is where to look to find our way out of our current "scorpions in a bottle" government.

MICHAEL WALLACE: If I may be indulged one more war story, I would like to recall the way the Reagan administration looked at its first congressional midterm elections. In 1981 Democrats in the House were afraid they would lose their seats, because fifty-two of their members had gone down in flames the fall before and reapportionment was coming up. This administration made what seems to me a conscious decision to go down the tubes on a Sunday morning in January 1982, when the chief of staff said on "Meet the Press" that the average loss for the president's party in off-year elections is thirty-eight House seats and if the Republicans lost fewer than thirty-eight seats they would be doing a pretty good job. What he did was to serve notice to the Democrats that they had nothing to fear. If the Democrats knew they had nothing to fear, the House Republicans that week were terrified. They wanted to know which were among the thirty-seven the White House was preparing to sell out. Congress understands the game—they know they are entitled to try to get a new president. But President Reagan took the position that he was not entitled to try to get a new Congress.

IRVING KRISTOL: There is something old and something new in the conflict we are witnessing between the legislative and the executive. The something old is that with separation of powers comes conflict of powers. Power wants to accrete more power to itself. If it is not doing that, it feels that it is losing power, and, indeed, that may be the case. This is a structural problem that has existed since the beginning of American democracy, but it is one that we coped with reasonably well until fairly recently.

Some twenty years ago, at the end of the Johnson administration, there began to be talk about the imperial presidency, and not all of it was misguided. There was genuine concern about the emergence of administrative agencies with enormous powers, apparently uncontrolled by anyone, and Congress began to take steps to achieve some degree of equality with the executive in certain areas. The president had the Council of Economic Advisers; so Congress set up the Congressional Budget Office. The president had special science advisers; so Congress set up the Office of Technology Assessment. Since Congress had no real research capacity, it expanded the General Accounting Office (GAO), which now gives the chairmen of congressional committees the studies they want with the conclusions they want. Never does a GAO study come forward with a conclusion that the chairman of a committee does not want. That is normal. That is how the game is played. These institutional changes are simply modern adaptations of the old pattern, in which institutional imbalances tended to be corrected over time.

What is new and what has radically transformed the whole situation is the ideological polarization of the political parties. There have always been ideological differences between the parties. But only in the past couple of decades have we seen something that can fairly be called ideological polarization. Yet the interesting fact is that this is not true only in the United States. It seems to be a feature of democracy itself. It is true in Western Europe, where the parties are far more ideological, where there is less civility, less comity, and far greater intensity of conflict than existed twenty or twenty-five years ago.

What is important about this is that as the political parties have become more intensely ideological, more intensely combative, more unprincipled in their combativeness, the people have not become more ideological. I know of no evidence that the people of the United States or Britain or France or Germany are more ideological today than they were twenty or twenty-five years ago. The people are just confused by this ideological intensification in the parties. It is the work of a relatively small number of educated, ambitious people who are committed more to ideas than to reality and who, because they are activist, play a dominating role in modern political parties.

The people are confused, and they resolve this paradoxical situation by splitting their votes at different levels of government in Europe and different branches of government in the American system. The consequence is that a further built-in conflict is emerging. People vote overwhelmingly for Ronald Reagan and strongly for a liberal Democratic Congress. It is the only way they can figure out to cope with ideological parties that they do not really want, at least not when they are intensely ideological parties. But the parties have lives of their own; the people who control them are not going to go away, and as a consequence we have government in which ideological polarization and ideological conflict exacerbate the normal conflict resulting from the separation of powers.

315

How does one cope with this? The president is a victim not just of Congress but of *this* Congress with *these* particular ideas, a Congress that wants to weaken the presidency to establish the supremacy of these ideas, in foreign policy and in domestic policy. I certainly agree that the president has to understand what game he is playing. He must understand what the issues are, and he must devise an appropriate strategy for this game. Our conservative Republican presidents over the past twenty-five years have been unable to do so, in part because they have not been intellectually alert. Republican administrations have generally been timid, thinking in legalistic terms and essentially permitting the other side to play the game while they try to lob the ball back. At some point the other side comes to the net with a smash, and that is that.

I have found it impossible to get the executive branch to take this contest seriously. I remember when James Miller became head of the Office of Management and Budget. I went to pay my respects and found him brooding over the budget. He had forty-eight hours to decide how the administration should respond to the congressional budget resolution—after that the government would run out of money. I said, let the government run out of money. The army will not be paid, civil servants will not be paid, welfare recipients will not get their checks. The president can then go to the people and explain what is happening. Miller smiled and said that was an interesting idea—but, of course, it was not about to happen. How can the president cope with a situation in which Congress holds all the cards?

There are two things the president can do. Here the president can learn from the example of Franklin D. Roosevelt. Roosevelt had a Democratic Congress but not a congenially liberal Congress, because the Democratic party in Congress was controlled by southerners who were quite often reactionary. Roosevelt got his program through by defining the presidency not as one branch of the government but as the tribune of the people. He got most—not all—of his program through by going to the people and using popular pressure on Congress to achieve his ends. That is the only way an executive under current circumstances can intimidate Congress.

Congress is a bullying institution, and like most bullying institutions it is also a cowardly institution. I am not speaking about individual congressmen, some of whom are good friends of mine. But as an institution Congress is both bullying and cowardly. The only way the president can cope with this is by being what we call populist. Roosevelt set the model for that by going to the people and building up popular support. This is not hard, especially in the most controversial area, foreign policy.

I cannot help laughing when I hear solemn discussion of the War Powers Act, which gives the president ninety days to send American troops abroad. Ninety days is quite enough. The president has absolute freedom of action if he has that much time to get started. If the president wanted to send troops to Panama—and I am not suggesting he should—it would not take ninety days to send the troops in, clean up a few things, and bring them home. Or not bring them home. If the president makes a mistake and the troops are still fighting and dying after ninety days, what is Congress going to do? What can Congress do? Congress may say bring the boys home, but if the president says no, Congress cannot do much about it.

If the president goes to the American people and wraps himself in the American flag and lets Congress wrap itself in the white flag of surrender, the president will win. If Lyndon Johnson had done that on Vietnam, he would have won. You have to go to the people on any kind of foreign policy issue involving the projection of American force and the use of American troops overseas. The American people always support the president in these circumstances—I can think of no exception in American history—whether the president is sending troops to Mexico, Vietnam, the Dominican Republic, as long as the president articulates exactly what he is doing and why he is doing it, and then does it, and as long as he has sense enough to know when to cut his losses and when to increase his commitment.

When it comes to foreign policy, the president of the United States today has as much freedom as he ever had—if only he would use it boldly. But he has to go to the people to use it. He has to tap the vein not only of patriotism but of nationalism, which is very strong in the American public. Look at the public response to the American landings in Grenada. If the president had waited to consult with Congress before acting there, Lord knows what would have happened. The media were 95 percent certain that the American public would be against sending troops to Grenada. But once it was done, there was 95 percent public approval. The American people had never heard of Grenada. There was no reason why they should have. The reason we gave for the intervention—the risk to American medical students there—was phony, but the reaction of the American people was absolutely and overwhelmingly favorable. They had no idea what was going on, but they backed the president. They always will. What we need is a president who understands this and does not listen to the Pentagon or the State Department—although in recent years the State Department has shown more understanding of the uses of force than the Pentagon—a president who understands that popular opinion is out there waiting to take effect and that it is his job to mobilize it, not to whine about the separation of powers, not to whine about congressional usurpation of his prerogatives. The president can reestablish presidential leadership only by being a leader, and in a modern democracy this means being a populist leader. François Mitterrand understands this. Ronald Reagan seems not to. My advice to the president is—do it and let Congress cope with it afterward. You may lose some, but that does not matter. As long as you are an activist president, as long as you attend to your relations with the American public, you will in the end be a popular and successful president.

MR. HOROWITZ: I agree with much of what Irving Kristol has said, but my experience is a little different. I was in the Reagan administration at the beginning of the first term, when the president was indeed using that bully pulpit and seemed to be mowing down all opposition. That was the popular view. Actually, there was less to our victories than met the eye and far more in the way of congressional maintenance of the status quo. Congress is a very potent institution and can do in the presidency, and the confrontational approach for the president is not necessarily and surely not always as winning an approach as Irving Kristol makes it out to be. His Grenada case, for example, is both good and misleading. There was great support for our Grenada policy, to be sure—but perhaps only because we won in two days. I am not so sure what the level of support would have been if we had been bogged down three months later and congressional hearings began in the middle of that kind of combat. That is not to say that the bully pulpit should not be used. But congressmen can be bullied a lot less than one might think, because what is really at stake for them is reelection, and no bully pulpiting from the president really threatens their increasingly ensured reelections under present conditions. Congressmen lie low when the president wins in two days, but boy, do they come back when the president falters. They have staffs with essentially lifetime civil service tenure—because they always win and they reappoint the same staffs—to sustain them. Until we deal with that issue, there is just too much unworkable macho in what Irving Kristol suggests. Presidents often have to accommodate Congress because congressional power is real, and it shoots real bullets.

MR. KRISTOL: The strategy I have outlined is not risk-free, but it is more realistic than the one you have outlined, which is, as I understand it, to reform the Democratic party. I don't know how to do that.

QUESTION: I believe President Reagan did pretty well in appealing to the people during his first term. But on Central America there is tremendous grass-roots organization by the left. When the president requested time for a televised appeal to the country before the last congressional vote on aid to the contras, the networks all refused because, they said, what he would say was "predictable." With this kind of situation, what is the power of the president to influence the people?

MR. MALBIN: It is a fair point that if the power of the presidency is essentially the power of public persuasion, isn't the president's ability to persuade being eroded? The president's persuasive powers are, in fact, limited, and that is something we have to address.

MR. KRISTOL: The president's powers of persuasion have not been eroded in areas of foreign policy, because there the instincts of the American people are all on his side, and the media can do practically nothing to insert themselves between the president and public opinion. On domestic issues, yes, it can be very difficult to mobilize public opinion behind presidential authority because domestic issues are often very complex. He cannot just wrap himself in the flag on most domestic issues. They are often hard to understand. But certain things are not so hard to understand, like an appropriations bill that weighs forty pounds. The president can get on television and say, I am vetoing it because it is absurd. Or he can take a tax bill running over a thousand pages and do the same thing—get on television to explain that he is vetoing the bill because he cannot understand it and the people who wrote it cannot understand it and the American people will never understand it. That sort of thing the American people can follow well enough.

Clearly, he has to choose his spots. The president cannot go to the people day after day. They would get bored if he did. But it does not really matter if the president loses some of the little games. After all, liberal Democrats are entitled to win some. They work at it. They are there, and they are going to win some. The important thing is not to lose the important fights. Then we might eventually end up with a decent Congress.

MR. HOROWITZ: Irving Kristol and I are agreed that the executive has much more power than it has used. Surely we suffered through the disuse of this power when the Reagan administration failed to take issues to the people as often as it might have. We agree that stupid appointments make this difficult and better appointments—like William Bennett at the Education Department—can do much to transform the terms of the debate. At the same time, the notion that the president can unhorse the existing Congress through his bully pulpit is so simplistic as to be just plain wrong. It will lead presidents into confrontations that they will lose far too often. It is true that the presidency is embattled and that it is embattled by Congress more than by its own mistakes. Much of the problem is structural. But unless we focus on the question of how congressmen can be made more vulnerable to a moderate electorate—and I think Irving Kristol is right about the moderate character of the electorate—we will miss the real target.

Appendix

FIGURE A–1

NEW LEGISLATIVE RESTRICTIONS ON EXECUTIVE CONDUCT OF FOREIGN AFFAIRS, PER PERIOD

Number of Statutes

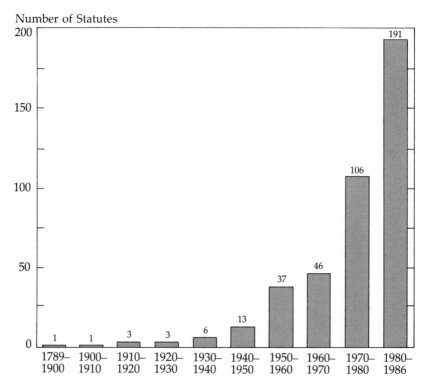

SOURCE: "Legislation on Foreign Affairs through 1986," Senate Committee on Foreign Relations.

FIGURE A–2

APPEALS FROM DECISIONS OF ADMINISTRATIVE AGENCIES TO U.S.
COURTS OF APPEALS, SELECTED YEARS, 1940–1986

Number of Appeals

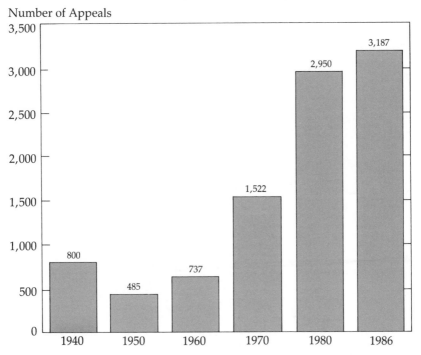

SOURCE: Annual Reports, Administrative Office of the United States Courts.

Index

A NOTE ON THE BOOK

This book was edited by Dana Lane,
Trudy Kaplan, and Janet Schilling of the
publications staff of the American Enterprise Institute.
The index was prepared by Patricia Ruggiero.
The text was set in Palatino, a typeface designed by Hermann Zapf.
Presstar Printing Corporation of Silver Spring, Maryland,
set the type, and Edwards Brothers Incorporated,
of Ann Arbor, Michigan, printed and bound the book,
using permanent acid-free paper.